THE ULTIMATE BOOK OF
Gardening
Hints & Tips

DK THE ULTIMATE BOOK OF
Gardening
Hints & Tips

Pippa Greenwood

LONDON, NEW YORK, MUNICH,
MELBOURNE, DELHI

Senior Editor Linda Martin
Project Art Editor Jayne Carter
Designer Helen Benfield
Managing Editor Stephanie Jackson
Managing Art Editor Nigel Duffield
Senior Managing Editor Krystyna Mayer
Senior Managing Art Editor Lynne Brown
Production Controller Sarah Coltman
DTP Designer Jason Little

This edition published in 2009
First published in Great Britain in 1996
by Dorling Kindersley Limited,
80 Strand, London WC2R 0RL

A Penguin Company

A CIP catalogue record for this book is available
from the British Library

ISBN 978-1-4053-4937-6

Reproduced by Chroma Graphics, Singapore
Printed and bound in Singapore by
Star Standard Industries Pte Ltd.

Discover more at
www.dk.com

CONTENTS

INTRODUCTION 6

RESTORING GARDENS 10

PLANTS AND PLANTING 38

CONTAINER GARDENING 62

INTRODUCTION

*T*HE KEY TO CREATING AND MAINTAINING *a beautiful and productive garden is regular, sustained care. Whether starting from scratch, renovating a neglected garden, or keeping a garden in good condition, this book is filled with common-sense solutions, sound advice, and helpful tips that minimize time and effort – giving you more time to relax and enjoy yourself in the garden.*

USING THIS BOOK

ESTABLISHING A GARDEN

Three sections cover the fundamental aspects of gardening – from sowing lawns to clearing overgrown borders or flowerbeds. *Restoring Gardens* offers advice on successfully renovating an unkempt garden without wasting precious time or money. *Plants and Planting* reveals the essential points to consider when selecting plants for a garden and supplies helpful tips on providing the plants with a healthy and promising start. *Lawns* is a comprehensive guide to creating, restoring, and maintaining a green, dense, and healthy lawn.

Planting bulbs
To find out how to plant bulbs so that you avoid unsightly, dying foliage after flowering, see page 56. For advice on planting bulbs in a lawn, see page 126.

MAINTAINING A GARDEN

A garden requires regular care and attention if it is to remain both attractive and fertile. *Plant Care* describes how to look after plants once they are established. *Pests and Diseases* helps you to identify and eliminate unwelcome visitors, while demonstrating that not everything that moves in the garden is harmful. *Propagating Plants* demystifies the satisfying and economical process of producing new plants from existing ones. *General Maintenance* features tips on repairing and brightening up the structural and practical elements of a garden – the walls, paths, fences, sheds, greenhouses, tools, and furniture.

Dividing clumps
For tips on digging up and dividing clumps of perennials, see page 60. For other methods of propagation, see pages 140-157.

ADDING NEW DIMENSIONS TO A GARDEN

Once a garden is established and thriving, additional features can create further exciting areas of interest. *Container Gardening* outlines the techniques for planting up pots, tubs, hanging baskets, and windowboxes, offers dozens of tips on maintaining containers with the minimum of effort, and gives innovative ideas for displaying pots to their best advantage. *Water Features* highlights the advantages of having water in gardens, with suggestions for introducing water to small gardens with limited space, and hints on attracting wildlife. Finally, the comprehensive index and chapter-by-chapter colour coding make it easy to find hints and tips throughout the book.

Saving compost
To find out how to stabilize tall containers and save on compost when planting up, see page 22.

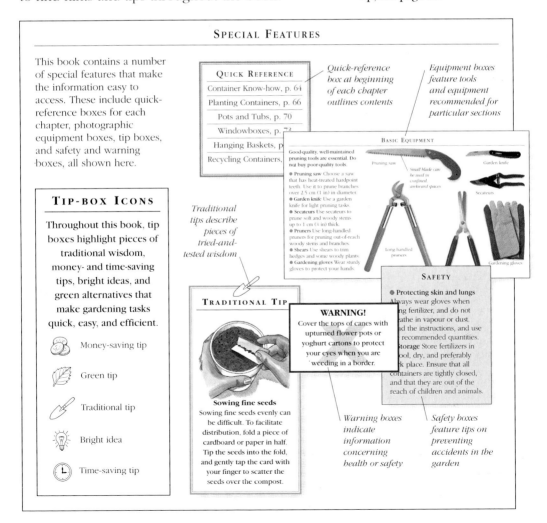

SPECIAL FEATURES

This book contains a number of special features that make the information easy to access. These include quick-reference boxes for each chapter, photographic equipment boxes, tip boxes, and safety and warning boxes, all shown here.

QUICK REFERENCE
Container Know-how, p. 64
Planting Containers, p. 66
Pots and Tubs, p. 70
Windowboxes, p. 72
Hanging Baskets, p.
Recycling Containers,

Quick-reference box at beginning of each chapter outlines contents

Equipment boxes feature tools and equipment recommended for particular sections

BASIC EQUIPMENT

Good-quality, well-maintained pruning tools are essential. Do not buy poor-quality tools.

● **Pruning saw** Choose a saw that has heat-treated hardpoint teeth. Use it to prune branches over 2.5 cm (1 in) in diameter.
● **Garden knife** Use a garden knife for light pruning tasks.
● **Secateurs** Use secateurs to prune soft and woody stems up to 1 cm (⅜ in) thick.
● **Pruners** Use long-handled pruners for pruning out-of-reach woody stems and branches.
● **Shears** Use shears to trim hedges and some woody plants.
● **Gardening gloves** Wear sturdy gloves to protect your hands.

Pruning saw — *Small blade can be used in confined awkward spaces* — *Garden knife* — *Secateurs* — *Long-handled pruners* — *Gardening gloves*

TIP-BOX ICONS

Throughout this book, tip boxes highlight pieces of traditional wisdom, money- and time-saving tips, bright ideas, and green alternatives that make gardening tasks quick, easy, and efficient.

Money-saving tip

Green tip

Traditional tip

Bright idea

Time-saving tip

Traditional tips describe pieces of tried-and-tested wisdom

TRADITIONAL TIP

Sowing fine seeds
Sowing fine seeds evenly can be difficult. To facilitate distribution, fold a piece of cardboard or paper in half. Tip the seeds into the fold, and gently tap the card with your finger to scatter the seeds over the compost.

WARNING!
Cover the tops of canes with upturned flower pots or yoghurt cartons to protect your eyes when you are weeding in a border.

Warning boxes indicate information concerning health or safety

SAFETY

● **Protecting skin and lungs** Always wear gloves when using fertilizer, and do not breathe in vapour or dust. Read the instructions, and use the recommended quantities.
● **Storage** Store fertilizers in a cool, dry, and preferably dark place. Ensure that all containers are tightly closed, and that they are out of the reach of children and animals.

Safety boxes feature tips on preventing accidents in the garden

CREATING A MANAGEABLE GARDEN

Gardening can be a time-consuming and labour-intensive job, but it need not be. With careful planning, a low-maintenance scheme can be put into effect. After the first year, it will require a minimum of work to keep the garden looking good. Consider paving an area and using plants in containers to create a colourful and manageable display. Cover walls and fences with fast-growing climbers that need little pruning, such as *Pyracantha*. Instead of choosing herbaceous borders, which may need constant care, select plants that need less attention, such as bulbs and shrubs. To deter weeds and conserve moisture in the soil, use groundcover, and apply a thick mulch of compost or bark chips.

Preventing weed growth
Removing weeds from a garden can be a tedious task; it is easier to prevent their growth in the first place. One of the most successful and attractive ways of achieving this is to deprive weed seedlings of light and air by using plants that will cover the soil with foliage.

GROWING FOOD IN YOUR GARDEN

More and more people are discovering the delights of growing their own vegetables, fruit, and herbs. Not only do these plants make attractive additions to borders and containers with the variety of foliage and flowers they offer, they also produce fresh, tasty, and nutritious crops. With the extensive choice now available through seed catalogues and garden centres, it is possible to experiment until you find your own favourite edible plants. Compact, fast-growing, and densely planted crops are ideal for a small garden, while fan-trained fruit trees can make productive and decorative screens for larger areas. For an aromatic, attractive display, consider planting a herb garden. Of use to every cook, herbs add a final, delicate touch to an edible garden.

Choosing crops
When deciding which vegetables to feature in a garden, make sure you choose cultivars that are resistant to disease. If possible, select a range of vegetables that will produce crops in succession and over a sustained period of time.

GARDENING ON A ROOF OR BALCONY

You can create a beautiful garden on a roof or balcony with an array of striking containers overflowing with suitable plants. In a location where weight is an important consideration, use plastic or fibreglass containers, and fill them with polystyrene crocks and lightweight potting mix. Assess the features of the site carefully so that you select plants that thrive in shady or exposed conditions. Train hardy climbers over trellis panels to form attractive screens for privacy or to filter the wind. Avoid tall plants that may be blown over, and choose some fragrant plants so that you can enjoy their scent from indoors as well as outdoors.

Planting containers
Use pots to grow vegetables and fruit, such as lettuce and strawberries.

Protecting your back
Make sure you use a tool of the correct length and weight when digging, and ensure that your back is kept straight.

MAKING THE GARDEN A SAFE PLACE

Although a garden is a place to enjoy and to relax in, some features and tasks require a certain amount of care in order to keep it a safe, accident-free area. When designing a garden from scratch, take into account the needs of those most likely to use it. If this includes young children, consider featuring water in a bubble fountain, rather than a pond. Read plant labels thoroughly before purchase to ensure that you do not choose any potentially hazardous plants. Always use electrical equipment and tools with care. Avoid trailing cables and, where possible, install a circuit breaker. Unplug power tools before repairing them, and never use them while watering, or during or just after rainfall.

WORKING WITH THE SEASONS

One of the pleasures of having a garden is knowing how to work with the seasons to maximum advantage. Differences in climate, soil type, and location will all affect the growth of plants and the timing of various activities. To be successful, a gardener needs to take all these elements into account before deciding when and what to do. However, there are a number of basic tasks that can be carried out at specific times through the year, and helpful suggestions are given on pages 174–181.

Storing apples and pears
Apples and pears may be kept for weeks, even months, if stored in cool, dark conditions. Wrap in tissue paper, taking care not to bruise the fruit.

RESTORING GARDENS

RENOVATING OR CHANGING A GARDEN does not have to be hard work. A little planning, the right equipment, some basic gardening knowledge, and enthusiasm are all that you need to transform your garden. Begin with a few improvements that will not take too much time or money (see below). These changes will help to make you feel positive about the garden and will inspire and encourage you to tackle it in more fundamental ways.

GARDEN PROBLEMS AND SOLUTIONS

GARDEN PROBLEMS	SIMPLE SOLUTIONS
LAWNS The shape is boring or simply does not appeal to you; the lawn edges are broken and dilapidated; the lawn is full of uneven areas, moss, weeds, and brown patches. Maybe there is too much of it.	Alter the shape; neaten lawn edges or remake them from scratch; level out humps and hollows; control moss and weeds; reseed bare areas; plant a specimen tree; make an island bed; make a path; create an ornamental divider.
FLOWERBEDS AND BORDERS Beds and borders are fine overall, but some plants are swamped by others; some plants are in poor condition; there are gaps in a border.	Divide overcrowded plants, removing some entirely; add climbers to leggy shrubs; use annuals, perennials, and bulbs to fill gaps; grow climbers or groundcover plants to cover bare slopes.
TREES Trees are dominant, overgrown, and out of shape; they are blocking light from shrubs and plants and the house; low branches restrict access around tree.	Create a garden or bed using plants that enjoy woodland conditions; plant spring bulbs and water and feed them to counteract competition; crown-lift or crown-reduce a tree to increase light levels.
PATIOS The area is untidy and covered in moss, algae, and weeds; there are broken and cracked slabs; you do not like the shape; it is stark and uninviting.	Clear up rubbish; control mosses, algae, and weeds; replace broken slabs or remove them; add plants; alter the shape; use pots, baskets, and other containers; make a barbecue or water feature.
PATHS AND STEPS They are too angular and harsh and do not fit in with the garden; they are slippery; they have loose slabs; weeds are growing in the cracks; they are breaking up; they look untidy.	Plant up with edging to soften harsh lines and to make them look more attractive; remove algae and mosses; mend loose or damaged areas; remove weeds and prevent their reappearance; liven them up with planted-up containers.
WALLS They serve a purpose but are damaged, discoloured, ugly, and do not provide any benefit to the garden; they are uninteresting.	Clean, whitewash, or paint; plant and train fruit trees; plant climbers; thin out existing climbers; tidy up old trellis, or erect new trellis; paint a mural; add a mirror; add a seat to make a bower.

A TRANSFORMED GARDEN

A garden that has been neglected over a long period of time can be a depressing sight. Restoring it may seem a daunting task, but you will be amazed at the transformation you can make in just one year. Make a start by clearing away any rubbish and cutting the grass.

IDEAS FOR RENOVATING AND RESTORING A GARDEN

Shape of tree is improved by pruning (see p. 18)

Tree is underplanted with wildflowers (see p. 15)

Shed has new roof and renovated cladding (see p. 160)

Planning renovation
Retain any features that are worth saving, such as a tree or a shrub that provides a focal point. Introduce immediate colour with pots of annuals, bedding plants, and fast-growing climbers.

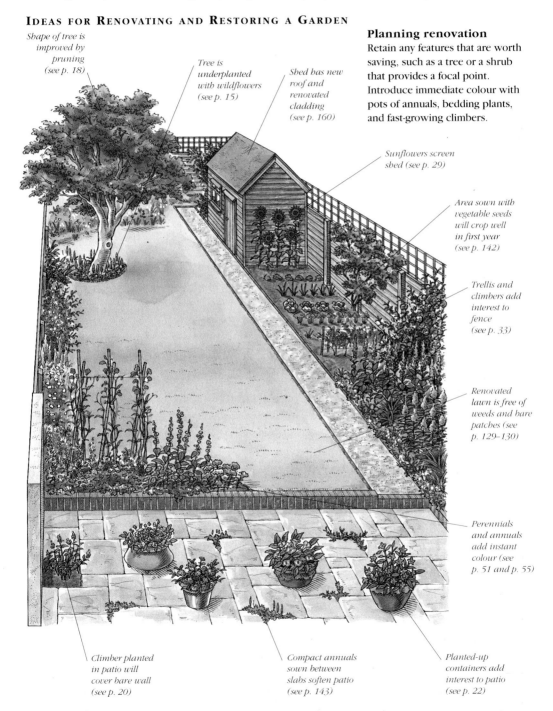

Sunflowers screen shed (see p. 29)

Area sown with vegetable seeds will crop well in first year (see p. 142)

Trellis and climbers add interest to fence (see p. 33)

Renovated lawn is free of weeds and bare patches (see p. 129–130)

Perennials and annuals add instant colour (see p. 51 and p. 55)

Climber planted in patio will cover bare wall (see p. 20)

Compact annuals sown between slabs soften patio (see p. 143)

Planted-up containers add interest to patio (see p. 22)

TRANSFORMING LAWNS

A LAWN OFTEN FORMS one of the most central parts of a garden and, in many cases, may take up the largest proportion of the garden area. If the lawn is dilapidated or uninspiring, this can make the rest of the garden look uninviting.

RESHAPING LAWNS

The shape of a lawn is fundamental to the way it affects a garden. It may impart a degree of formality, or it may have a casual, relaxed effect. Changing a lawn's shape need not be too difficult and does not necessarily involve the expense of buying more turf or grass seed.

CURVED LAWNS
● **Marking out** Use string and pegs (see p. 125) to mark regular curves. For complicated curves, use a flexible hose pipe.

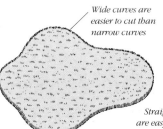
Wide curves are easier to cut than narrow curves

Using curves
Create a curved lawn to give your garden a casual look. Combine this with informal planting. Bear in mind that curves are more difficult to mow than straight edges.

STRAIGHT LAWNS
● **Marking out** Draw string tightly between pegs driven into the lawn. Cut along the edge of a plank (see p. 128).

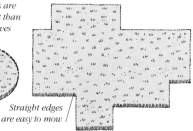
Straight edges are easy to mow

Using straight edges
Use straight edges and right angles to create a formal, elegant look. To retain the effect, keep the lawn edges neat and well maintained (see p. 128).

PLANNING SHAPES
● **Viewing the effect** After marking out the proposed new shape of a lawn, view the plan from several different places before starting to make the changes. If possible, check to see what the new shape looks like when viewed from an upstairs window.

PLANTING FOR EFFECT
● **A formal look** Plant neatly clipped *Buxus* shrubs in beds and borders to increase the formal appearance of a straight-edged lawn.
● **An informal look** Allow herbaceous plants with rounded shapes to overhang the edges of a curved lawn.

MAKING AND SHAPING ISLAND BEDS
● **Adapting to conditions** Turn any areas where grass does not grow well – perhaps because the ground is too dry, too wet, or too shaded – into an island bed. Use plants that are suited to the prevailing conditions (see p. 44).
● **Alternative planting** Instead of planting herbaceous and annual flowers or shrubs in an island bed, try filling it with some attractive vegetables and fruit. Rhubarb, chard, runner beans, lettuce, raddiccio, and strawberries – or a selection of herbs – will all look good, and will provide fresh produce throughout the year.

● **Scale** Create an island bed to break up a lawn. Make sure that the scale of the bed is in proportion to the lawn size.

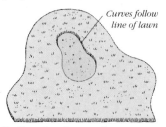
Curves follow line of lawn

Following lawn shapes
To create a coordinated and balanced look in a garden, make a curved island bed in a curved lawn, and make a straight-edged bed in a formal lawn.

TRADITIONAL TIP

Making a focal point
Transform an expanse of green by planting a specimen tree. Choose one that will grow to a suitable size. A large tree looks confined in a small setting, and a tiny tree is lost in a large area.

BREAKING UP LAWNS

An alternative way to alter an existing lawn is to divide it up. There are many ways of doing this, both by altering the structure of the lawn itself and by using plants, paths, or stepping stones. Dividing a lawn into sections can often make a long garden look wider.

DIVIDING LAWNS

● **Different uses** If a lawn is large enough, consider dividing it into two distinct areas – perhaps one for children to play on, and one for adults to relax on.

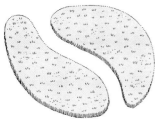

Shaping lawn areas
To create continuity between divided areas of lawn, shapes should complement each other. Make sure that the edges between the areas are easy to mow, and that any dividing borders are in proportion to the grassy areas.

USING PATHS

● **Ideal width** Make sure that a new path crossing a lawn is unobstructed and that it is wide enough for at least one person to walk along easily.
● **Curved path** If laying a path across a curved lawn, make sure that the path follows the shape of the existing curves.
● **Direction of path** Try to make sure that a path leads either to a particular object, such as a shed or greenhouse, or to a different section of the garden. A path that obviously leads nowhere can look odd and out of place.
● **Fruit edging** Plant stepover apples, trained to grow to roughly 45–60 cm (18–24 in) above ground level, to create interesting edges on a straight path that crosses a lawn.

USING HEDGES

Creating garden rooms
Use hedges to divide a large lawn into a series of different "rooms". Each area can have its own distinctive character. Divisions can add interest to a garden, as well as making it seem larger. Screens made up of shrubs planted at generous intervals, and arranged informally or trained over supports, can be used to the same effect (see p. 29).

MAKING STEPPING-STONE PATHS

If your planned garden path is not going to be subjected to heavy use, paving slabs – laid either in a line to make a symmetrical path or informally as a stepping-stone path – can look attractive. If the soil beneath is compacted, the slabs can be laid on sand rather than hardcore.

LAYING A STEPPING-STONE PATH

1 Mark out the position of the slabs by cutting around them, and remove enough soil to sink each slab just beneath the level of the grass. Allow for at least 1 cm (½ in) of sand or hardcore for bedding in.

2 Note the depth required, and repeat for each slab along the path. Thoroughly compact the soil, add the sand or hardcore, and bed each slab firmly in. Check the level, and adjust the slabs if necessary.

POSITIONING SLABS

● **Arranging slabs** Experiment with different positions for a series of slabs before cutting and removing turf. Check that the slabs are conveniently spaced for walking on.
● **Tools** Use a half-moon edger for cutting turf and a spade or trowel to remove soil.
● **Depth of slabs** Make sure that paving slabs are sunk sufficiently deep into turf to ensure that they present no obstruction to a lawnmower.
● **Secondary path** Use stepping stones to provide access from the main pathway to a play area, garden seat, or arbour.

LEVELLING LAWNS

If the look of a garden is informal, a few minor hollows or humps in a lawn may not matter too much. If, however, hollows and humps become numerous or obvious, the uneven areas will benefit from levelling out. Small hollows can be improved with a sandy top-dressing.

LEVELLING A HOLLOW OR HUMP IN A LAWN

1 Using a half-moon edger, cut a deep cross through the centre of the uneven area. Cut right through the soil and beyond the problem area. Carefully peel back the sections of turf, and fold them back.

2 Fork over the soil lightly with a hand fork. To fill a hollow, add sandy topsoil a little at a time. To remove a hump underneath the turf, remove as much soil as necessary. Firm down the soil.

3 Carefully lower the turf back into position. Firm gently, and check that the area is completely level. Firm thoroughly, and sprinkle top-dressing into any gaps. Water the area thoroughly.

ESTABLISHING CAUSES OF HOLLOWS AND HUMPS

● **Poor drainage** Hollows may be caused by poor drainage, which may be indicated by the presence of moss. Make sure that the soil used to re-establish the level contains plenty of grit. Use a sandy top-dressing mixture.
● **Hidden causes** Check that uneven areas are not caused by any underlying debris or buried tree roots. If necessary, dig out the cause of the problem, and re-establish the level using topsoil or a sandy top-dressing mixture.

● **Burrowing moles** Severe hollows in a lawn can be caused by the collapse of mole runs. If so, the runs must be excavated and filled in. To prevent further damage, deter moles from coming into your garden (see p. 113).

PLANNING REPAIRS

● **Best time** If possible, level out uneven areas in autumn or spring when turf will re-establish quickly. Water the lawn frequently and thoroughly to encourage rapid rooting.

PROTECTING REPAIRS

● **Regular use** If children use a lawn regularly, it may be worth fencing off repaired areas with canes and string until the turf is re-established.

BRIGHT IDEA

Making turf resilient
For a long-lasting repair to an area that develops hollows due to heavy use, add finely chopped car tyres to the top-dressing. The rubber will make the turf more resilient to regular pounding.

LEVELLING WITH TOP-DRESSING

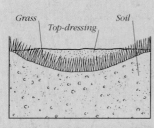

Grass   Top-dressing   Soil

Slight hollows in a lawn can be rectified with a sandy top-dressing. The grass will grow through and then root into the top-dressing. Use this method only for shallow hollows, since excessive quantities of top-dressing may smother the grass and prevent growth.

ENHANCING TREES IN LAWNS

A tree planted in a lawn can provide a natural central feature for a garden, especially if it has an attractive and interesting shape. A tree that has particular seasonal interest, perhaps spring blossoms or striking colour in autumn, can also form a stunning focal point.

PROVIDING SEATING

Adding a seat
Put an old, large tree to good use by placing a bench or seat around or under it. Make sure that there is enough room for the tree trunk to expand without being constricted by the bench.

LOOKING AFTER TREES
● **Trees in lawns** Leave a circle about three or four times the diameter of each tree's rootball free of grass. This makes feeding easy and minimizes competition from the grass.
● **Soil level** If making a flowerbed under a tree, try not to raise the soil level more than about 5–8 cm (2–3 in). If the bed is any deeper than this, the tree roots may be suffocated.

PLANTING GROUNDCOVER
● **Bulbs under trees** Bulbs form decorative groundcover under trees. Choose bulbs that flower mainly in spring, when the tree will not cast much shade.

FEEDING TREES

● **When planting** Give a new tree a good start. Mix plenty of bulky organic matter, with added fertilizer, into as large a planting hole as possible.
● **Stimulating growth** Foliar feed a newly planted tree throughout its first and second growing season. This will help to speed up the tree's establishment by stimulating root growth.
● **Feeding area** When feeding an established tree, lift squares of turf around the outermost spread of the branches, and fork fertilizer into the soil. Replace the turf, and water well.

CREATING WILDFLOWER AREAS

G rass growing directly beneath a tree rarely thrives. Although it may occasionally be possible to cultivate a reasonable area of green if you choose a suitable grass seed mixture or turf, it may be easier to plant flowers instead. Choose plants that are tolerant of shade and dryness.

PLANTING WILDFLOWERS UNDER TREES

Flowers will attract pollinating insects

Self-seeding foxgloves quickly establish in shade of tree

Small groundcover plants at edges keep weeds down

Choosing appropriate plants
Choose any plants that grow naturally in the conditions found under trees. Because suitable plants all enjoy the same habitat, they will not look out of place together. Groundcover plants, such as periwinkle, are easy to maintain and keep weeds down.

SELECTING PLANTS
● **Correct choice** Choose from the following plants and bulbs, which will all grow well under a tree: *Anemone* x *hybrida, Anemone nemorosa,* Bergenia spp., *Brunnera macrophylla, Convallaria majalis, Cyclamen, Galanthus nivalis, Geranium macrorrhizum, Hyacinthoides non-scripta, Iris foetidissima, Lamium* spp., *Liriope muscari, Tiarella cordifolia, Viola.*

MAINTAINING PLANTS
● **Watering** Although plants that grow under a tree do not require much water, you will need to water them regularly during dry periods, when little rain penetrates the canopy.

RESTORING BORDERS

A BADLY PLANTED BORDER, or one that has become too crowded, can spoil the look of a garden. If, however, the basic design is good, it may be possible to transform a border by some careful thinning out or additional planting.

THINNING OUT BORDERS

It is very easy to overplant a border. Planted at the correct spacing, a border invariably looks sparse until the plants have grown and developed. When they have, you may need to remove a number of complete plants, or simply divide existing plants into smaller pieces.

DEALING WITH AN OVERCROWDED BORDER

Rapidly growing, vigorous shrub　*Plant too large for space*　*Perennial clump*

Small shrub suitable for this border　*Gap between plants allows for growth*　*Replanted perennial clump*

Border before thinning
Rapidly growing shrubs create competition and shade and are best removed. This allows more space for other plants to grow and develop properly. Herbaceous perennial clumps become congested and need to be divided every two or three years.

Border after thinning
Divide congested herbaceous perennial clumps (see p. 60). Keep some sections for the border, and use others to fill gaps elsewhere in the garden. Move some shrubs (see p. 59) to another site, and prune back others as required.

USING CLEMATIS

Reviving a shrub
Instead of digging up a straggly, leggy shrub, plant a clematis close by, and allow it to scramble through the shrub. This will soon mask any sparseness and will also provide colour.

IMPROVING BORDERS
● **Starting again** If a border is beyond repair, move the plants into a spare piece of ground. Replan the area, and replant.
● **Improving the soil** If you clear a border, take the opportunity to revitalize the soil. Incorporate compost and well-rotted manure, and use a general fertilizer (see p. 84). If the soil is heavy and sticky, dig in grit to improve the drainage (see p. 42).
● **Digging in winter** Do not carry out radical work on a border with heavy soil during a wet winter; this could damage plants. Wait until spring.
● **Mulching** Cover any bare areas between plants with a 5–7 cm (2–3 in) deep layer of mulch to retain moisture and suppress weeds (see p. 90).

MOVING AND PLANTING
● **Recycling** If moving shrubs from a mixed border to other areas of the garden, do this in late autumn, when the roots are dormant (see p. 58–59).
● **Dividing perennials** Use only the vigorous sections of divided perennials. If you have any spare clumps, you can plant them in containers as well as in other areas of the garden.
● **Planting distance** When planting, always check a plant's potential height and spread (see p. 51), and group plants together accordingly. This can save a lot of time and effort later.
● **Roots** Always check the roots of any plant you are moving. If they are congested, soak the rootball in water for a few hours, then tease the roots out.

FILLING GAPS IN BORDERS

If planted correctly, it takes several years for a mixed or herbaceous border to develop its full potential. The planting will look sparse for the first few years. Rather than overplant in the first place, fill gaps between plants temporarily, until they are well established and fully mature.

SPRING COLOUR

Planting bulbs
Use bulbs to fill gaps in a newly planted or thinned out border. Spring-flowering bulbs, such as *Narcissi*, are useful because they look their best when shrubs and herbaceous plants are bare.

SUMMER COLOUR

Planting perennials
Use herbaceous perennials and a few annuals in spaces between young shrubs in a border to give an immediate, full look. As the shrubs mature, remove the plants as necessary.

SOWING ANNUALS
● **Planting times** Try sowing some traditionally spring-sown annuals in autumn instead. This can often result in a long, sustained flowering period.

USING CONTAINERS
● **Planting pots** Bring temporary colour to a border with planted-up containers. Bury the pots up to their rims in the soil, or stand them in the border, making sure that the bases are hidden by the foliage of nearby plants.
● **Autumn colour** Use pots of autumn crocus and *Colchicum* to brighten up borders in late summer or autumn.

COVERING SLOPES

Sloping areas often help to add interest to a garden and can provide useful and unusual opportunities for planting. If your garden varies in level, use this to your advantage. Slopes do, however, need careful planning and planting to avoid soil erosion and slippage.

DEALING WITH SLOPES
● **Terraces** One way of dealing with a steep slope is to terrace it. Build a series of retaining walls to support the soil.

Planting up a slope
If access to plants on a slope is difficult, choose plants that do not need much maintenance. You may need to use groundcover plants initially to help keep the soil in place (see p. 44).

STABILIZING SOIL
● **Retaining walls** Make sure that any wood you use to make retaining walls has been pressure-treated, and that it is sturdy enough to bear the weight of the soil.
● **Netting** Keep soil on a steep slope in place with netting (see p. 44). This is best left in place, although you can cut it away when plants are established if you prefer.
● **Adding mulch** Use a layer of mulch to disguise netting. The mulch will also help to keep the soil in place.

CHOOSING PLANTS
● **Wet soil** Consider planting moisture-loving plants at the bottom of a slope that is usually damp (see p. 44).

TIME-SAVING TIP

Disguising rubble
Instead of disposing of an unwanted pile of rubble, plant a climber to disguise it. Many climbers, including roses and clematis, grow well horizontally. If the rubble includes concrete, do not use lime-hating plants.

CREATING A WOODLAND GARDEN

Rather than struggling to radically alter a garden that is planted with trees, it may be more sensible to work with the trees and develop a woodland-style garden. If you have trees growing in a border, underplant them with suitable, dry shade-loving plants.

DEVELOPING A WOODLAND GARDEN

Tree trunk adds to woodland atmosphere

Foxgloves self-seed to produce more plants each year

Thick undergrowth provides shelter for wildlife

Looking natural

For a natural, woodland look, aim for plants that multiply by self-seeding. Include bulbs in your planting scheme, too. Choose plants with small, simple flowers and plain leaves.

PLANNING SHADY BEDS

● **Shrubs** Underplant large trees with shade-tolerant shrubs. Take care not to damage the trees' roots as you dig.
● **Groundcover** Choose herbaceous plants that thrive in shade. Some make useful groundcover for what would otherwise be bare ground.
● **Graduated shade** Ground at the edge of a tree canopy receives more light than that closer to the trunk. Choose your plants accordingly.

THINNING TREES

A large, mature tree in a garden is something very special. If, however, a tree causes problems by creating excessive shade, or due to branches that encroach too far towards a building, it may be possible to improve the situation without having to spoil the tree.

PRUNING TREES

● **Professional help** Always employ a specialist tree surgeon to carry out any tree surgery. This type of work can be dangerous and the outcome disastrous if it is carried out by somebody who has not been properly trained.
● **Height and spread** If a tree has outgrown its position and its lower branches are casting shade, it may be possible to have it "crown-reduced" to decrease both its height and its spread. If this is done properly, the tree will retain its natural shape after pruning but will be significantly smaller.

THE EFFECTS OF CROWN-LIFTING A TREE

Lowest branches have been removed

Low branches cast shade

An unpruned tree
This large tree may cause problems, especially if low branches are casting shade over an area of the garden, and access around the tree is restricted.

A crown-lifted tree
This tree has been crown-lifted. The lower branches only have been removed, which will improve access and allow more light into the garden.

RENOVATING PATIOS

A NEGLECTED PATIO can be very uninspiring. Common patio problems include weed infestation and loose, cracked slabs, which may be covered with slippery mosses and algae. Even subtle alterations can have a surprising impact.

CLEARING AND CLEANING PATIOS

B efore deciding exactly how you want to change a patio, remove any debris that has accumulated, and deal with stains and algal deposits. You will also need to eliminate weeds. This initial, basic work will go a long way towards the renovation of the patio.

TIDYING, CLEANING, AND REPAIRING PATIOS

● **Debris** Place any organic debris on a compost heap for future use in the garden.
● **Drips** If you have an external tap on a patio wall, check that it is not dripping constantly. The algal growths that cause slippery, green patches are often caused by drips or leaks.
● **Green slime** Clean unsightly and dangerous slippery slabs with a stiff brush and soapy water, or use a proprietary algae- and moss-killer.

● **Weeds** Always check the label before using a weedkiller, and carry out a test on a small piece of slab in an obscure corner. Old or porous stone or concrete slabs may be stained by certain products. If in doubt, handweed the area.
● **Repairs** If possible, mend or replace any cracked slabs (see p. 167). If you cannot buy matching replacements, swap damaged slabs in prominent places with perfect ones from less noticeable areas.

REMOVING WEEDS

Using weedkillers
Weeds may appear between patio slabs – or in cracks in broken slabs. Use a watering can with a special attachment to apply liquid weedkiller (see p. 97).

SOFTENING PATIOS

A n established patio that is very angular can look harsh and uninviting. Slabs on a new patio that have not yet mellowed as a result of weathering can also have a similar effect on the area as a whole. A few plants, and a variety of materials, can make all the difference.

COVERING A WALL

Planting in a patio
Bring colour and shape to a bare patio wall by lifting a nearby slab and planting a climber or wall shrub. Fix a support to the wall, and tie in any young stems.

CHOOSING MATERIALS

Mixing and matching
Try combining different materials for a soft, interesting effect. Bricks, paving stones, and gravel, or bricks and cobble stones, look good together.

ADDING INTEREST

● **Containers** Use pots, tubs, and other containers to brighten up and soften a patio, particularly one that has no plants growing in it.
● **Focal point** Add a small statue or a water feature (see p. 133). Bubbling or cascading water, or a striking statue, will draw the eye away from plain, stark areas.
● **Wall shrubs** Choose shrubs that benefit from the protection of a wall. Wall shrubs will soon add colour and interest, and are generally more suitable for small patios than wide-spreading climbers.

PLANTING IN PATIOS

Broken slabs or sections of a patio can be removed with a spade or trowel, enabling you to plant directly into the soil beneath.

Undamaged paving may also benefit from selective planting, introducing new colours, shapes, and textures to liven up a bare patio.

PLANTING BETWEEN PATIO SLABS

● **Removing mortar** Use a chisel or a screwdriver to scrape out any debris, moss, or old mortar that remains between paving slabs.

● **Forking soil** Remove any hardcore with a spade, then fork over the soil beneath lightly to relieve compaction. This will aid drainage.

● **Adding scent** Try to include some plants with fragrant flowers or scented foliage. Choose plants that grow happily in a confined space.

1 Insert the blade of a spade or trowel in a gap between paving slabs. Work the blade so that it digs in lower than the base of a slab, ease it beneath, and lever out the slab. Dig out any hardcore or sand.

2 Loosen the soil around the edges of the hole, and dispose of it. Add plenty of good garden soil, together with compost or well-rotted manure and some general fertilizer. Mix together well.

3 Plant shrubs or perennials following the normal method (see p. 47). Make sure that they are at the correct depth, and tease out the roots if necessary. Add a few bulbs if you wish, and water well.

CARING FOR PLANTS

Patio plants need special attention. Many patios are in sunny positions, which means that temperatures can become high during the summer. Additionally, patio paving quickly depletes the area of moisture and nutrients.

● **Watering** To keep patio plants fresh, water them regularly and thoroughly. Add mulch to help retain moisture around the plants' roots.

● **Feeding** Feed patio plants throughout the growing season with a weak liquid fertilizer. Alternatively, apply a granular general fertilizer once a year (see p. 86).

● **Pruning** Occasional pruning may be necessary to keep a plant's growth in check once it is established.

TRANSFORMING A PATIO

● **Improving soil** Never skimp on soil preparation before planting in a patio. Any soil beneath a patio will probably contain very few nutrients or beneficial microorganisms (see p. 42). The soil may also be badly compacted.

● **Winter interest** Include a few evergreen plants with variegated leaves for added interest during winter.

● **Unsuitable plants** Do not choose plants that are too invasive, or any that may cast unwanted shade. Avoid plants with vigorous root systems, since roots may start to push up the patio in future years. Steer clear of thorny plants and those that are prone to aphid infestations in places where people gather.

BRIGHT IDEA

Ageing a patio
If you want to give your new patio a weathered look, paint the paving slabs with natural yoghurt or liquid manure. This will encourage the growth of mosses and algae on the surface of the slabs.

USING RAISED BEDS

Break up the monotony of a large patio area with a permanent raised bed. This can be planted with climbers and trailing plants to introduce both height and colour. By selecting the appropriate soil, you will be able to grow plants that would not thrive in your garden soil.

MAKING RAISED BEDS ON PATIOS

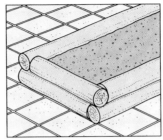

Using bricks
If you are building a raised bed with bricks, make sure that they are frostproof. Choose bricks that match any others that are nearby so that the bed blends in well with its surroundings.

Using logs
Logs that have been pressure-treated with clear wood preservative make a long-lasting, rustic-style raised bed. Use rustproof galvanized nails to join the logs together.

MAKING AND PLANTING

- **Using concrete** Make an inexpensive raised bed with concrete blocks. If you want to grow lime-hating plants, line the sides of the bed with butyl or heavy-duty polythene. Alternatively, paint the interior with several coats of bitumen.
- **Drainage** Always make drainage holes in the base of a raised bed, and line the sides to prevent soil from spilling on to the patio.
- **Choosing plants** To disguise hard edges, select a number of plants that will trail down the sides of a raised bed.

ENHANCING SUNKEN PATIOS

Create planting areas around a sunken patio by building retaining walls and planting in on top of them. Use materials that are the same as existing materials in that part of the garden. Ensure that there is good access between the sunken patio and the rest of the garden.

PLANTING AREAS AROUND SUNKEN PATIOS

- **Grass or flowers** Use a small, raised bed behind a retaining wall for planting annuals and perennials, or for grassing over.
- **Colour** Use trailing plants to mask patio edges. Choose evergreens for interest all year around, and select other plants to provide seasonal colour.

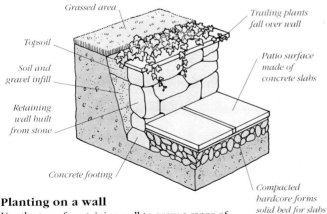

Grassed area

Topsoil

Soil and gravel infill

Retaining wall built from stone

Concrete footing

Trailing plants fall over wall

Patio surface made of concrete slabs

Compacted hardcore forms solid bed for slabs

Planting on a wall
Use the top of a retaining wall to grow a range of plants, but first make sure that there is a decent depth of topsoil on top of the infill behind the wall. For best results, choose shallow-rooting plants.

TRADITIONAL TIP

Providing drainage
Retaining brick walls do not allow excess water from the soil to drain away. Prevent waterlogging by making a "weep hole" in the lowest layer of bricks. To do this, leave a few joints empty of mortar. Ensure that weep holes are kept clear of debris.

CREATING TEMPORARY PLANTINGS

Containers of every size or shape, whether made from plastic, terracotta, stone, or lead, can be used to transform a patio instantly.

Containers can be moved around with each new season and planted up to provide colour, interest, and fragrance (see p. 70–71).

PLANTING A TALL CONTAINER

Make good use of unsightly rubble to stabilize container

1 Stabilize a tall container by placing rubble or large stones at the bottom. This is important when a container is to be used on a patio, because it is likely to be knocked over if not weighted down.

2 To save on compost, find a separate plastic pot that fits snugly into the top of the container. Fill it with compost, and plant it up (see p. 66). The pot can be removed easily for replanting when necessary.

USING CONTAINERS
● **Maintenance** Most shrubs, and some small, slow-growing climbers, can be grown in containers on a patio. To keep them in good condition, water and feed them regularly (see p. 69). You may also need to prune the plants frequently.
● **Moving containers** As soon as the plants in a container are past their best, move the container to an inconspicuous or hidden part of the patio. Position another container that is full of flowering plants in the same place.
● **Introducing water** Use a large, watertight half barrel to make a water feature that you can position in a corner of the patio (see p. 134).

USING BROKEN AND EMPTY POTS

There is no need to throw away broken containers. You can put them to good use by planting them up and using them on a patio or in the garden. If you plant them up in the correct way, and use the right kind of plants, cracks and missing chunks can be disguised.

DISGUISING DAMAGE
● **Positioning pots** Hide scratches, a missing piece, or a crack on a large pot by positioning a smaller, planted-up container in front of it.
● **Trailing plants** Use trailing annuals such as *Lobelia erinus* or perennials such as *Aubrieta* to conceal any broken or chipped edges on pots. Give them a foliar feed (see p. 86) after planting up to encourage them to grow quickly.

USING EMPTY POTS
● **Decorated pots** Try grouping glazed, painted, or stencilled pots (see p. 79) together for an effective display of empty pots.

USING A BROKEN POT

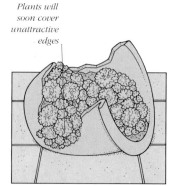

Plants will soon cover unattractive edges

Planting a broken pot
Lay a broken pot on its side, and plant it up with *Sempervivum*. These plants grow well in sparse, dry conditions and will soon grow over any broken edges.

GROUPING EMPTY POTS

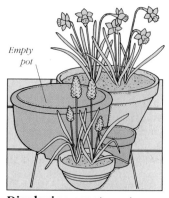

Empty pot

Displaying empty pots
Use empty pots – either on their own or grouped with planted-up containers – to create an original display. Change the arrangement from time to time.

BUILDING A BARBECUE

A patio can be an ideal place for a barbecue. Although you can buy a barbecue from a shop or a garden centre, building your own is a simple and cheap alternative. It also allows you to incorporate features that many barbecues do not have, such as a good-sized worktop.

CONSIDERING BARBECUE FEATURES

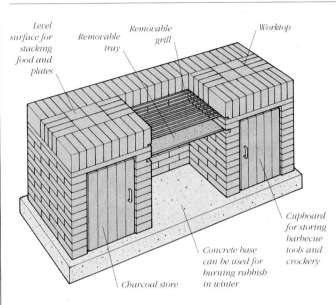

Level surface for stacking food and plates

Removable tray

Removable grill

Worktop

Concrete base can be used for burning rubbish in winter

Charcoal store

Cupboard for storing barbecue tools and crockery

Constructing and siting a barbecue
A sturdily constructed barbecue is useful on any patio. Choose the right spot and the right materials to ensure that it blends in with its surroundings.

DESIGNING A BARBECUE
- **Grilling racks** Build your barbecue to fit standard-sized metal grilling racks so that they can be replaced easily.
- **Access** Position a barbecue so that there is easy access to the house and to any seating area. Do not site it in the middle of a patio where children may play.
- **Support** If you are not sure how well a patio was laid, build the barbecue on a concrete plinth to ensure that it will not sink into the patio.
- **Size** Always build a barbecue a little larger than you think you need it to be. A large barbecue will allow you to cater for a large outdoor party.
- **In-built incinerator** Design your barbecue so that it can also serve as an incinerator for burning leaves in winter. Lift off the grilling rack, and transfer it to the front of the barbecue to retain the rubbish.

LOCATING A BARBECUE
- **Reducing smells** Do not position a barbecue very close to the house; smoke and cooking smells may filter in.
- **Avoiding trees** Do not build a barbecue directly under a tree, which may be scorched if the heat becomes too intense. Trees may also attract insects, which could be a problem.
- **Considering others** Position a barbecue away from dividing walls or fences so that neighbours are not bothered by noise and smoke.
- **Seasonal use** Do not site a barbecue in a central position, since it may be used only for a small proportion of the year.

ADDING LIGHTING
- **Electricity supply** Install an electricity supply from the house to a weatherproof, sealable socket on the patio. This will enable you to install lighting for a barbecue.
- **Safety** To avoid potential dangers, bury an electricity cable underground. If this is not possible, run the cable along an outside wall – do not string it along a fence or hedge.

WARNING!
Always take great care when lighting a barbecue. Follow instructions, and stand well back after lighting. Never use petrol to light a barbecue.

MAINTENANCE

To keep a barbecue hygienic and in good condition, you need to clean it thoroughly after each use. Clear up all fat spillages and ash, and throw away any debris that may attract vermin.

- **Removing fat** Scrub off fat deposits with a stiff brush and a strong solution of washing-up liquid.
- **Caring for metal** As soon as the barbecue season is over, clean the racks and tools thoroughly. When dry, rub them with a rag soaked in cooking oil. Store them in a dry place to minimize rusting. Scrub well before reusing.

TRANSFORMING PATHS AND STEPS

WELL-CONSTRUCTED PATHS AND STEPS should be looked after, since rebuilding them can be time-consuming. If they are unsightly, there are a number of ways to alter their appearance that do not require you to start from scratch.

SOFTENING EDGES

The severe edges and straight lines of some paths and steps can look out of place among the gentle, natural shapes of a garden. These structures may benefit from a new, fresh design or inspirational planting, transforming them into useful and attractive garden features.

PERFUMING A PATH

Planting a lavender hedge
To add scent and shape to a garden path, plant a low hedge of lavender along its edge. If brushed against or crushed slightly, the foliage will perfume the air. Plant in a sunny, dry site.

SUITABLE PLANTS FOR EDGING

Arenaria spp. (most),
Armeria maritima,
Aubrieta deltoidea (and cvs.),
Aurinia spp.,
Campanula poscharskyana,
Dianthus deltoides,
Draba spp.,
Erinus alpinus,
Helianthemum spp.,
Iberis sempervirens,
Phlox (dwarf spp.),
Portulaca grandiflora,
Salvia officinalis,
Saxifraga (including
'Hi Ace' and 'Penelope'),
Sempervivum montanum,
Thymus spp. and cvs.
including *T. x citriodorus*
'Anderson's Gold',
Viola odorata.

PLANTING ALONG A PATH

Creating gentle shapes
Make a rippling, gentle path by planting bushy, sprawling plants in adjacent borders. Consider plunging terracotta pots at the edge of the path to break up straight lines further.

LOOKING AFTER EDGES

● **Repairing edges** Damaged paving can be dangerous, particularly if located in the centre of a path or steps. Repair promptly (see p. 166).
● **Raising edges** Construct a raised edge along the sides of a gravel path to prevent gravel from flicking on to a lawn and damaging a lawnmower. It will also stop soil from borders from spilling on to a path.
● **Planting edges** Path edges may become damaged with use. Remove the broken brick or slab, scoop out the soil beneath, add a new layer of compost, and plant a bushy, trailing evergreen in the space. The plant will spread and conceal the area below.

DISGUISING EDGES

● **Featuring stones** Conceal damage or alter the outline of a path by using large, rounded, or coloured stones to create an attractive edging.
● **Planting seasonally** Planting along a path's edge need not be permanent. Replace seasonal bedding at least twice a year to ensure constant colour and to prevent plants from becoming too invasive.
● **Adding colour** Lighten a gloomy, dark path or steps by filling the surrounding borders with evergreens with cream, yellow, and brightly variegated foliage for year-round colour.

TRADITIONAL TIP

Laying brick edges
Make an inexpensive, striking edging to a path with bricks. Dig a small trench along both sides of the path. Place each brick in its trench on its side, so that it rests on the point of one corner and leans on the neighbouring brick. Pack soil tightly around the bricks.

MAINTAINING GRAVEL PATHS

Gravel paths are inexpensive, easy to lay, and do not require specialist equipment to maintain. However, they can be difficult to walk on, are prone to invasion by weeds, and are not suitable for pronounced slopes because of the looseness of their surfaces.

LAYING A NEW PATH

Fitting a polythene base
Compact the soil, then create a raised edge with a strip of treated wood. Lay a polythene sheet over the soil to prevent the appearance of weeds. Spread gravel over the polythene with the back of a rake.

RENOVATING A PATH

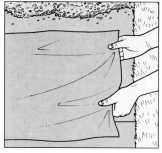

Removing gravel
Renovate an old path by laying sheets of polythene beneath the gravel. Work in sections along the path's length, raking the gravel away. Position the polythene sheets so that their edges overlap.

WORKING WITH GRAVEL

● **Selecting gravel** If children are likely to use a path, ensure that you lay smooth gravel that consists of well-rounded stones, such as pea gravel.
● **Creating drainage** Polythene underlay may prevent a path from draining properly, leading to waterlogging in wet weather. If this is a problem, replace the polythene with a layer of woven synthetic material that acts as a barrier against weeds but allows water to drain to the soil beneath.
● **Raking** Regularly rake gravel to level the surface of a path and redistribute the stones.

BRIGHTENING CONCRETE STEPS

Concrete forms a hardwearing and resilient surface, making it a popular material for the construction of steps. However, its bare, angular shape can look harsh and unattractive, and it rarely fits in well with surrounding garden features. Lighten this effect with clever planting.

IMPROVING STEPS

● **Featuring alpines** If steps are wide, plunge a few pots of cushion-forming alpines into piles of gravel at intervals along the length of the steps. Planting in the pots ensures that growth is restricted and makes it easy to remove the plants.
● **Stacking terracotta** Break up a long, wide flight of steps by stacking planted-up, weathered terracotta pots in groups along the edge of the treads.
● **Creating form** Add an air of formality to the base of steps with two carefully chosen container plants placed on either side of the step. Spiral or cone-shaped box plants and standard bay or rose trees planted in Versailles tubs or large, terracotta pots will make a striking, memorable display.

PLANTING FOR EASE

● **Using small pots** If steps are used infrequently, or the treads are deep, add colour with a number of small pots, which are portable and easy to move.

Planting containers
Place seasonal bedding plants – such as bulbs, annuals, and tender perennials – on steps. Replace these at intervals for year-round interest. Alternatives are clipped shrubs and herbs.

PLANTING FOR EFFECT

● **Softening steps** Plant up around steps to permanently soften their outline. Make sure that you choose plants that will not become too invasive.

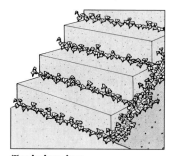

Training ivy
Plant small-leaved ivies in the soil adjacent to steps. Train the ivy along pieces of garden wire secured against the risers. Trim the ivy regularly to prevent it from growing over the treads.

TRANSFORMING WALLS

W ITH A LITTLE IMAGINATION, a wall can be transformed from a functional boundary marker into an exciting, vertical growing space, literally adding a new dimension to a garden. Train climbers and fruit trees for the best results.

COVERING WALLS

W hen building a wall, the height and shape of the design and the choice of building material will all affect how the finished structure blends in with its surroundings. If an old wall is unsightly, young fruit trees can be trained to make an attractive, productive covering.

FAN-TRAINING A FRUIT TREE AGAINST A WALL

Pruned laterals tied in to canes

New side shoots tied to canes and attached to wires

New side shoots are tied in

Stems have been pruned out

1 In early spring, select two laterals on a young fruit tree that are 30 cm (12 in) above ground level to form the main arms. Prune each one to 38 cm (15 in) and tie to a cane at a 40-degree angle. Prune the leader to just above the laterals.

2 The following year, in early spring, prune arms by a third to an outward-facing bud. In early summer, tie new side shoots to canes. Prune out any stems that develop below the two main arms or that point down or away from the wall.

3 In early summer, thin out excess stems to leave them 10–15 cm (4–6 in) apart. During summer, tie in side shoots, and pinch out any that overlap the main framework of arms. Prune fruiting shoots back to a new shoot at the base of the tree.

CREATING WALL SPACE

Designing a wall
Be adventurous when planning a wall. Consider incorporating a porthole or a gate that is large enough to walk through. This will introduce light to new areas of the garden and could encompass distant views.

IMPROVING WALLS
● **Stains** Discoloured bricks make a wall look unsightly. Scrub over the surface (see p. 164) before deciding if any further action is necessary.
● **Tending climbers** Thin out and prune back climbers. If they are straggly and not responding to care, replace them with young plants.
● **Screening a wall** Cover a wall with more than one climber. Choose plants with different flowering times – evergreen and deciduous – to ensure that the wall is screened for as much of the year as possible.
● **Fruit trees** If a wall is in a shady site but you would like to fan-train a fruit tree, plant a Morello cherry tree.

BRIGHT IDEA

Creating a new shape
To make a new climber that has put on uniform growth look more established and natural, trim it back unevenly to create an irregular, informal outline.

USING TRELLIS PANELS

Fixing trellis panels on to the side or top of a wall can be the answer to a variety of problems in a garden. They will provide privacy from neighbours, conceal eyesores, disguise damaged or discoloured surfaces, and increase the potential planting space in a garden.

INSTALLING TRELLIS

● **Material** If using trellis in a garden, choose a wooden frame. It will look good, is long lasting, and can support a greater weight than most plastic or plastic-coated frames.
● **Supports** Use planks of tannalized or pressure-treated timber to support a trellis. After cutting the timber or trellis, paint the surfaces with wood preservative.
● **Fittings** Use galvanized nails, screws, and other fittings to prevent rust.
● **Paint** Before fixing trellis on to a painted wall, apply a fresh coat of paint to the surface, and carry out any necessary repairs.

PROVIDING EASY ACCESS TO A WALL

1 To provide easy access to a wall for maintenance, attach pieces of timber, called battens, to the trellis and the wall. Fix hooks to both ends of the wall battens, and eyes to the ends of the trellis battens.

2 To secure the base of the trellis to the wall, fix hinges to the bottom of the trellis panel. Alternatively, fix a pair of hooks and eyes to the lower battens to make the complete removal of the panel easy.

PLANTING UP TRELLIS

Main shoots tied to trellis

Stable container of good depth

Supporting a climber
Use a triangular trellis to support a climber growing in a container. Before planting, place the trellis in the pot, then pack soil firmly around its base. Tie the top of the trellis to a wall, if necessary.

DESIGNING WITH TRELLIS

● **Adding colour** Brighten up a standard, golden-yellow wooden trellis by painting it with a coat of coloured wood preservative. Alternatively, mix together emulsion paint and clear wood preservative to create a unique colour.
● **Selecting colour** When painting a trellis, select a colour that either complements or dramatically contrasts with the garden furniture, structures, and nearby plants.
● **Choosing shape** Be adventurous when selecting new trellis panels. They are available in many different shapes and sizes. Alter the line of the top of a wall or screen with concave and convex panels, or use alternate square- and diamond-shaped pieces to bring variety to a garden.
● **Dividing trellis** Bring an air of formality to a garden by using ornamental trellis posts.

COVERING NEW TRELLIS

● **Annuals** In its first year, plant up a new, bare trellis with annual climbers. These will provide a good covering while the long-term planting is given time to become established. Just one season's growth of sweet peas and morning glory will have the desired effect.

Using a temporary display
Screen a new trellis with a selection of containers planted up with climbers, trailers, and tender perennials. These can be used elsewhere once any permanent planting has covered the trellis.

DESIGNING WITH SPECIAL EFFECTS

An ugly wall can be transformed by training climbers and fruit trees to cover it. Other clever devices can be used to make an area look perceptibly different. Use coloured paint, mirrors, and decoratively shaped trellis to create changes in a garden, both real and imaginary.

BRIGHTENING WALLS

● **Whitewash** If a garden is dark and gloomy, paint fences and walls with whitewash to bring light to the area.

● **Murals** Add a dimension to a garden by painting a mural on a flat, vertical surface. To increase the false sense of perspective, place a real pot by a painted one and match the colours of the plant with those in the mural.

● **Mediterranean style** Put sunny walls and fences to use by planting climbers that require the protection and warmth they provide. Add terracotta pots of geraniums, pelargoniums, and nasturtiums to create a Mediterranean feel.

ADDING DEPTH

Fixing decorative trellis
Add a sense of depth to a garden by fixing a trellis with a false perspective to a wall or other flat, vertical surface. Plant up the trellis with a sprawling climber, and position shrubs around it to increase the illusion of reality.

REFLECTING SPACE

Using a mirror
Fix a mirror to a wall or fence to increase light in a garden and give the impression of size and space. Ensure that its position offers an attractive reflection. Disguise mirror edges with timber, or plant with evergreen climbers.

USING ARCHES

An arch is often erected in the middle of a garden to link one area to another. It may also be randomly positioned, acting principally as a support for climbers. Fix an arch to a wall and create an arbour, immediately bringing shade, seclusion, and privacy to a garden.

POSITIONING AN ARCH

Creating an arbour
Place a metal or wooden arch against a wall, and train climbers up it to make an attractive garden feature. Convert it into an arbour or secluded seating area by placing a bench inside.

WORKING WITH AN ARCH

● **Outside room** Convert part of a garden into an outside room by including seating space for two or four in a sheltered arbour. Consider adding a small table if space permits.

● **Selection** Choose an arbour carefully if it is to be located in a prime position all year round. A wooden arch can look good in its own right and need not be covered with climbers. Treat regularly with wood preservative (see p. 162).

● **Position** Situate an arbour according to the amount of sun desired at the time you are most likely to use the garden – perhaps in the morning to eat a summer breakfast, or to enjoy the evening sun.

TRANSFORMING AN ARCH

● **Fragrance** When planning an arbour, include scented climbers in your summer planting scheme. If you are likely to use the area only in the evening, ensure that you select plants that remain fragrant during the evening.

● **Illusion** Add a mirror to the wall behind an arch to increase the feeling of space.

● **Hiding place** Link two arches together to create a miniature hideaway or summer play area for children.

● **Using evergreens** If an arbour is to be used in early spring, late autumn, or winter, make sure that it has a covering of attractive evergreens as well as seasonal climbers.

CONSTRUCTING SCREENS

A BEAUTIFUL GARDEN can be spoiled by an ugly view or the intrusion of other houses. Necessary but unattractive items, such as dustbins, clotheslines, and sheds, can have the same effect. With planning, these can be screened from view.

CONCEALING UNSIGHTLY FEATURES

Take a considered and objective look at your garden from a variety of positions, including inside the house, on the patio, and at the back door. Make a list of all the objects you would like to conceal or obscure; this can be achieved in a number of different ways.

DECORATING A DIVIDER

Covering a screen
Plant up both sides of a trellis or fence panel to make the most of the growing area and to create an effective and attractive screen.

LOOKING AFTER PLANTS

● **Positioning** Stagger plantings along the two sides of a dividing screen to reduce possible interference between the root systems. This will also help to reduce competition for water and nutrients.
● **Maintenance** Feed the soil at the base of a densely planted screen, and ensure that it is always kept moist. Mulch regularly to provide the best possible soil conditions for plant growth.
● **Growth** Keep plant growth in check to ensure that a dividing screen does not become too wide and encroach into adjacent areas.

SUITABLE PLANTS

Berberis darwinii,
B. thunbergii,
Corylus avellana,
Cotoneaster franchetii,
C. lacteus,
Crataegus monogyna,
Euonymus japonicus,
Forsythia x *intermedia,*
Fuchsia magellanica,
Garrya elliptica,
Ilex aquifolium,
Pittosporum tenuifolium,
Potentilla fruticosa,
Prunus spinosa, Pyracantha,
Rosa 'Nevada',
Rosa 'Roseraie de l'Hay',
Rosa rugosa,
Viburnum opulus
'Compactum'.

MONEY-SAVING TIP

Growing an annual screen
Plant a cheerful annual screen using sunflowers. Grow runner beans up the stems to add density and provide a source of fresh vegetables.

HIDING A TREE STUMP

Planting a climber
Always try to remove a tree stump, since it may encourage diseases such as honey fungus. If this is impossible, treat the stump with a proprietary solution. After 12 weeks, plant a climber to scramble over the stump, covering it in flowers and foliage.

CREATING A SCREEN

● **Appearance** Use sections of trellis to make a screen around dustbins and unsightly household objects (see p. 30). Make sure that the enclosed area is large enough for easy access once climbers have grown to their full size.
● **Scent** When screening potentially noxious objects, such as compost heaps, wormeries, and liquid-manure containers, plant up a selection of scented climbers to act as natural air fresheners.
● **Bamboo** To create a striking screen of foliage, plant up clumps of bamboo. Their densely packed stems make them ideal for screening.

CONCEALING SERVICE AREAS

No matter how large a garden is, you will probably want to fill every spare corner of it with plants. However, there will inevitably be items that take up valuable gardening space and create potential eyesores. Use temporary and permanent screens to conceal these objects.

POSITIONING AND PLANTING UP SCREENS

● **Using trellis** Position trellis panels to hide unsightly items, ensuring that they are strong enough to support climbers. To add strength, construct a frame around the structure, using wooden posts and battens.

● **Using evergreens** Trellis can be used on its own, but it is most effective and attractive if plants are scrambling over it. Include evergreens in your planting scheme to ensure year-round concealment.

Partitioning

Use trellis panels and a trellis door to partition off a large, unsightly area in a garden. Plant up the trellis lightly so that the screen and the area beyond merge in with the rest of the garden.

SELECTING A DISGUISE

● **Metal covers** Use containers to conceal metal service covers. Make sure they are lightweight so that they can be moved quickly in an emergency. If you would like to feature a heavy container, make it easy to move by fixing wheels to its base, or stand it on a wheeled platform.
● **Pipes** Group several different pots together to hide a cesspit or septic tank pipes.
● **Large eyesores** Obtrusive oil tanks and gas cylinders are often situated close to houses. Use trellis, wattle hurdles, or fence panels as screens, and plant up with climbers.

CONCEALING DUSTBINS

Most buildings have at least one dustbin, sometimes more. Both these and large, unsightly, wheeled plastic bins can be easily disguised. When using screens, remember to avoid the temptation to thoroughly conceal dustbins, since access must be unrestricted.

MAKING SCREENS

● **Small screen** To make a simple and effective screen, hiding a single dustbin from view, attach one wattle hurdle or trellis panel at right angles to an existing fence or wall.
● **Large screen** Use trellis, wattle hurdles, willow panels, or fence panels to make an open-ended partition behind which dustbins can be stored. Ensure that the area is densely planted in the summer, to keep the sun off the bins.
● **Scented screen** Plant up a bin area with fragrant flowers. Mix strongly scented roses, jasmine, and honeysuckle with other climbers, and complete the colourful and perfumed effect with an annual sowing of sweet peas.

DESIGNING WITH BRICKS

Building for permanence

Construct a permanent dustbin screen from bricks, leaving holes for ventilation. Allow for access, but keep the top low to prevent animals from removing lids. Build a trough above, and plant up with trailing or fragrant foliage.

LOCATING A CONTAINER

Using temporary colour

To create an attractive, temporary display, use a large, planted-up container to partially hide a dustbin. Slip a section of wattle hurdle or a trellis panel between the container and the dustbin for additional concealment.

USING HEDGES AS SCREENS

In some cases, a natural, living screen or divider will be more appropriate to a particular area than a constructed one. A hedge makes an attractive and long-lasting screen. However, to look good, it is essential that a hedge is correctly planted, maintained, and clipped.

CONCEALING THE SPARSE BASES OF HEDGES

● **Using a trellis** If the base of a hedge becomes sparse and leggy, construct a low trellis to hide the area. This can then be used as a support for climbers.

● **Partial screen** If you do not want to completely conceal the area beneath a hedge, partially obscure it with a selection of herbaceous plants.

Positioning a screen
Position a fence so that it screens only the bare base of a hedge. When digging holes for the support posts, make sure that you avoid the roots of the hedge.

Selecting plants
If the soil beneath a hedge is dry, plant drought-tolerant plants and bulbs. Water and feed regularly to ensure that the plants and hedge do not compete for nutrients.

PROMOTING GROWTH

To promote even and sustained growth in a formal or informal hedge, it is essential that careful trimming is regularly carried out.

● **Deciduous hedges** To achieve an attractive, dense deciduous hedge, ensure that it is trimmed twice annually with shears or an electrical hedgetrimmer, taking care to keep the flex out of the way.
● **Coniferous hedges** Treat conifers with care. When pruning in the first years, remove only the lateral branches until a hedge reaches its desired height. Do not cut back hard, since the inner, often dead, brown foliage may be revealed. With little replacement growth from these stems, it will be difficult to disguise the damage.

TRIMMING HEDGES

● **Nests** Avoid trimming a hedge when birds are nesting. Wait at least two weeks, until the nesting period is over. The hedge will not suffer, and you will help to preserve the next generation of garden birds.
● **Shaping** Formal hedging looks messy if cut unevenly or at the wrong angle. Use a taut piece of string tied between two upright posts to check that a hedge is level, and use a template to shape the top.
● **Clippings** Put clippings to good use by incorporating them into a compost heap. Do not do this if a hedge is known to be diseased.
● **Silver hedges** If a hedge such as laurel or *Prunus* spp. is prone to silver leaf disease, restrict its annual trim to the summer months.

LOOKING AFTER HEDGES

● **Maintaining** Feed and water hedges regularly, since they are constantly clipped and grow rapidly, using up large amounts of energy.
● **Trimming** To ensure that the top of a hedge is cut flat and level, keep shear blades parallel to the line of the hedge.
● **Roadside hedges** Before winter, position polythene screens around any hedges that are planted along a road. This should prevent the roots from taking up de-icing salt and the foliage from being scorched.
● **Climbers** Erect a system of straining wires between posts spaced at intervals along the length of a sparse hedge. Train twining climbers along them to create a curtain of colour and foliage.

MONEY-SAVING TIP

Restoring a hawthorn
To rejuvenate a hawthorn hedge that has become sparse and leggy at the base, bend a number of pliable stems downwards. Peg these into the soil using small metal hooks. In time, these stems will take root and fill out the base of the hedge.

SCREENING SHEDS

A shed is a practical and often essential addition to a garden, offering a work area and storage space for tools, bulbs, seeds, and other items. However, even if in good condition, a shed is a potential eyesore and may detract from the overall effect of garden planting.

CREATING A SCREEN USING TRELLIS PANELS

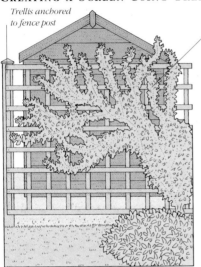

Trellis anchored to fence post

Climber trained to cover trellis

Building a screen
Erect a trellis panel to create a perfect screen for a functional shed. Use fence posts to support the structure, and ensure that it is positioned clear of the sides of the shed, allowing access for maintenance. When planting, choose a climber that will not outgrow the trellis.

MAKING SCREENS
● **Using chicken wire** Create a freestanding, column-shaped screen by rolling up a length of galvanized chicken wire. Train climbers over and through it.
● **Using natural materials** Use willow panels or hazel-wattle hurdles to make a functional and attractive screen. Although expensive, these are well suited to an informal or cottage-style garden.

PREVENTING WOOD ROT
● **Protecting screens** Ensure that the base of a wooden screen is raised 5–7.5 cm (2–3 in) above the soil to avoid damp and prevent wood rot.

ENHANCING SHEDS

Screening a shed can be impractical if access is limited in any way. In such a situation, consider highlighting the shed rather than hiding it. With careful planting and grouped selections of striking containers, an old shed can become an attractive, integral part of a garden.

MAINTAINING SHEDS
● **Reroofing** Sustain the usefulness of an old shed and improve its appearance by reroofing using new felt and galvanized fittings (see p. 160).
● **Renovating** Scrub off algae and other debris from the timber, and allow the shed to dry thoroughly before painting with a coat of wood preservative. Consider using a coloured preservative or adding paint to camouflage discoloured areas and create a brand new look.
● **Cleaning** Check for wood decay, and treat and refill the wood if necessary (see p. 162). At the same time, wipe the glazing with a proprietary cleaning agent to remove the build up of debris.

PLANTING FOR COLOUR

Positioning containers
Decorate a shed with hanging baskets and windowboxes packed full of annual flowers and trailing foliage. Strategically placed terracotta pots and other containers will help to hide damaged and discoloured areas.

TRAINING CLIMBERS

Creating shapes
Grow a climber directly up and over the roof of a shed. This will look striking but, since it may encourage deterioration of the timber, is best kept for old sheds that have a limited function and life expectancy.

OBSCURING UNSIGHTLY VIEWS

Even when every effort is made to design, create, and maintain an attractive garden, the surrounding environment often presents a permanent and unsightly view. Counter this effect by hiding and obscuring unattractive objects with natural and constructed screens.

PLANNING A SECLUDED GARDEN

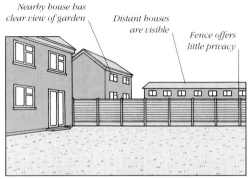

Nearby house has clear view of garden

Distant houses are visible

Fence offers little privacy

Assessing the surrounding area
Neighbouring buildings sometimes overlook a house and have a clear view into the garden. These buildings may also be prominently visible from the garden, despite a high, wooden fence. Privacy and a sense of seclusion are required in a built-up area.

ADDING HEIGHT AND SHAPE

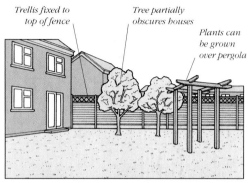

Trellis fixed to top of fence

Tree partially obscures houses

Plants can be grown over pergola

Positioning permanent structures
Trees give shape to a garden and conceal unsightly views. A pergola and trellis panels fitted along the top of a fence bring shelter and seclusion to a garden. These permanent structures can be planted up for additional shape and colour.

ADDING TRELLIS EXTENSIONS

Raising the height of a garden's boundaries is an inexpensive and relatively easy way to conceal unsightly views and ensure privacy. Trellis sections can be attached to the top of a wooden fence or brick wall, then planted up with annual and evergreen climbers.

PERMANENT EXTENSION

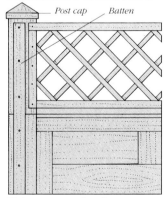

Post cap *Batten*

Using a wooden batten
To extend a fence using wood, remove the post cap, and nail the fence and an extension post together with a strip of wooden batten. Using galvanized nails, attach the trellis panel to the post, and replace the cap.

REMOVABLE EXTENSION

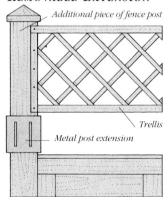

Additional piece of fence post

Trellis

Metal post extension

Using a metal fixture
Metal post extensions are quick to fit and allow easy replacement of trellis panels. Remove the post cap, and slide the extension on to the post. Insert the additional piece of fence post, attach the trellis, and refit the cap.

WORKING WITH TRELLIS
- **Changing outlines** Alter the outline of a fence or wall by fixing concave or convex trellis sections to its top.
- **Limiting shade** Before extending the height of a garden boundary, assess how much light will be lost. Limit the amount of shade by fitting trellis panels and planting a few small-leaved climbers. Avoid creating a wall of foliage.
- **Protecting wood** Once trellis is in place, treat the fence with a coat of wood preservative to help blend the new timber in with the old.
- **Planting** To conceal the joints connecting a fence and trellis, plant up fast-growing climbers along with the permanent planting scheme.

PLANTING TREES

An established tree will bring a sense of stability and permanence to a garden. Its height will create shade and privacy, and its shape can significantly alter the overall look. When planting a tree, position it with care where it is least likely to cause damage.

USING TREES FOR SHADE AND PRIVACY

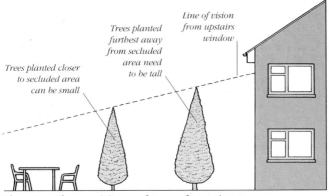

Line of vision from upstairs window

Trees planted furthest away from secluded area need to be tall

Trees planted closer to secluded area can be small

Planning the positions of trees for privacy

Carefully consider the position, shape, and overall design of your garden before planting trees. Take into account the direction and path of the sun, and decide whether you want to divide one section of the garden from another, create a secluded, shaded seating area, or conceal part of the garden from the house. Conversely, you may want to screen certain rooms in the house, such as bedrooms or bathrooms, from general view.

SELECTING TREES

● **Seasonal use** Plant up deciduous trees in an area that is used only in the summer. These will provide screening from late spring to autumn.
● **Size** To partially obscure objects from view, use small trees and shrubs to create a manageable natural screen.
● **Roots** Check the growing habit of a tree before purchasing it, particularly if your garden soil is clay-based. In certain conditions, tree roots can cause major damage to structural foundations.
● **Suckers** Some trees look good but produce suckers. If you cannot spare the time required to remove suckers, avoid planting *Prunus* spp. and cvs., lilac, and sumach.

USING PERGOLAS

A pergola adds height and diversity to a garden and can provide an attractive area for vertical planting. At the same time, it will create a decorative division in the garden that can also serve as a screen to conceal functional areas, damaged surfaces, and unsightly features.

CREATING COLOUR

Planting climbers

Heavily plant up a pergola with foliage and flowers. The climbers may take several years to become fully established but, if they are given adequate attention and care, it will be worth the wait.

FEATURING PERGOLAS

● **Purchasing** When buying a pergola, make sure that its construction is strong enough to support the climbers in your planting scheme.
● **Constructing** Use pressure-treated or tannalized timber for a pergola. Transform the appearance of the completed structure with a coat of non-toxic, coloured wood preservative, which will not damage plants.
● **Renovating** When replanting an old pergola, take the opportunity to replace timber that is broken or rotten, and consider painting the repaired structure a different colour.

SUITABLE PLANTS

*Akebia quinata,
Berberidopsis corallina,
Campsis grandiflora,
C. radicans,
Celastrus,
Clematis* spp. and cvs.,
*Hedera,
Humulus lupulus* 'Aureus',
*Jasminum officinale,
Laburnum,
Lardizabala biternata,
Lonicera* x *americana,
L.* x *brownii,
Passiflora caerulea,
Rosa* spp. and rambling and climbing cvs.,
*Tropaeolum speciosum,
Vitis coignetiae,
Wisteria.*

ADDING HEIGHT AND PERSPECTIVE

THERE ARE MANY DIFFERENT ISSUES to be considered when planning a garden. Introducing height adds a new dimension to a garden, while adjusting the perspective can make a garden appear narrow and long or wide and short.

INTRODUCING HEIGHT WITH ARCHES

Trees and large shrubs can be used to add height and shape to a garden. Alternative permanent features, such as arches, pergolas, and decorative posts, can also be arranged to create points of interest. In a small garden, just one feature may alter the look.

SELECTING AN ARCH STYLE

Horizontal beams provide support for climbers

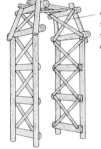

Diagonal struts strengthen arch

Pointed arch
Construct a pointed, rustic arch from unplaned timber. Use galvanized nails or screws to fix the timber pieces to each other.

"Cottage-style" arch
Diagonal struts of unplaned timber add strength and support to an arch. Its "cottage-style" look is suitable for an informal garden.

PLANNING ARCHES
● **Height** When building an arch, make sure that it is tall enough for a person to walk through in comfort. Consider the types of flower that you are intending to plant up. If they are pendulous, incorporate this into the measurements, and make the arch even taller.
● **Width** If a garden arch is to be walked through, make sure that it is wide enough to allow two people to pass through side by side.
● **Planting** Use cross beams to increase the strength of an arch, making it suitable for supporting heavy climbers.

PLANTING A WALKWAY

Training climbers
Create an attractive walkway by training lightweight climbers over a series of wooden or plastic arches. Consider planting annuals or ornamental, runner, or edible climbing beans.

CREATING NEW ARCHES
● **Building** To prolong the life of an archway, assemble with tannalized or pressure-treated timber. Stabilize an upright arch post by setting it in concrete, or use galvanized metal supports (see p. 163).
● **Transformation** Transform a new arch with fast-growing annuals such as *Eccremocarpus scaber, Ipomoea, Rhodochiton atrosanguineum,* and *Thunbergia alta.*
● **Planting beans** To make an "edible" arch, plant up runner or climbing beans with different flower colours.
● **Planting roses** When buying a rose for an arch, select a rambler; this has more flexible stems than a climbing rose.

TRADITIONAL TIP

Dividing a garden
Use a trellis arch to divide a garden into two distinct sections. Plant a screen of evergreen shrubs on either side.

USING PLANT SUPPORTS

Most climbing plants need to be trained on supports, such as tree trunks, bamboo-cane wigwams, and obelisks. Whether these supports occur naturally or are added to a garden, their height and shape can be used to create high points and enhance existing features.

USING A WIGWAM

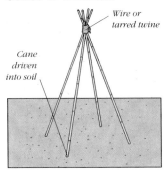

Wire or tarred twine

Cane driven into soil

Creating a pillar of colour
Bamboo-cane wigwams are used traditionally to support runner beans. Plant up a wigwam with annual climbers to bring pillars of striking colour to a border.

USING AN OBELISK

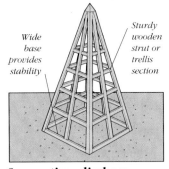

Wide base provides stability

Sturdy wooden strut or trellis section

Supporting climbers
An obelisk will look good in its own right and can be left outside through the winter. Use it to support climbers and create a permanent, attractive display.

MAINTAINING WOOD
● **Preserving** Treat a wooden structure regularly with a coat of wood preservative. Use pressure-treated timber and galvanized fittings for repairs to further extend its life.
● **Painting** Enhance the appearance of a plant and help to make its support attractive in winter by applying a brightly coloured paint to the support.

CREATING SHAPES
● **Planting** Use a dense climber with attractive foliage, such as a variegated ivy, to create a solid, three-dimensional shape or screen.

PLANTING CLIMBERS

Evergreen and annual climbers can be used both to emphasize the height of an object and to conceal or alter the appearance of an eyesore. Some climbing plants need support in the form of trellis panels or wires, while others may be grown over an object without support.

COVERING A TREE

Transforming a dead tree
Always try to remove a dead or dying tree, which may pose a hazard. If this is not possible, cut away the branches, leaving only the trunk standing. Grow a climber or two over the tree, adding wire supports if necessary.

CHOOSING SUPPORTS
● **Temporary** Form an arch from chicken wire, and use it to support lightweight, annual climbers for a colourful, temporary summer display.
● **Long-term** Use a sturdy wire frame to train climbers or create unusual topiary shapes. Although not an instant or even quick effect, the frame will form a stylish, long-term plant support.
● **Using hose pipe** To support a lightweight plant, make a small arch using two wooden pegs and a length of old hose pipe. Place a peg into one end of the pipe, and push in so that only a third of the peg remains visible. Repeat with the second peg. Drive one end into the ground, form an arch with the hose, and secure the other end.

GREEN TIP

Transforming a post
If an old metal post or clothesline is embedded in concrete and cannot be removed easily, use it as a vertical support for a climber. The denseness of the climber's growth will hide the post.

DECEIVING THE EYE WITH DESIGN

When designing a garden, consider the effect you wish to create, and decide whether you would like to alter the shape and the perspective of the garden.

● **Divisions** To make a long garden seem wider and shorter, partially divide it up with trellis sections. Alternatively, use shrubs and other bushy plants to create a natural divider.

● **Rooms** Divide a garden into a series of different "rooms", each with a different theme or style. A garden will seem to be larger than it really is if it is not possible to see all areas from one spot.

● **Hedges** To alter the perspective in a short garden bordered by a hedge, cut the top of the hedge slightly lower along the back or far end of the garden. This will give the illusion that the hedge is further away than it actually is.

● **Secret places** Create alcoves and arbours around walls or fences to increase the sense of hidden and unexplored areas.

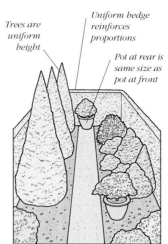

Trees are uniform height

Uniform hedge reinforces proportions

Pot at rear is same size as pot at front

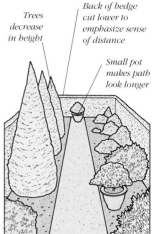

Trees decrease in height

Back of hedge cut lower to emphasize sense of distance

Small pot makes path look longer

Planting for a natural view
Retain the natural perspective of a garden by considered repetition of heights and shapes. Lay a parallel-sided path, and flank it with trees of an equal height. Position a planted-up container near the house, and position another at the end of the garden.

Exaggerating distance
To exaggerate the natural perspective of a garden, lay a tapering path, and plant it up with trees that are progressively shorter towards the back of the garden. Position a pot in the background that is the same style but smaller than a pot in the foreground.

USING PLANTS TO SUGGEST SIZE

The design of a garden can create illusions, and the apparent size of an area can be altered inexpensively by careful planting. When purchasing a plant, make sure that you consider its colour and shape, since these characteristics can increase or decrease the sense of space.

INCREASING LENGTH

Working with colour
To increase the apparent length of a border, position brightly coloured flowers and foliage in the foreground, and frame these against darker colours. Plant pale colours at the back of a garden.

CREATING SPACE

Featuring foliage shapes
To suggest space in a small garden, position plants with large, flamboyant foliage and bold outlines at the front of a border. Where possible, vary the colours for additional emphasis.

CHOOSING PLANTS

● **Pastels** Locate pale or pastel colours at the back of a border to create a sense of distance.
● **Greys** To make a border seem large, include a variety of plants with grey foliage.
● **Hot colours** Reduce a sense of distance in a garden by planting fiery, hot-coloured flowers. This will bring these plants to the foreground.
● **Glossy foliage** Brighten a dull corner with glossy foliage that reflects the light, such as that of *Ajuga, Fatsia,* and *Mahonia.*
● **Strategic planting** Scatter distinctive plants through a border to draw it together and make the area appear smaller.

PLANTS & PLANTING

IF A PLANT IS TO SUCCEED, you need to do your homework before planting it. Is the plant suited to the type and texture of soil present in the site you have chosen for it? Will it receive the right amount of sun or shade? Will the plant fit the site, or will it grow too large? Will it look good alongside its new neighbours, or would its size, shape, and flower colour be better suited to a different part of the garden? When you know you have the right plant, invest time and care in preparing the soil.

SOIL CONDITIONERS

Digging and forking will improve soil texture to some extent, but to improve the texture, nutrient content, drainage, or moisture retention considerably you need to incorporate suitable materials before you begin to plant.

● **Soil texture** Use coarse sand and gravel to open up and improve the texture of soil. Always use horticultural sand and gravel, since builders' materials sometimes contain harmful contaminants.

● **Soil pH** Lime and peat can be used to alter a soil's acidity or alkalinity. Lime will raise soil pH and help to break up a heavy or compacted soil. Peat or a peat alternative lowers soil pH and improves moisture retention, which makes it especially useful on light soils.

● **Soil improvers** Cocoa fibre, organic matter, leafmould, and composted bark all improve moisture retention, texture, and drainage. Manure improves soil texture and fertility because of its nitrogen content. Always use well-rotted manure (see p. 49).

Peat

Cocoa fibre

Organic matter

Leafmould

Manure

Composted bark

Lime

Coarse sand

Gravel

BASIC EQUIPMENT

Before you buy any tools, test them for size and weight, and check that they are comfortable to handle. Stainless steel tools will not rust but are more expensive than coated steel tools.

● **Cultivation** A hand fork and hand trowel are excellent for planting or weeding around small plants, and for moving them. Use a Dutch hoe for weeding between young and established plants and vegetable rows, and for marking out drills for planting. A large fork and spade are essential for digging and turning over the soil. Use a garden rake to collect up debris, to break up the soil surface, and to rake the soil level before sowing seed.

● **Pruning** Use secateurs for most pruning jobs. A sharp knife is good for light pruning tasks and is useful for cutting string. Wear gloves to protect your hands.

● **Watering** Choose a watering can that is large enough to carry a useful amount of water, but not so large that it is too heavy when full of water.

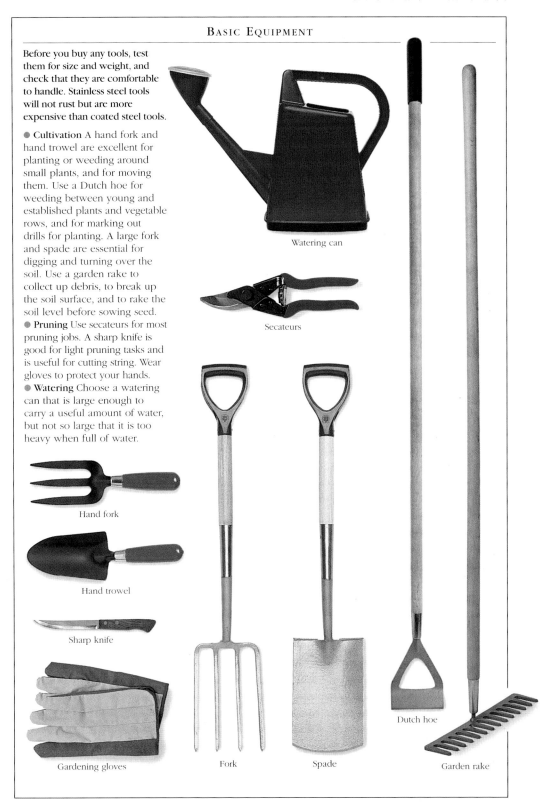

Watering can

Secateurs

Hand fork

Hand trowel

Sharp knife

Gardening gloves

Fork

Spade

Dutch hoe

Garden rake

PREPARING TO PLANT

Good PREPARATION SAVES you time and effort later, so find out about your garden before planting up beds and borders. Plants that are positioned in optimum conditions perform well and are equipped to resist attack from pests and diseases.

DETERMINING SOIL TEXTURE

You can find out a lot about your soil simply by feeling it. Its texture affects the amount of work you need to do on it and the types of plant you can grow successfully. The ideal soil is loam, which is a mixture of the two extreme soil types – sand and clay.

CHECKING SOIL
● **Local research** To gain a general idea of your soil type, and the plants you will be able to grow most successfully, find out what is growing in your neighbours' gardens. Make a note of the plants that are doing well and those that are struggling.
● **Soil compaction** Check for localized areas of compaction – perhaps a path trodden into a lawn, or an area next to a barbecue or under a child's swing. These need to be prepared by spiking (see p. 131) or digging over.

CLAY SOIL

Clay soil feels smooth and sticky

Sticky and smooth
Clay soil is made up of tiny particles, making it heavy, sticky, and moisture retentive. Although clay soils are often difficult to work, they are usually fertile.

SANDY SOIL

Sandy soil feels dry and gritty

Dry and loose
A sandy soil can dry out rapidly and does not retain nutrients well. It usually needs more maintenance than clay soil but is easy to work initially.

TESTING SOIL pH

The acidity or alkalinity of your soil (the soil pH) is one of the factors that most influences the plants you can grow. Some plants will suffer, and may even die, if grown in an unsuitable soil. Choose a testing kit to find out which kind of soil you have, and grow plants suited to the pH.

COLOUR TESTING KIT

Yellow-orange indicates acid soil

Bright green indicates neutral soil

Dark green indicates alkaline soil

Acid result

Neutral result

Alkaline result

Using a colour testing kit
Take a small sample of garden soil, and mix it with the chemical solution in the kit.

Leave the mixture to stabilize. Match the resulting colour against the pH chart in the kit.

ADJUSTING SOIL pH

● **Alkalinity** Increase the alkalinity of your soil by applying horticultural lime at the recommended rate. Most mushroom compost, which usually contains a lot of lime, may have a similar effect.
● **Acidity** Making soil more acidic is difficult. Add sulphate of ammonia or sulphur.
● **Treatments** Try to change the acidity of your soil before you start planting. Recheck it frequently to see how much it has altered.

CHOOSING THE RIGHT PLANTS

Putting the right plant in the right place is essential to your success as a gardener. When deciding on a planting scheme, remember to consider your soil texture and pH, as well as the aspect of the site (see p. 44). Use this chart to help you to choose which plant to put where.

SOIL TEXTURE	SUITABLE PLANTS	
CLAY SOIL A clay soil is able to retain moisture and food materials efficiently. However, during very dry weather it may crack – while during wet periods it can become waterlogged. The erratic moisture levels can cause plants to suffer.	*Acer* spp., *Aucuba, Bergenia, Campanula* spp., *Celastrus scandens, Clematis, Cornus* spp., *Cotoneaster, Euonymus fortunei, Forsythia,* hardy herbaceous geraniums,	*Helleborus* spp., *Hosta* spp., *Kerria, Laburnum, Lathyrus, Lonicera* spp., *Malus* spp., *Philadelphus, Prunus* spp., roses, *Rudbeckia, Sedum* spp., *Syringa, Viburnum, Vitis coignetiae, Wisteria.*

Syringa

SANDY SOIL A sandy soil is light and free-draining. It is prone to drying out and generally does not remain as fertile as a clay soil. A sandy soil is much easier to dig but, because it does not retain nutrients well, plants may need extra attention, especially during dry weather.	*Abutilon* (some), *Achillea* spp., *Artemisia, Ceanothus, Cercis siliquastrum, Cistus, Cotinus, Cytisus, Elaeagnus, Jasminum*	(hardy types), *Kerria, Laburnum, Lavandula, Mahonia, Perovskia, Rosmarinus, Sorbus, Verbascum, Wisteria.*

Verbascum

SOIL pH	SUITABLE PLANTS	
ALKALINE SOIL The types of plant you can grow on an alkaline soil are limited, largely because of the effect that the high soil pH has on nutrient availability. Unsuitable plants often show deficiencies of iron and manganese, resulting in a distinct yellowing between the veins on the new leaves.	*Acanthus, Acer* (some), *Achillea, Aesculus, Alcea, Alchemilla, Allium, Alyssum, Anemone, Aquilegia, Arabis, Artemisia, Aubrieta, Bergenia, Campanula, Caryopteris, Ceanothus,*	*Ceratostigma, Chaenomeles, Clematis, Crataegus, Crocosmia, Fuchsia, Gypsophila, Kerria, Lavatera arborea, Lonicera, Matthiola, Pyracantha, Silene, Syringa, Tulipa, Verbascum, Viburnum, Weigela.*

Tulipa

ACID SOIL An acid soil may have a sandy, clay, or loam (a mixture of the two) content. Most plants are able to survive in a typically acid soil, while there are others that will not flourish in any other kind of soil.	*Arctostaphylos, Berberidopsis corallina, Calluna, Camellia, Daboecia, Enkianthus, Eucryphia, Fothergilla, Gaultheria, Hamamelis, Kalmia,*	*Lapageria rosea, Lithodora, Magnolia* spp. (some), *Nomocharis, Nyssa, Pernettya, Philesia magellanica, Phyllodoce, Rhododendron, Trillium, Vaccinium.*

Rhododendron

IMPROVING SOIL

Before planting up your garden, invest some time in working on the soil. Both its texture and its fertility can be improved considerably, and it is easy to do this before the beds are full of plants. Precisely what you need to do depends upon the kind of soil you have.

ADDING ORGANIC MATTER TO SOIL

● **Adding life** Bring your soil to life by adding organic matter (see p. 38). This contains a whole host of microorganisms that help to keep garden soil in good condition.

● **Different types** Each type of organic matter has slightly different properties. These may alter the moisture retention, pH, aeration, and nutrient levels of the soil (see p. 40).

Saving time Instead of digging in organic matter, spread it evenly over the soil in autumn. Winter temperatures help to break it down, enabling worms and other organisms to incorporate it into the soil for you.

(see p. 38)

MAKING LEAFMOULD

Collect fallen leaves, and place them into a large, black polythene bag. Make a few holes in the bag, and loosely fold over the top. The leaves should have thoroughly decomposed after 6–12 months, when the leafmould will be ready to use.

WORKING THE SOIL

● **Using frosts** Dig heavy, clay soils in late autumn. Any frosts will help to improve the soil's texture by breaking it down into small pieces.

● **Digging soil** Try to avoid digging heavy soils when the soil is very wet, since this causes compaction of the soil. Reduce compaction by standing on a board to spread your weight (see p. 142).

● **Forking soil** After digging or forking, the surface of the soil may be rough and lumpy. To produce a fine tilth before planting or sowing, dig or fork the soil over again, breaking up any lumps of soil on the surface with a rake.

● **Using organic matter** Make organic matter to work into the soil by composting down almost any organic garden waste. Leaves, grass clippings, shredder by-products, prunings, and annual weeds can all be used (see opposite).

CLAY SOIL

● **Improving drainage** Always use a fork on a clay soil. A spade may seal the edges of the holes as it is driven in, making it even harder for water to drain through.

Opening up clay soil Incorporate horticultural gravel to a depth of at least 30 cm (12 in) into a clay soil. This helps to improve drainage, but does not affect nutrient levels. Do not use gravel obtained from a builders' merchant (see p. 38).

STONY SOIL

● **Removing stones** Remove as many large stones as possible before planting, especially if you intend to grow root crops. Their shape and development can be spoiled by stones.

Enriching stony soil Fork in leafmould or compost to enrich a dry, stony soil. Choose a dry day to do this work, if possible. Start at one end of the bed and work backwards so that you do not step on the soil you have just forked over.

MAKING COMPOST

Making your own compost is an easy, quick, and environmentally friendly way of disposing of organic garden and kitchen waste. It also provides a very inexpensive, high-quality material that will greatly improve the quality of the soil in your garden.

COMPOST INGREDIENTS

Almost any organic kitchen or garden waste can be composted, but avoid any diseased material or perennial weeds. Natural-fibre pillows, carpets, and knitted items can be composted down, as can old, shredded newspapers. Avoid pungent kitchen waste and meat, since these attract vermin. Turn the compost once a week.

Grass
Grass clippings should be used sparingly.

Clippings
Pruning clippings are made from chopped twigs.

Weeds
Mix annual weeds with drier materials.

Waste
Kitchen waste, such as peelings, can be used.

Knitted items
Cut up natural-fibre items and add to compost.

Carpets
Old carpet should be cut up into small squares.

Feather pillows
Old feather pillows are a useful ingredient.

Newspapers
Paper should be shredded or cut into strips.

TENDING COMPOST

● **Layering** Add compost to the heap in thin layers – never use very much of any one ingredient at once. Try to intersperse moist, leafy material with drier ingredients such as pruning clippings.

● **Adding nitrogen** Green material has a high nitrogen content, which speeds up the composting process. Avoid using too much moist greenery, since it can soon turn to strong-smelling slime rather than good, broken-down compost.

● **Cooling** Add water to the compost during very hot, dry weather, or if you are using lots of dry material. Moisture encourages the materials to break down.

● **Insulating** Keep the compost well insulated during cool weather so that the rotting process does not slow down too much.

MAKING YOUR OWN CONTAINER

● **Plastic bin** Use a plastic barrel to make a compost bin. Cut off the top and bottom, drill 2.5-cm (1-in) holes around the sides, and use one end as a lid.

● **Recycled wood** Make a compost container from sturdy corner posts and old floor boards nailed together with galvanized nails.

Chicken wire is attached with galvanized nails

Old carpet used as lid

Old tool handles make effective stakes

Using old materials
Make a low-cost compost or leafmould container using galvanized chicken wire held in place with wooden stakes driven firmly into the ground. Use a piece of old carpet to form a warm, insulating lid.

ALLOWING ACCESS

Removing a panel
Choose or make a compost container that has a removable front panel. This allows easy access to the compost when you need to turn it (which you should do regularly) or need to remove some of it for use in the garden. Make sure that the compost is well rotted.

PLANTING FOR SPECIFIC SITES

The aspect of a garden is the direction in which it faces, and this determines how much sun or shade various areas in the garden will receive. The aspect is influenced by the site, the soil type, and any overhanging trees, high walls, slopes, or nearby high-rise buildings.

ASSESSING GARDENS

● **Careful planning** Study your garden carefully before planting. Notice where shade falls throughout the day, and remember that evergreen trees cast shade all year round. Establish whether shady areas are moist or dry, and choose appropriate plants.

● **Sunny walls** Soil at the base of a sunny wall is particularly prone to being hot and dry. Improve the soil's ability to retain moisture (see p. 38), and choose suitable drought-resistant plants (see p. 89).

DEALING WITH SLOPING FLOWERBEDS

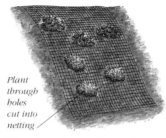

Plant through holes cut into netting

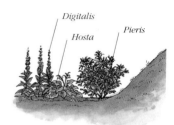

Digitalis
Hosta
Pieris

Planting through netting

Groundcover plants stabilize the soil on a slope. Plant through plastic netting secured with pegs. This will retain the soil while the plant roots are growing.

Choosing the right plants

Choose moisture-loving plants for the base of a slope, since water will run down to the bottom. *Digitalis*, *Hosta*, and *Pieris* are all suitable plants for this situation.

PLANTS FOR DIFFERENT ASPECTS

ASPECT OF GARDEN	SUITABLE PLANTS		
SUNNY AND DRY There are numerous plants well suited to a fairly dry, sunny site. However, even these plants will need plenty of water in their first year to encourage healthy, sturdy growth while they become fully established.	*Achillea* spp., *Arabis* spp., *Aster* spp. and cvs., *Aubrieta*, *Campsis radicans*, *Cistus*, *Cytisus* spp., *Eryngium*, *Fremontodendron*, *Genista* spp.,	*Hypericum* spp., *Iberis* spp., *Phlomis* spp., *Rosmarinus*, *Santolina*, *Sedum* spp, *Senecio* spp., *Tamarix*, *Vitis coignetiae*, *Weigela*, *Yucca gloriosa*.	*Aster novae-angliae*
DRY SHADE Dry shade is common on light soils and beneath trees and hedges. Walls or fences can shelter an area so that it receives little or no rain. A brick wall will absorb moisture from the soil. Fortunately, a number of plants will tolerate dry shade.	*Alchemilla mollis*, *Anemone nemorosa*, *Aucuba*, *Cyclamen* spp., *Daphne laureola*, *Epimedium* spp., *Euonymus* spp., *Hyacinthoides non-scripta*, *Hypericum* x *inodorum* and cvs.,	*Ilex aquifolium* and cvs., *Iris foetidissima*, *Lonicera japonica* 'Halliana', *Mahonia* spp., *Pulmonaria* spp. and cvs., *Ranunculus ficaria* and cvs., *Ruscus aculeatus*, *Vinca* spp.	*Ilex aquifolium*
MOIST SHADE This occurs in gardens that have a naturally moisture-retentive soil. It can also occur at the base of a shaded slope or in areas that are overshadowed by trees. Many plants will not flower well in shade, so foliage is an important consideration.	*Anemone blanda*, *Aucuba*, *Camellia japonica* and cvs., *Convallaria majalis*, *Digitalis*, *Eranthis*, *Erythronium*, *Fritillaria* (most), *Galanthus nivalis*, *Helleborus* spp.,	*Hosta* spp. and cvs., *Lonicera* spp., *Paeonia suffruticosa*, *Pieris* spp. and cvs., *Primula* spp. (most), *Rhododendron* spp. and cvs., *Skimmia japonica*, *Vinca* spp.	*Primula vulgaris*

CHOOSING PLANTS

SELECTING THE BEST POSSIBLE PLANT is one of the surest ways of increasing your chances of success. Whether you buy your plants from a local market or from a reliable garden centre or nursery, always check that they are in good condition.

USING PLANT LABELS

Check colour

Peony
Paeonia 'Sarah Bernhardt'

SEASON OF INTEREST In late spring to mid summer, this beautiful plant produces masses of large, scented, double flowers that have papery, rose-pink petals with pale edges.

HEIGHT 1 m (3 ft)

SPREAD 1 m (3 ft)

HARDINESS Generally fully hardy, but young growth can sometimes be damaged by late spring frosts.

SOIL TYPE Rich and well-drained.

ASPECT Prefers full sun, but will tolerate light shade.

Check plant information

- **Season of interest** Find out when the flowering period is, and whether the flowers are fragrant.
- **Potential size** Use the label to check what the plant's potential height and spread will be.
- **Hardiness** Check whether the plant is fully hardy. If it is not, it will need protection from harsh winds and low temperatures throughout the winter months.

POISONOUS PLANTS

- **Plant safety** If a plant is potentially hazardous, the label should indicate the degree of risk and whether skin reactions or poisoning are a potential problem – most important if children play in the garden.

SELECTING PLANTS FOR YOUR GARDEN

Before buying a plant, check that it is suitable for the spot you have in mind. Knowing the range of different growing conditions in your garden will help you to decide what to buy. You should also consider what the plant will look like with its neighbours.

BUYING GOOD PLANTS

- **When to buy** Avoid buying plants during or just after an extremely cold spell. Even the rootballs of hardy plants may freeze if unprotected, and this can prove fatal. Delay buying until spring, when a plant's state of health is apparent from the state of its foliage.
- **Clean compost** Select plants with compost that is free from weeds, algae, moss, and liverworts. These all indicate that the plant may have been in its pot for too long.
- **Damaged plants** Avoid wilting plants and those with blotched leaves. If plants have been kept hungry, or if they have suffered from drought or waterlogging, they may well have suffered permanent damage.
- **Fragrance** Try to include some plants chosen specifically for their scented blooms.

CHOOSING FOR A SPECIFIC SITE

- **Narrow bed** Choosing plants suitable for a narrow bed can be tricky. If the bed is adjacent to a wall or fence, choose plants that can tolerate dry shade. If the bed is next to a path, avoid plants with thorns or prickly leaves.
- **Island bed** If the bed is wide, choose tall plants that require little maintenance for central areas where access is difficult. If the bed is in a lawn, choose plants that will not flop over the grass.

Planting in corners
A corner bed often needs plants that can thrive in a relatively dry soil. Choose tall plants for the back and small, trailing plants for the edges.

- **Easy border** Choose shrubs that require little pruning, and combine these shrubs with perennials that need no winter protection. Avoid plants that must be supported, and try to buy drought-resistant plants (see p. 89). Bulbs are useful, but plant only hardy ones that do not need lifting and storing throughout the winter.

Tall plants at back of bed

Small, trailing plants at edges

STORING PLANTS

Always aim to transfer plants into the ground as soon as possible after purchasing them. If extremes of cold or wet make the soil totally unsuitable at the time, or if you cannot plant everything in one day, you may need to store plants. Do not do this for more than a few days.

STORING PLANTS OUTDOORS

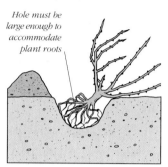

Hole must be large enough to accommodate plant roots

Heeling in
Heel in bare-root shrubs and trees to keep the roots moist and in good condition. Place the plant at an angle in a hole in the ground. This reduces the effect of wind on the stems, which can rock the roots. Backfill the hole.

Planting in a pot
Plunge a container-grown plant into the ground while it is still in its pot. This will help to protect the plant's roots from extremes of temperature and will decrease the risk of the compost drying out.

BRIGHT IDEA

Storing short-term
Put evergreen shrubs and conifers in a sheltered spot, where they will be protected from the sun, wind, and freezing temperatures.

LOOKING AFTER STORED PLANTS

● **Protecting roots** The roots of a stored plant are very susceptible to damage. Extremes of temperature can cause root death. Protect the rootball by insulating it with soil, hessian, or bubblewrap.
● **Preventing growth** Never feed a plant while it is being stored. This could stimulate growth at a time when the plant needs a resting period.

● **Watering** Keep roots moist, but do not overwater. Roots confined to a plunged pot or a temporary planting hole are easier to overwater than those on an established plant in open ground.
● **Dormant plants** Plants that are dormant adapt to storage conditions much more successfully than plants that are still actively growing.

STORING PLANTS INDOORS
● **Sheds and garages** Do not allow temperatures to rise high enough to encourage growth. This will make it difficult for a stored plant to become established once outside.
● **Rodents** Make sure there are no mice around. They will soon eat any stored plants.

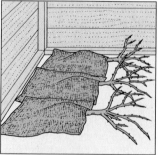

Covering roots
Store bare-root plants for a few days in an unheated garage or shed. Cover the roots loosely with moist hessian or polythene to prevent them from drying out.

STORING BULBS

● **Dry conditions** Stand bulbs on dry sand or newspaper in a tray, and position them so that they do not touch each other. Label each box with the date and the type of each bulb.
● **Moving air** A cool but frost-free shed, greenhouse, or garage makes an excellent store for bulbs. Air movement helps to prevent diseases that affect the bulbs, but avoid draughts.

PLANTING SUCCESSFULLY

PROVIDING YOU CHOOSE WELL and pay attention to your planting technique, your plants should have a healthy and promising start. Follow up with good aftercare to ensure that your plants stay vigorous and healthy (see p. 80).

PREPARING TO PLANT

Do not risk putting a pot-bound plant in the ground without first improving its condition. Tease out any girdling roots, and use secateurs to prune back damaged or very restricted roots. Once planted, water your plants regularly until they are well established (see p. 92).

BEFORE PLANTING

● **Digging a hole** Prepare a planting hole before you take a plant out of its container.
● **Releasing roots** If congested roots are difficult to release, first soak the rootball in a bucket of water for several hours, or even overnight. This makes it easier to move the roots, and limits the damage you cause in the process.
● **Planting conditions** Choose suitable weather conditions for planting whenever possible. Do not plant when the soil is excessively dry, waterlogged, or frozen.

CONTROLLING WEEDS

Removing weeds
Remove any weeds from a pot. This both limits their spread and prevents them from competing with the plant for water.

WATERING EFFICIENTLY

Positioning a pipe
Position a section of drainpipe or wide-bore hose in a planting hole. This will allow you to direct water straight to a plant's roots.

BASIC PLANTING TECHNIQUE

Whatever you are planting, treat it with the care it deserves, and it should respond positively. One of the most common mistakes is to plant too deeply. Make sure that the top of a planting hole is level with the surface of the pot compost.

CORRECT PLANTING PROCEDURE

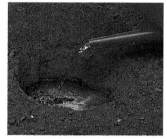

1 Dig a planting hole about twice the size of the plant's rootball. Water the hole well to ensure that it is thoroughly moist, and to check that the soil drains freely (see p. 42).

Soak plants thoroughly

2 Place plants waiting to be planted in a bowl of water. Position each plant at the correct depth in its hole, then backfill the hole with a mixture of compost, fertilizer, and soil.

Leave stem area clear

3 Firm the soil, and water the plant thoroughly to settle the soil around the roots. Lay 5–7 cm (2–3 in) of mulch all around the root area, leaving the stem area clear.

PLANTING SHRUBS

Sᴴᴿᴜʙs ꜰᴏʀᴍ ᴛʜᴇ ᴘᴇʀᴍᴀɴᴇɴᴛ sᴛʀᴜᴄᴛᴜʀᴇ of a garden. Making sure that you choose the best specimens and that these are given a really good start is very important and well worth your investment of time, money, and care.

CHOOSING SHRUBS

Yᴏᴜ can buy shrubs that are container grown, containerized, rootballed, or bare rooted. If you buy a shrub that is not in leaf, concentrate on examining the roots and general shape of the plant. It should have a healthy, well-developed root system and evenly distributed stems.

CONTAINER-GROWN SHRUB

Foliage is not yellow or withered

Healthy, well-spaced top-growth

Stems are free from damage, pests, and diseases

Roots are firm and white or pale brown

Checking roots
Remove the pot carefully to check the root system. The compost should be firm with healthy, fibrous roots visible on the outside. If there is a mass of congested roots, the shrub is pot-bound.

CONTAINERIZED SHRUB

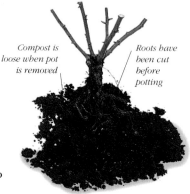

Compost is loose when pot is removed

Roots have been cut before potting

Identifying a specimen
A containerized shrub is one that has been lifted from open ground and potted up recently, making it slow to establish.

ROOTBALLED SHRUBS

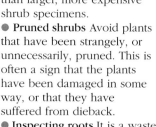

● **Checking soil** Gently squeeze the soil around the rootball to check that it is moist and firmly packed.
● **Good value** Rootballed shrubs are less expensive than container-grown shrubs and often grow better than bare-rooted specimens.

CHECKING SPECIMENS
● **Young shrubs** Young, small shrubs are generally easy to establish. They grow more rapidly and more successfully than larger, more expensive shrub specimens.
● **Pruned shrubs** Avoid plants that have been strangely, or unnecessarily, pruned. This is often a sign that the plants have been damaged in some way, or that they have suffered from dieback.
● **Inspecting roots** It is a waste of your time and money to buy a plant that has an inadequate root system. Do not hesitate to remove the pot to check the condition of the roots if necessary.

BARE-ROOT SHRUBS

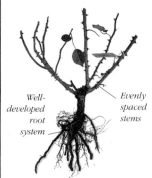

Well-developed root system

Evenly spaced stems

Finding good specimens
Look for shrubs with sturdy stems and no distorted, crossing growth. Any buds should be plump, and the roots must be healthy and unbroken.

GIVING SHRUBS A GOOD START

Always try to plant shrubs during autumn or spring so that they have time to become established before the dry summer weather. Container-grown shrubs can be planted at any time, but even these shrubs often perform best after autumn or spring planting.

PREPARING TO PLANT

● **Preparing roots** Soak roots in tap water before planting. This helps to ensure that they are really moist, which will make it easy to tease out any congested roots.
● **Dry soil** If planting in a dry spot, make a slight depression in the soil around the shrub. This will ensure that water soaks into the soil instead of running off the soil surface.
● **Heavy soil** If planting in a heavy, wet soil, do not put moisture-retentive organic matter in the planting hole. This may act like a sump and draw water in from the wet soil, making a dangerously wet area around the roots.

CHECKING DEPTH

Graft union

Using a cane
Place a cane across the planting hole, and hold the rose in the centre of the hole with its roots well spread. The graft union should be a maximum of 2.5 cm (1 in) below the cane.

PRUNING FOR SHAPE

Pruning out dead wood
Use sharp secateurs to prune out any dead, diseased, damaged, crossing, or straggly stems. Make sure that the remaining stems form an even shape. Cut back to a healthy, outward-facing bud.

PLANTING SHRUBS SUCCESSFULLY

● **Avoiding sickness** Never use the same, or a closely related, plant to replace one that you have removed. If planted in the same spot, the new shrub may suffer replant sickness and fail to thrive.
● **Correct depth** Check that all roots are covered, but that the stem base is no deeper than it was before planting.

● **Planting hole** Make sure that the planting hole is at least twice the size of the rootball, and prepare it well with organic matter and fertilizer.
● **Underplanting** Underplant new shrubs with small bulbs for seasonal interest – or choose bulbs to coordinate with the form and colour of the shrubs' foliage or flowers.

USING MANURE

● **Avoiding scorch** Always use fertilizer and well-rotted manure in the planting hole. Mix both into the soil so that they are not in direct contact with any of the roots.

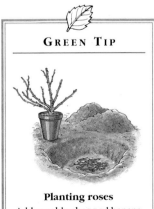

GREEN TIP

Planting roses
Add roughly chopped banana skins to the soil when planting roses. This improves texture and moisture retention, and also adds potassium.

Newspaper placed on moist soil

Cover newspaper with soil, which will prevent rapid evaporation

Mulching
Use newspaper as a low-cost, efficient mulch. Ensure that the soil is really moist, and lay very wet newspaper on the soil surface around the shrub. Spread soil over the newspaper to disguise it.

PLANTING PERENNIALS

ALTHOUGH PERENNIALS ARE AVAILABLE throughout the year, it is best to buy them in autumn or spring, when they will establish rapidly once planted. If your soil is heavy and wet, it is best to delay buying and planting perennials until spring.

CHOOSING PERENNIALS

Small perennial plants are generally better value than large specimens, but larger plants are more useful for providing an instant effect. You will be getting very good value for your money if you choose large plants that are ready to be divided (see p. 60).

SELECTING A CONTAINER-GROWN PERENNIAL

Top-growth is green and healthy

Crown has sturdy new shoots

No weed growth visible on compost surface

Strong roots free from signs of dieback

Checking a crown
When choosing a perennial plant, look for signs of new growth at the crown. If the plant is dormant, check that the crown is firm and undamaged.

BUYING HEALTHY PLANTS
● **Wilting** Choose plants with a compost surface that is neither very wet nor very dry. Never buy wilted perennials. If they have been allowed to dry out once, it has probably happened many times before, and the plant will have suffered considerably.
● **Moss** Choose plants that do not have any surface growth of algae, moss, weeds, or liverworts. This is a sign that the plants have been in their pots for too long.
● **Cracked containers** Ensure that the container is intact. If it is cracked, the roots may have been damaged.

ROOTS IN MESH

Some perennials have mesh bags around their roots. The roots should be able to grow out of the mesh and become established in the compost. However, if a plant is lacking in vigour, this may not happen, in which case the roots will remain restricted.

Mesh may be visible at surface of soil near base of stem

Cutting mesh
Before planting, carefully cut through the mesh in several places with sharp scissors, a knife, or secateurs, taking care not to cut through the plant's roots. Cutting the mesh will allow the roots to grow out into the surrounding soil easily.

MONEY-SAVING TIP

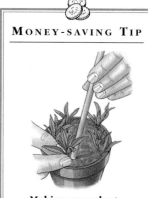

Making new plants
Pot cuttings from tender perennials in late summer to ensure that you have plenty of plants for use in the following year (see p. 153).

WHEN AND HOW TO PLANT PERENNIALS

Perennials can be planted at any time of the year, except during extreme conditions. They should grow rapidly and usually perform well within their first year. Use the chart below as a guide to the ideal planting distances for planting some perennials.

REMOVING A PLANT

Slide fingers between stems

Tapping a pot
Turn a plant's pot upside down, and firmly tap the base with your hand or the handle of a trowel. The plant should slip out of the pot quickly and easily, with the rootball left intact.

REDUCING STRESS

Use secateurs to remove large leaves and flowers

Preventing moisture loss
To reduce stress on a plant if planting during dry or hot weather, prune off flowers and large leaves before planting. Shade the plant with a "tent" of netting supported on sticks.

GREEN TIP

Adding bracken
Incorporate a handful of coarsely chopped bracken into a planting hole to improve the texture of the soil. Do not use bracken with lime-loving plants, since it is slightly acidic.

PLANTING DISTANCES FOR PERENNIALS

PLANT	DISTANCE	HEIGHT
Acanthus mollis	60 cm (24 in)	90 cm (36 in)
Ajuga reptans	30–45 cm (12–18 in)	10–30 cm (4–12 in)
Alchemilla mollis	40 cm (15 in)	30–45 cm (12–18 in)
Anaphalis spp.	30–45 cm (12–18 in)	30–60 cm (12–24 in)
Aruncus sylvester	30–45 cm (12–18 in)	120–180 cm (4–6 ft)
Coreopsis grandiflora	45 cm (18 in)	30–45 cm (12–18 in)
Dicentra spectabilis	45 cm (18 in)	30–75 cm (12–30 in)
Doronicum spp.	30 cm (12 in)	60 cm (24 in)
Geranium endressii	45 cm (18 in)	30–45 cm (12–18 in)
Geum chiloense	30–45 cm (12–18 in)	45–60 cm (18–24 in)
Gypsophila elegans	30 cm (12 in)	60 cm (24 in)
Gypsophila paniculata	60–90 cm (24–36 in)	90 cm (36 in)
Helenium autumnale	30–45 cm (12–18 in)	120–180 cm (4–6 ft)
Heuchera sanguinea	45 cm (18 in)	30–45 cm (12–18 in)
Liatris spicata	45 cm (18 in)	60–90 cm (24–36 in)
Lychnis coronaria	22–30 cm (9–12 in)	45–60 cm (18–24 in)
Monarda didyma	40 cm (15 in)	60–90 cm (24–36 in)
Lupinus	60 cm (24 in)	90 cm (36 in)
Penstemon barbatus	60 cm (24 in)	90 cm (36 in)
Penstemon hartwegii	30–45 cm (12–18 in)	60 cm (24 in)
Potentilla garden cvs.	30–45 cm (12–18 in)	30–60 cm (12–24 in)
Pulmonaria saccharata	30 cm (12 in)	30 cm (12 in)
Rudbeckia fulgida	45 cm (18 in)	30–90 cm (12–36 in)
Tiarella cordifolia	30 cm (12 in)	15–35 cm (6–14 in)
Verbascum	45–60 cm (18–24 in)	90–150 cm (3–5 ft)
Veronica spicata	30–60 cm (12–24 in)	15–45 cm (6–18 in)

PLANNING DISTANCES
● **Width and height** Check the potential heights and spreads of plants before planting to ensure that you leave the correct distance between them. Use the chart on the left as a guide. Remember, different cultivars can vary considerably.
● **Filling in gaps** A correctly planted herbaceous border can look very sparse when newly planted. Use bulbs and temporary seasonal bedding to fill in any gaps (see p. 17).

FOLIAGE AND FLOWERS
● **Winter appearance** Consider the season of interest of each perennial, and its appearance in winter. Most perennials die back in winter, but some retain many of their leaves.
● **Grouping plants** For an effective display, plant several of each type of plant together, rather than dotting individual plants throughout a border.

SUPPORTING CLIMBERS

Covering walls and fences with perennial climbers brings an extra dimension to a garden. Some climbers are self-clinging, so need no support, but most need trellis or wires to keep them in place. Before planting, check that the support is both stable and strong.

USING NETTING
● **Light support** Use plastic or wire netting to support lightweight or annual climbers. Pigeon netting or plastic fruit-tree netting is ideal.

Stapling netting
Galvanized stock netting is suitable for lightweight, permanent climbers. Use rustproof, galvanized, U-shaped, staples to hold the netting slightly away from a fence.

USING WIRE
● **Strong support** Galvanized wire makes a good supporting structure for vigorous climbers. A system of horizontal wires works best for heavy climbers.

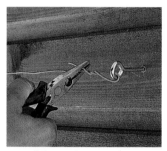

Attaching wire to vine eyes
Use vine eyes to hold heavy-duty wire in place on a fence or wall. Screw in a vine eye, wind one end of a length of wire around its head, pull it tight, and secure the wire to another vine eye.

LOOSE FITTINGS

Wall plug

Vine eye

Sound area

● **Repairing supports** If a few vine eyes, nails, or staples are loose, drill a new hole in a nearby sound area, insert a wall plug, and refit the fixture. Always try to repair supports with the plant in place.
● **Replacing wire** If one of your supporting wires breaks, it is probably a good idea to replace all of them, since other wires may break soon after the first one.

USING TRELLIS
● **Wooden support** Trellis makes a good support for light or medium-weight climbers, and can be cut to size.

Attaching a trellis
To ensure that you can easily repair or maintain the wall behind a trellis, and to avoid causing damage to the trellis, attach it to wooden battens with hinges on the lower section (see p. 27). You can then swing the trellis down.

BASIC EQUIPMENT

Always buy good-quality fixings; they are durable and save a lot of time, money, and frustration in the long run. Do not skimp on the number you use. Too few may cause a support to fail.

Garden twine for tying in plants

Vine eyes for holding wires

Flat vine eyes

Plastic netting for lightweight support

Staples

Galvanized wire

PLANTING CLIMBERS

Most roses are bought bare-root in late autumn or winter and should be looked after like any other bare-root plant (see p. 49).

A much smaller selection of container-grown roses is available throughout the year. Treat these as container-grown shrubs (see p. 48).

PROVIDING SUPPORT

Garden twine

Tying in new stems
Container-grown roses may have some leafy stems. Tie these to supporting wires with garden twine (or use proprietary fixings) to ensure that the stems are not damaged by supports.

PREVENTING DAMAGE
● **Flaky walls** Avoid planting self-clinging climbers against a wall that has a flaky surface or loose mortar. These plants are likely to make the problem worse and may cause extensive damage to the wall.

PROVIDING COVER
● **Temporary cover** Newly planted climbers may take a few years to grow to a useful size. Create a temporary covering with rapid-growing annual climbers such as *Ipomoea purpurea* or *Lathyrus*. You may decide you like them so much that you keep them – even when the permanent climbers are larger.
● **Hiding bare bases** Many climbers become rather sparse at the base as they get older. If they do not respond to feeding or other maintenance (see p. 86 and p. 102), plant decorative shrubs at the base to hide the straggly stems.

CONSERVING MOISTURE

Using mulch
After planting, water a rose well. Apply a 5-7.5 cm (2-3 in) layer of mulch over the moist soil. Keep this clear of the base of the support and of the rose stems, since it can rot both.

AVOIDING RAINSHADOW
● **Planting measurements** Make a planting hole for a wall-trained climber 30–45 cm (12–18 in) away from a wall or fence so that its roots are not in an area of ground sheltered from the rain.

Cane provides temporary support for young stems

Planting at an angle
Plant a climber at an angle to encourage it to grow towards its support. Use a cane as a temporary support for young, fragile stems. Train a few of the larger stems into position low down on the support.

COMPANION PLANTING

Deterring pests
Try companion planting around the bases of your roses with marigolds. These may deter several rose pests and, although not scientifically proven, the technique is worth trying.

PLANTING CLEMATIS

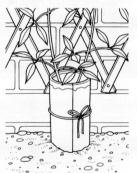

● **Protecting the base** Plant clematis several inches deeper than it is in its container. Use a cylinder of strong cardboard or plastic to protect the base from slugs and snails. Secure with twine.
● **Extra precaution** Smear a band of grease around the top of the cylinder. Slugs and snails will not be able to climb over this, so they will not reach any young stems and cause them damage.

PLANTING ANNUALS

ANNUAL BEDDING PLANTS bring colour and shape to a garden, and are relatively easy to grow from seed. If you lack time, space, or equipment, an excellent alternative to seeds are the many plantlets available near their flowering time.

CHOOSING ANNUALS

Most annuals are grown for the colourful displays they provide during the summer months. They are available from mid spring. Some, such as *Viola* x *wittrockiana* and *Bellis,* are grown as annuals for winter colour and are best bought in late summer or autumn.

IDENTIFYING HEALTHY ANNUALS

Compact, green foliage

Sturdy growth

Moist compost

SELECTING PLANTS
● **Quality** Always check that you are buying a full and healthy tray of annuals. Reject poor-quality plants.
● **Colour and type** To brighten up your garden with minimal expense, buy the same annual in bulk. For the best effect, restrict the colours you use to two or three at most.

Buying plants
Choose plants that are strong and sturdy, with no signs of diseases, pests, or nutrient deficiencies. Avoid old plants, which rarely transplant satisfactorily and have little flowering potential left.

ORDERING BY MAIL
● **Saving time** Save both time and space by ordering annuals from one of the many companies now offering a mail-order service. Annuals are available at various growth stages, from seedlings to plantlets, and should be despatched with protective packaging and full instructions.

INTRODUCING SCENT
● **Planting annuals** Most annuals release only a limited amount of perfume. Plant one of the exceptions, *Matthiola bicornis,* for a strong scent in the evening. Try training *Lathyrus odoratus* among other border plants, or use the dwarf forms in pots.

PURCHASING SEEDS
● **Catalogues** Most garden centres stock a good selection of seeds, but it is worth looking through the catalogues produced by major seed suppliers, which usually offer a wide choice of varieties.
● **Early ordering** Whether you buy your seeds from garden centres or catalogues, make sure you do your seed shopping early. New ranges are available from autumn, and the most popular varieties are liable to sell out quickly.
● **Heat damage** Garden centres can become very hot during the summer. Avoid buying seeds at this time, since extreme temperatures can damage seeds.

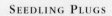

SEEDLING PLUGS

Many annuals are available as seedling "plugs", each supplied with its own plug of compost. When planted, the well-developed root system suffers little damage and transplants readily, ensuring rapid subsequent growth.

ESTABLISHING ANNUALS

The lifespan of an annual is no more than a year. In order to ensure that these plants look their best for the little time that they are in flower, it is essential that they are well planted. A moist soil, a good supply of nutrients, and regular deadheading are the keys to success.

REMOVING ANNUALS

Hold firmly, and push base with thumb

Rootball

Releasing rootballs

Water trays well before removing the plants. Release the rootballs by pushing up from the base of the tray and easing the plants out. Plant only on cool days or when the area is shady. Early evening is best, so that the plants can settle before the heat of midday.

FEEDING ANNUALS

Ensure all leaves are sprayed

Applying a foliar feed

Shortly after planting, spray the leaves with a foliar feed. This stimulates the roots to grow and speeds establishment. Apply another foliar feed if at any time the plant leaves begin to turn yellow; this is an indication of nutrient defiency.

BRIGHT IDEA

Tying canes

When constructing a wigwam support for a climber, use an elastic band to hold the canes in place temporarily. This allows you to keep both hands free, enabling you to tie the canes in position easily.

CONSIDERING HEIGHT AND COLOUR

The charm of an annual flowerbed is often dependent on an irregular planting scheme, with one colour flowing into another. Graduate the plant heights, introducing as many levels as you can, and – unless you have a very large flowerbed – keep to two or three colours.

PLANTING ANNUALS IN A FLOWERBED

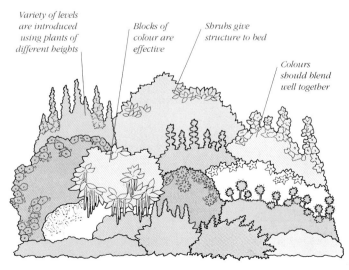

Variety of levels are introduced using plants of different heights

Blocks of colour are effective

Shrubs give structure to bed

Colours should blend well together

SELECTING COLOURS

● **Blocks of colour** Group bold blocks of annuals in a limited range of colours together to show this kind of planting off to its best advantage.

● **Combinations** Warm yellows, reds, and oranges, soft-coloured pinks and mauves, and rich blues toned with pinks are all good colour combinations.

Designing for impact

A variety of textures and shapes makes an eye-catching display. Use different plants and foliage to add texture to your planting scheme. Annual foliage plants can also be used for contrasting or harmonizing colour.

PLANTING BULBS

ALTHOUGH MOST BULBS are fairly inexpensive, those that are fully hardy can provide a display of flowers for many years. All they need is an adequate supply of food and water, and a little maintenance (see p. 57 and p. 156).

CHOOSING BULBS

Try to choose bulbs that show no signs of new root development. However, if bulbs have just started into growth, check that the growth tips are firm and healthy. If you choose twin-nosed bulbs, remember that the smaller of the two bulbs may not flower for a year or two.

PURCHASING BULBS

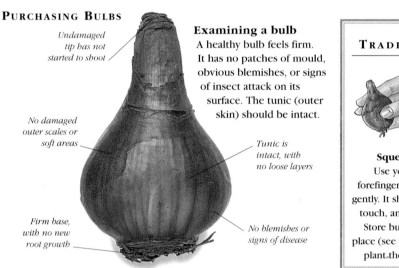

Undamaged tip has not started to shoot

No damaged outer scales or soft areas

Firm base, with no new root growth

Examining a bulb
A healthy bulb feels firm. It has no patches of mould, obvious blemishes, or signs of insect attack on its surface. The tunic (outer skin) should be intact.

Tunic is intact, with no loose layers

No blemishes or signs of disease

TRADITIONAL TIP

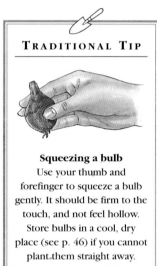

Squeezing a bulb
Use your thumb and forefinger to squeeze a bulb gently. It should be firm to the touch, and not feel hollow. Store bulbs in a cool, dry place (see p. 46) if you cannot plant them straight away.

PLANTING BULBS IN BASKETS

Flowering bulbs look good until the flowers and foliage start to fade. Removing the foliage too soon prevents the bulbs from performing properly next year. Plant bulbs in a basket, which you can lift and put in an inconspicuous place while the leaves die down.

USING CONTAINERS

● **Recycling containers** Use any suitable household container for planting bulbs. A pond basket is also ideal.

● **Adding holes** Good drainage is essential. If a container does not have many holes, make extra holes in the base.

● **Non-hardy bulbs** Use basket planting as an easy way of dealing with non-hardy bulbs. When temperatures fall, lift the basket, and put it in a cool but frost- and mouse-free shed or garage for the winter.

PREPARING AND PLANTING A BASKET OF BULBS

Position bulbs at random

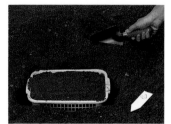

1 Fill the bottom third or quarter of a basket with garden soil. Plant the bulbs as you would normally (see p. 57), and fill the container to the top with soil.

2 Dig a hole slightly deeper than the basket, and lower the basket into it. Backfill the hole with soil, and water. Hide a label in the container so that it stays with the bulbs.

PLANTING BULBS IN BEDS

Most bulbs need sun, but a few prefer shade, so take care to select the right bulbs for the particular spot you have in mind. Choose small bulbs for the fronts of beds and for planting next to paths or a lawn. Their small size does not cause problems with obtrusive foliage.

PLANTING IN WET SOIL

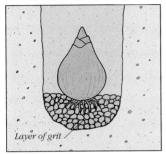

Layer of grit

Improving drainage
Most bulbs prefer a well-drained position. To improve drainage if planting in a wet, heavy soil, put a 2.5-cm (1-in) deep layer of coarse grit in the bottom of each planting trench or individual planting hole.

GROUPING BULBS
● **Odd numbers** Bulbs look best planted in groups of odd numbers. Most will start to multiply after a few years, creating a miniature drift.
● **Set patterns** As a general rule, avoid set patterns and straight lines. However, some bulbs, such as gladioli, will suit a formal planting.

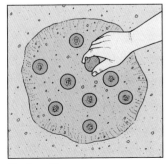

Saving time
Plant several bulbs in one large hole to save time and effort. Bulbs planted in this way look less formal than those that have been planted individually.

PLANTING IN DRY SOIL

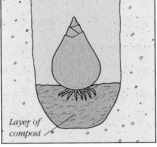

Layer of compost

Retaining moisture
Bulbs may not flower properly in very dry soil, and may even die. To improve the soil's moisture retention, place a 3.5-cm (1½-in) deep layer of moist compost in the bottom of each planting hole or trench.

BULB MAINTENANCE
● **Regular watering** Adequate moisture throughout the year is essential if flower buds are to form properly. Be sure to water bulb areas regularly throughout a dry summer.
● **Unsuitable conditions** Do not risk planting bulbs if weather conditions are not suitable and the ground is very wet or frozen. Store the bulbs (see p. 46) until conditions improve, or plant them loosely in boxes full of compost for their first year.
● **Avoiding disease** To avoid tulip fire, a fungal disease that attacks tulips, do not plant tulip bulbs until late autumn.
● **Pot bulbs** Plant hardy pot bulbs out in the garden when they have finished flowering. These bulbs are often crammed together, so make sure you divide the contents into individual bulbs.
● **Bulb boost** Give a foliar feed to dying foliage (see p. 156).

MEASURING DEPTH

Bulb planted at three times its depth

Bulb planted at five times its depth

Checking planting depth
Most bulbs are planted at a depth between three and five times their height. Always check the instructions on the packet. If winter temperatures are very cold, or summers very dry, plant the bulbs slightly deeper.

LILY BULBS

● **Drainage** Place a 2.5-cm (1-in) layer of gravel in a planting hole when planting lilies. This will encourage any excess water to drain away.
● **Planting position** Lily bulbs are notoriously prone to rotting in damp weather conditions. If water gathers around the scales, the bulbs will die off rapidly. Reduce the likelihood of rotting by planting each lily bulb on its side, so that water is unlikely to remain around the crown.

MOVING PLANTS

DO NOT BE AFRAID TO MOVE a plant that is not thriving because it is in the wrong place. It probably has a better chance of survival if it is moved than if it is left in its original site. Spring and autumn are the best seasons for transplanting.

CHOOSING PLANTS TO TRANSPLANT

The most important factor in transplanting is to avoid damage and disturbance to plant roots as much as possible. Young, small plants are invariably easier to transplant than older, more established ones. Use this information to help you decide which plants you can transplant.

EASY TO MOVE	RISKY TO MOVE	DIFFICULT TO MOVE
Most herbaceous perennials and shrubs that have not been planted in open ground for more than two or three years can be moved easily and successfully. Good aftercare is essential, or the initial effort is soon lost.	Old, well-established plants are generally more difficult to move than young plants because they have wide-spreading roots. Specimens that are only three or four years old should have a reasonable chance of success, but accept that moving them is a risk.	Generally speaking, plants of Mediterranean origin, which usually have a very fine and wide-spreading root system, do not transplant successfully. The following plants are best left alone if possible.
Azaleas, Bamboos, *Camellia,* *Gaultheria,* Heathers, *Kalmia,* *Pieris,* *Rhododendron,* *Vaccinium.*	Buddleias, *Chaenomeles,* Peonies*, *Rosa* spp. and cvs., most conifers, all climbing plants unless they are young with little root growth. *To increase your chances of transplanting peonies successfully, it is best to undercut them (see opposite).	*Cistus* spp., *Cytisus,* *Eucalyptus,* *Lavandula,* *Magnolia* spp., *Mahonia* spp., Poppies, Rosemary.

TRANSPLANTING CHECKLIST

● **Time of year** Move plants in autumn or early spring, never when they are growing actively.
● **Time of day** Whenever possible, move plants late in the day when temperatures have dropped. This minimizes the possibility of transplanted plants losing moisture.
● **Weak plants** Avoid transplanting a plant that is already showing signs of distress. Try to improve its growing conditions before moving it.
● **Insurance** In case of failure, take several cuttings from a shrub or plant before moving it.

● **Watering** Water the ground thoroughly before digging up a plant. If possible, do this for several days before transplanting.
● **Stems** Tie back foliage and stems before transplanting; the process is much easier if you do not have to contend with floppy branches. This also reduces the risk of damage to a shrub.
● **Spreading roots** The roots of shrubs and trees usually extend past the outermost spread of the branches. Try to move as much of the root system as possible, even if this means persuading several friends to help.

● **Soil level** Make sure you position a transplanted plant so that the soil level in the new planting hole matches the original soil level.
● **Pruning** After transplanting, prune back foliage to reduce stress from moisture loss.
● **Water loss** After transplanting, consider using an anti-transpirant spray to reduce water loss from the leaves. This is especially effective on large leaves.
● **Mulch** After transplanting, water, mulch with a deep layer of organic material, and protect the plant from sun and wind.

TRANSPLANTING SMALL SHRUBS

Small shrubs are usually fairly straightforward to move. Their rootballs are compact so are easy to lift with the minimum of disturbance. If they have wide-spreading roots, they are more difficult to move. Keep a shrub well watered and mulched after it has been replanted.

ASSESSING CONDITIONS
● **Soil condition** Do not attempt to transplant a shrub if the ground is either waterlogged or frozen.

PREPARING TO PLANT
● **Planting hole** Prepare a new planting hole before lifting a shrub. Transfer the plant as quickly as possible.

CONSERVING MOISTURE
● **Moisture loss** If a delay between lifting and planting is unavoidable, wrap the rootball in polythene or damp hessian.

TYING AND DIGGING UP A SMALL SHRUB

Use string or raffia to tie branches

Tie lower branches to aid digging

Ease roots out of the ground

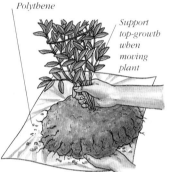

Polythene

Support top-growth when moving plant

1 Loosely tie up the branches. This makes the shrub easy to dig around and reduces the risk of stems being broken.

2 Dig a circle around the rootball. Angle the spade at about 45 degrees so that you can dig out the lowermost roots.

3 Lift the plant on to a sheet of polythene to transport it. Steady the top-growth to minimize root damage.

TRANSPLANTING LARGE SHRUBS OR TREES

Moving a large shrub or tree is risky, but it is often worth the effort and may be the only chance you have of saving a particularly precious specimen. If you are able to plan a few months ahead, a two-step process called undercutting is the most reliable method.

REUSING SHRUBS
● **Making a screen** If you are digging up specimens no longer required, group them to screen a shed or compost heap.

LOOKING AFTER PLANTS
● **Evergreens** Spray the foliage of evergreens every day for two weeks after transplanting.
● **Securing** If a shrub seems loose in its new position, drive three stakes into the ground around the planting hole. Secure the shrub's main stem to each stake with plastic string. To protect the shrub's bark, thread the string through a section of old garden hose.

UNDERCUTTING A LARGE SHRUB

Branches tied together

Dig trench outside rootball

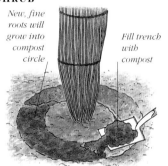

New, fine roots will grow into compost circle

Fill trench with compost

1 Tie all the branches together firmly with twine or garden wire. The autumn before you want to move the shrub, dig a circular trench around the outer edge of the rootball.

2 Fill in with compost, and water thoroughly. Keep this area moist at all times. Next autumn, dig around the outer edge of the circle so that the plant is lifted with its new roots.

TRANSPLANTING PERENNIALS

Although most perennials are easier to transplant than trees or shrubs, it still pays to transplant them with care, and at a time of year when they are least likely to resent disturbance – in autumn or spring. When lifting a plant, check whether it also needs dividing.

MOVING AND DIVIDING A WELL-ESTABLISHED PERENNIAL PLANT

Use thumbs to split plant

1 Choose as cool a day as possible, and try to wait until early evening. Use a large fork to dig up a well-established clump. Limit damage by digging deep, and by taking up as much of the root system as you can.

2 Divide the plant (see below), ensuring that each section has its own piece of the root system. Discard sections that are weak or badly damaged. The centre of a clump often contains the older, less vigorous parts of the plant.

3 Replant divided sections immediately. Considerable moisture can be lost through the leaves. To minimize this, trim off any old, damaged, or very large leaves, but make sure you do not cut back into the crown of the plant.

MOVING PERENNIALS

● **Ideal conditions** Autumn and spring are the traditional times for moving and dividing perennials. However, if your soil is particularly heavy and wet, restrict this job to the spring. If subjected to very wet soil, newly transplanted perennials are likely to suffer over the winter.

● **Summer transplanting** If a plant has to be moved or divided in the summer, choose as cool a day as possible. Water the plant thoroughly beforehand. Move it late in the day, preferably just before dark, so that it has time to recover before being subjected to midday temperatures.

● **Division points** Take a close look at the clump – you should be able to see where to separate it. Use your fingers to feel where the natural division points are. Divide the plant at these points.

DIVIDING METHODS

The most appropriate way to divide a perennial plant depends upon the type of plant involved. Small, fibrous-rooted perennials can be divided with two hand forks used back to back. You may need to use a spade for tough, fleshy-rooted plants.

Ensure that each section has at least one visible bud

Dividing with forks
Drive a fork into the clump, then drive a second fork in so that the two are back-to-back. Ease the forks up and down before pulling them apart gently and slowly. Repeat this method in order to divide up the plant into a number of pieces.

Dividing with a spade
Cut down through the centre of fleshy roots with a spade to divide the roots into sections. Some buds will be damaged in the process, but this is unavoidable. Use a sharp knife to neaten up the cut surfaces before replanting.

CARING FOR NEWLY PLANTED PLANTS

All too often, newly planted, vulnerable plants are abandoned to the elements. The care and attention taken up until this point is soon wasted if not followed by good aftercare. Anything that is newly planted, or recently replanted or divided, needs special attention.

SHADING A PLANT

Shade sunny side only

Erecting a shelter
A new plant does not have a well-established root system, so it is unable to replace lost moisture easily. Provide temporary shading using netting stapled around bamboo canes.

RETAINING MOISTURE
● **Mulching** Regular and thorough watering is essential. Limit moisture loss from the soil surface, and competition from weeds, by mulching.

Leave stem area clear

Mulching with carpet
Old carpet makes an excellent mulch. Cut a square or circle of carpet slightly larger than the root system. Cut a slit in it so that you can put the carpet around the plant. Once in place, disguise the carpet with a thin covering of mulching material, such as chipped bark or soil.

STAKING A PLANT

Making a twig support
Twigs make unobtrusive supports for tall, multi-stemmed plants. Drive them into the ground early in the year, before the plant has put on much growth. Tie them together with garden twine.

AVOIDING PROBLEMS
● **Critical period** Lavish attention on a transplanted or new plant during its first year. It is during this period that a new plant is most prone to problems and less able to cope in adverse conditions than at any other time during its life.

WATERING AND FEEDING
● **Organic matter** Improve the moisture retention of light soils by incorporating bulky organic matter before replanting (see p. 38).
● **Moisture retention** Use polymer granules to improve moisture retention in a localized area. These absorb water and slowly release it as conditions become drier.
● **Fertilizers** Regular feeding is essential. Never let granular fertilizers or manure come into direct contact with a plant because the leaves may be scorched (see p. 49).

TYING A PLANT

Tie string loosely

Tying in a tall plant
Tall flower spikes or stems often require support, especially in exposed places. Attach them to canes using string, tied loosely in a figure-of-eight, plant ties, or strips cut from a pair of old tights.

DEADHEADING

● **Rhododendrons** Remove faded flowers at regular intervals using a clean movement to limit damage to surrounding buds. Remove any dry, dead, or diseased buds at the same time.
● **Long-stemmed plants** When deadheading plants with long stems, cut each stem back to the next growth point or set of leaves.
● **Reducing stress** Minimize the stress to plants after planting by removing faded flowers and several of the new buds as well.

CONTAINER GARDENING

ONTAINER GARDENING is understandably popular. Not only does it give you the freedom to create and control your planting environment, it also makes it possible for each plant to have the most suitable growing medium as well as the optimum position for healthy growth. Containers can be used for long-term plantings in permanent positions, or moved around depending on the season.

BASIC CONTAINER TYPES

Containers are available in several materials: plastic, terracotta, stone, and wood. Weight is an important factor, especially if a container is for a balcony or roof. Size is another consideration; small pots dry out quickly, but large ones can be difficult to move.

● **Plastic containers** These are relatively inexpensive and very easy to maintain. They are lightweight and weather resistant. Plastic is available in a range of colours that can be coordinated with buildings, garden furniture, and plants.
● **Hanging baskets** These are available in a range of sizes and are best suited to seasonal planting. Carefully planted, they look equally good from all angles. They can be used on all kinds of vertical surfaces.
● **Terracotta and stone** For year-round use, choose frost-resistant containers. Stone pots are generally heavier and more expensive than other containers. They may not be suitable for lime-hating plants.
● **Wooden containers** These require regular maintenance and can be heavy, but they provide good insulation for plant roots in cold weather.

Plastic windowbox with built-in drip tray

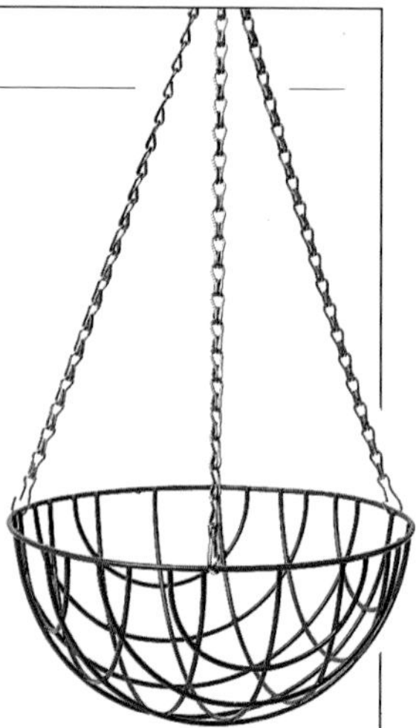

Plastic-coated wire hanging basket

Terracotta pot

Stone urn

Wooden half barrel

BASIC EQUIPMENT

The items shown here are useful for planting up, maintaining, and decorating containers.

● **Planting up** To plant up your containers you need a few key items: a good-quality hand trowel for filling and emptying containers, and for planting; a watering can for watering plants before and after planting; a layer of crocks or broken-up polystyrene to provide drainage; and windowbox feet, pot feet, or bricks to help prevent drainage holes from becoming blocked.

● **Maintaining** A hand fork is good for weeding the surfaces of established containers. You will need sharp secateurs and scissors for trimming and deadheading plants.

● **Decorating** Use a paint brush to paint your containers with gloss, matt, or plastic paint, and water-based preservative, depending on the material.

Hand fork   Hand trowel

Reversible rose for fine and coarse sprays

Watering can

Secateurs

Scissors

Crocks made from broken flowerpots

Paint brush

Windowbox feet

Pot feet

Broken-up polystyrene plant trays

Bricks

TYPES OF PLANTING SUBSTANCE

It is essential to choose the correct growing medium for your plants and their containers.

● **Composts** Lightweight peat, or peat-substitute, composts are suitable for short-term use. Heavier, loam-based composts are useful for stabilizing pots, but only when weight is not a factor.

● **Granules** Slow-release fertilizers gradually release nutrients according to soil temperature. Water-retaining granules absorb then release water when compost dries out.

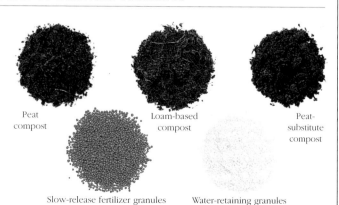

Peat compost

Loam-based compost

Peat-substitute compost

Slow-release fertilizer granules   Water-retaining granules

CONTAINER KNOW-HOW

WHATEVER TYPE OF CONTAINER you choose, the preparation, planting up, and maintenance are basically the same. All containers require adequate drainage, suitable compost, and an appropriate selection of plants.

MAKING THE MOST OF CONTAINERS

By choosing plants carefully, you can create a display that will last throughout the year. A shrub or perennial and some bulbs can be left undisturbed to come up year after year. You can complete the planting with seasonal plants around the edges of your container.

PLANTING AND REPOTTING
● **Compost** Use a peat-based, or peat-substitute, compost for large containers. It is lighter than a loam-based compost.
● **Permanent plants** Permanent container plants need feeding and watering regularly. You should repot them if their roots become congested.

Using seasonal plants
The larger the container, the more you can plant in it, especially if bulbs are planted at several depths. Put a shrub or perennial in the centre of the container, where it has most room to spread its roots, and add seasonal bedding plants around the edges.

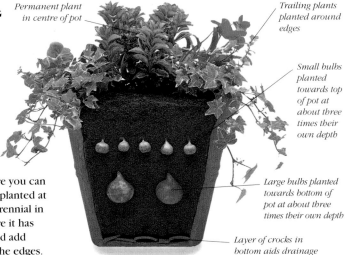

Permanent plant in centre of pot

Trailing plants planted around edges

Small bulbs planted towards top of pot at about three times their own depth

Large bulbs planted towards bottom of pot at about three times their own depth

Layer of crocks in bottom aids drainage

CREATING DRAINAGE

Adequate drainage is just as fundamental to a healthy container as adequate watering. A container that does not have proper drainage holes is virtually useless – unless you want to grow marginals or water plants. It is essential to keep all drainage holes completely clear.

CHECKING HOLES

Use high-speed drill to push through holes

Pushing through holes
Check that the drainage holes in your container have been punched out properly. If not, use a drill to do this yourself.

USING CROCKS

Teabag

Creating a drainage layer
Try using a layer or two of used teabags instead of traditional crocks. Teabags are readily available and easy to recycle.

USING DRAINAGE FEET

Keeping holes clear
Prevent drainage holes from becoming blocked with garden debris by standing your container on bricks or pot feet.

PLANNING SEASONAL PLANTING

All too often containers are full of plants during the summer but empty for the rest of the year. Use this chart to help you choose plants that will thrive in all seasons, and which can either be part of a permanent display or be planted up during the appropriate season.

SEASON	SUITABLE PLANTS		
SPRING Brighten up walls, patios, and gardens with cheerful spring containers. The warmth from the house may bring spring flowers in hanging baskets and windowboxes into life even earlier than similar plants in open ground in the garden.	*Azalea, Bellis* ('Pompette Mixed'), *Chionodoxa, Erica,* crocus, hyacinths, variegated *Hedera helix* cvs.*, dwarf irises, *Muscari azureum,* dwarf narcissus ('Hawera', 'Tête-à-Tête, 'Peeping Tom', 'February	Gold', 'February Silver), polyanthus, *Primula, Scilla sibirica* and cvs., dwarf tulips *(Tulipa kaufmanniana), Viola* x *wittrockiana, Vinca minor* 'Variegata', violas, wallflowers. * = Trailing	*Tulipa*
SUMMER There is almost no limit to the range of plants suitable for planting up in summer containers. New species and cultivars are available every year, so the choice is unbeatable. There are so many colours to choose from that you can coordinate your container in almost any way you want.	*Anisodontea capensis, Argyranthemum frutescens* and cvs., *Brachycome, Cineraria* x *hybrida, Convolvulus sabatius* cvs.*, *Dianthus chinensis, Fuchsia* (some*), *Helichrysum petiolare, Heliotropium,*	*Impatiens, Lobelia erinus* (some*), *Nicotiana alata* cvs., *Osteospermum, Pelargonium, Petunia* x *hybrida, Portulaca grandiflora, Thunbergia alata*, Tropaeolum, Verbena* x *hybrida, Viola.* * = Trailing	*Helichrysum petiolare*
AUTUMN Some summer plants will still be going strong in early autumn, but all the plants listed here can be either used on their own or combined with large plants that have good autumn colour.	*Ajuga reptans* cvs., *Callistephus chinensis, Dendranthema, Chrysanthemum koreanum, Chrysanthemum morifolium, Chrysanthemum rubellum, Cyclamen cilicium,* dahlias,	(bedding cvs.), *Euonymus fortunei* cvs., *Gazania, Hedera* cvs.*, *Lamium maculatum* cvs., *Oxalis floribunda, Lobelia siphilitica, Sedum spectabile.* * = Trailing	*Cyclamen*
WINTER Although the choice is more limited for winter than for the other seasons, you can still create gorgeous splashes of colour with what is available. You can enjoy perfume, too, by including some winter-scented shrubs such as *Daphne odora*.	*Buxus,* conifers, *Cotoneaster, Cyclamen* cvs., *Daphne odora, Eranthis hyemalis, Erica carnea* cvs., *Euonymus fortunei* cvs., *Euonymus japonicus, Galanthus nivalis, Hedera helix* cvs.*, *Helleborus, Ilex,*	*Iris unguicularis, Laurus, Mahonia* cvs., *Ophiopogon planiscapus, Pieris, Senecio maritima, Solanum capsicastrum, Vinca minor, Vinca major* cvs., *Viola* x *wittrockiana* cvs. * = Trailing	*Daphne*

PLANTING CONTAINERS

IT IS SURPRISING HOW MANY bedding plants you can squeeze into a container. Generally, the more you use, the better the end result. Buy good-quality plants, and keep the container well fed and watered for perfect results.

PLANTING FOR BEST RESULTS

Use a combination of upright, trailing, and bulky plants to create a full effect. For a dramatic look, try a single, large plant such as a shrub or small tree. After planting, leave the container in a sheltered spot for a few days before putting it in its final position.

PREPARING AND PLANTING UP A CONTAINER

Soak container with water

Upturned plastic flowerpot

Experiment with arrangements before planting

Empty plastic pot

Soaking a container
Terracotta and stone absorb water. To stop the compost from drying out, water both container and plants well before planting.

Saving compost
Deep pots are not necessary for shallow-rooted plants. Put an upturned pot inside a large container to save compost.

Positioning a pot
If a plant is prone to drying out, position a plastic pot near it. Water into this, and the water will flow directly to the plant's roots.

BASIC PLANTING METHOD

Once you have chosen a suitable compost and container for the types and number of plants you want to use, the basic planting method used for all containers is the same. Remember to bury plant labels in the potting mix next to their plants so that you have a record of your successes and failures.

Mix well before planting

Tease out congested rootball with your fingers

Firm compost between plants

1 Make maintenance easier by mixing slow-release fertilizer and water-retaining granules in with the compost before you plant up your container.

2 Start working from the centre outwards, planting your largest plant first. Check that the plants are level, and gently tease out any very congested rootballs.

3 Use your fingers to firm the compost between plants, leaving no spaces. Water well, and leave the plants to settle in a sheltered spot for a few days.

MAKING HERB GARDENS

A container allows you to have a miniature herb garden full of the herbs you use the most in a convenient place. It also makes it possible for you to move the herbs around so that they receive the summer sun and the winter protection they require in order to thrive.

PLANTING A HERB CONTAINER

Oregano

Chives

Flat-leaved parsley

Variegated sage

Trailing lobelia
will add
extra colour

Trailing
silver thyme

Golden
lemon
thyme

Planting to look good
Herbs in containers look attractive and smell delicious. Use variegated or coloured leafed forms for extra interest.

CARING FOR HERBS
● **Tender herbs** Plant frost-tender herbs in their own small pots within a container so that you can replace them easily if they become damaged in cold weather.
● **Large herbs** Herbs such as rosemary and bay need to be planted individually, since they can grow much larger than other herbs.
● **Pesticides** Avoid pesticides whenever possible. If you must use them, select those suitable for use on edible crops and that have short persistence. Check for pests and diseases regularly, and deal with them promptly.

MAINTAINING HERBS

Trimming regularly
To prevent small plants from being swamped, trim vigorous herbs with sharp scissors to remove straggly growth.

STORING HERBS

Add chopped
herbs to water

Freezing to preserve
Store chopped herb trimmings in ice for use in the winter when herbs are scarce. Thaw, and drain them if necessary, before use.

BRIGHT IDEA

Controlling mint
Mint is an invasive herb that can soon swamp less vigorous plants in the same container. Restrict its root growth by planting it in its pot when it is still small.

SUITABLE HERBS

Most herbs are suitable for containers, providing they have well-drained compost and a sunny position. Small herbs such as chives, basil, marjoram, oregano, parsley, and sage are particulary suited to container cultivation. Larger herbs such as rosemary need regular trimming. Tender herbs such as coriander and basil are fairly easy to grow in a container, provided they are given winter protection, but – since these herbs often deteriorate over winter – they are best resown annually to ensure a new crop of vigorous plants. Rosemary

COMBINING FRUIT AND VEGETABLES

Pots, windowboxes, and even hanging baskets can all be used for growing vegetables and fruit, providing you feed and water them very well. You do not need to restrict a container to just fruits or vegetables – some fruits and vegetables can be combined.

PLANTING FRUIT AND VEGETABLES IN A CONTAINER

Early cropping lettuces are most suited for growing with strawberries

Strawberries planted around edges of container

Looking good
Strawberries and lettuce grow well together in a container. For visual impact, plant red and frilly-leafed lettuces with the strawberries.

IDEAL FRUITS

Strawberries grow well in containers, and most other fruits can be container grown quite successfully as long as they are well maintained. Choose apples, pears, plums, nectarines, or other tree fruit on a dwarfing rootstock.

IDEAL VEGETABLES

French beans, tomatoes, courgettes, radishes, beetroot, aubergines, peppers, carrots, lettuce, and spring onions can all be grown in containers.

Peppers

MONEY-SAVING TIP

Making grow bags
Save money by making your own grow bags from large, plastic carrier bags filled with inexpensive compost. Water before inserting the plants. These work especially well for crops that prefer their own container.

GROWING CROPS

● **Attracting pollinators** Create a mixed container with runner beans and sweet peas trained up the same support. The sweet peas will help to attract pollinating insects. The container must be large and deep, and will need regular and thorough watering.
● **Intercropping** Grow a quick-maturing crop such as lettuce or radishes between slower crops that are most demanding late in the season.
● **Avoiding evaporation** Avoid windy sites for your fruit and vegetable containers, since wind causes rapid evaporation. Check that rainfall is not intercepted by any overhanging trees or nearby walls and roofs.
● **Mulching** Mulch containers with a 5-cm (2-in) deep layer of cocoa shell, gravel, stones, or similar material to conserve as much moisture as possible.

STRAWBERRY POTS

● **Pot size** Choose large pots, which are much easier to maintain than small ones.

Position pipe in centre of pot

Watering strawberry pots
Make some small holes in a length of hose, and put this in the pot before planting up. Water through the hose to make sure that all the strawberry plants get their share of water.

MAINTAINING YOUR PLANTS

Maintenance for container-grown plants is far more intensive than that for plants grown in the open ground. Because container plants do not have direct access to the garden soil, they are completely dependent on you for all their food and water requirements.

LOOKING AFTER PLANTS

● **Feeding** Start feeding from six to eight weeks after planting, and continue for as long as the plants are still growing. Choose a high-potash feed to encourage flowering. For a rapid effect, use a foliar feed.

● **Pruning** Large plants may need regular pruning and reducing if they are to remain in their containers. Occasional repotting into a slightly larger container also is advisable.

● **Pests and diseases** Deal with pests and diseases promptly. The close proximity of plants in a container can result in a minor infestation rapidly becoming a serious outbreak.

TRIMMING PLANTS

● **Controlling growth** Some plants are inclined to take over an entire container. Trim vigorous plants regularly to keep them in check.

Encouraging bushy growth
Use sharp scissors to prune any straggly stems. This will encourage bushy growth. Cut any flowerheads off trailing plants to encourage the growth of new foliage.

RENEWING POTTING MIX

Use trowel to remove compost

Maintaining fertility
Top-dress permanent plantings in spring to maintain compost fertility. Carefully scrape away the surface compost, making sure you do not damage any plant roots, and replace it with new compost or well-rotted manure.

REMOVING LEAVES

● **Fallen leaves** Remove fallen leaves from overhanging trees and other plants promptly, since they encourage rotting and deterioration.

Pinch out with thumb and fingers

Keeping plants healthy
Remove diseased leaves, or even whole plants, regularly to prevent the problem from spreading further. Always pinch out, or cut back, into perfectly healthy growth.

DEADHEADING PLANTS

Encouraging flowers
Pinch out, or use secateurs to cut off, fading flowerheads, or any that are beginning to form seed pods. This will stimulate the plant to produce more flowers of a better size, and over a longer period of time.

GREEN TIP

Saving water
Save water and liquid feeds from being wasted by putting pots or other containers directly underneath your hanging baskets. Any overflow from the baskets will then drip into the containers below.

POTS AND TUBS

THERE IS AN EVER-INCREASING RANGE of pots and tubs available – from the very basic and inexpensive to the extremely elaborate and expensive. Some can take only one small plant, while others are suitable for a good-size shrub or tree.

TYPES OF POT AND TUB

Pots and tubs are available in different colours, shapes, and materials. It is important that your pot is the right size for what you want to plant in it, and that it has good drainage.

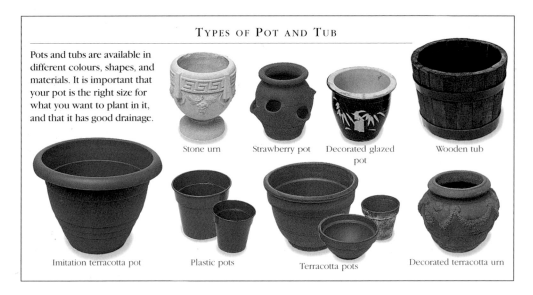

Stone urn   Strawberry pot   Decorated glazed pot   Wooden tub

Imitation terracotta pot   Plastic pots   Terracotta pots   Decorated terracotta urn

USING POTS AND TUBS

An unattractive container can be hidden by clever planting but, wherever possible, you should try to use pots, tubs, and windowboxes that complement their surroundings for a pleasing, coordinated look. They should also be the right size and style for the plants you choose.

USING ONE PLANT

Creating a focal point
Make an eye-catching focal point for your garden by planting a single specimen in a large container. For year-round interest, choose an evergreen or shrub that has highly coloured leaves or berries in the autumn.

GROUPING POTS

Softening hard edges
Group pots to hide ugly, hard edges or to make a feature of a boring part of your garden. Plant tender plants in small pots so that they can be easily moved to a sheltered area for protection during winter.

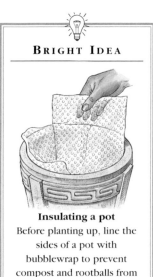

BRIGHT IDEA

Insulating a pot
Before planting up, line the sides of a pot with bubblewrap to prevent compost and rootballs from freezing over winter.

DISPLAYING POTS AND TUBS

Pots and tubs are used conventionally to soften and brighten up paved areas, but they can also add a whole new dimension to an established garden. You can move your pots to wherever they are needed in order to create different focal points throughout the season.

IMPROVING GARDENS

● **A friendly garden** Brighten up a new garden, or one that you are renovating, with temporary pots and tubs. They will make the garden a more encouraging and friendly place to work in.

● **Rotating pots** Make a flowerbed full of colour and interest throughout the year by introducing pots and tubs that are packed with flowers. As soon as they are past their best, change the displays for others that are in full flower.

● **Hiding eyesores** Use a carefully positioned, colourful pot or tub to hide an eyesore in your garden (see p. 30) or to protect a damaged area of lawn edging (see p. 130).

POSITIONING POTS AND TUBS

Stacking pots
Create a living statue of plants by stacking several pots on top of each other. This arrangement forms a dramatic garden ornament and looks especially striking if you restrict yourself to a limited range of colours.

Filling a gap
Rather than overplanting a new border, plant at the correct spacings, and use pots as temporary gap fillers until the border plants have matured. This will allow you to experiment with different plant combinations.

GARDENING ON BALCONIES AND ROOFS

Gardening above ground level very often means gardening in pots and tubs. This need not be too restricting, since a wide range of plants of all types can be grown in suitable pots – allowing you to fill even the bleakest balcony or roof with colour and scent.

MAKING A WINDBREAK

Protecting tender plants
Create a windbreak on a balcony or roof by growing climbers or wall shrubs up a trellis. As well as providing shelter for less hardy plants, it looks very attractive – especially if painted to fit in with the overall colour scheme.

MINIMIZING WEIGHT

Broken-up plant trays

Lessening the load
To keep weight to a minimum, use lightweight plastic pots and pieces of broken-up plant trays instead of crocks or stones. If you are planting shallow-rooted plants, you can fill up to a third of the pot with polystyrene.

ASSESSING A SITE

● **Checking weight** Always check the load-bearing capacity and suitability of a balcony or roof before using it to create a garden. Use lightweight potting mix and pots.

● **Tub size** Where space is limited and weight restricted, use a few large containers rather than a selection of small ones. Large containers support just as many plants, but do not dry out quickly.

FRESHENING THE AIR

● **Scented plants** Include scented plants in your selection so that you can enjoy their perfume from inside or outside the house.

CREATING ALPINE TROUGHS

Make your own trough with hypertufa, a mixture of cement, sand, and peat. Use two boxes as a mould – one inside the other – and stand the inner box on a few small, wooden blocks to allow the base to form. When these are removed, they will form drainage holes.

MAKING A HYPERTUFA TROUGH

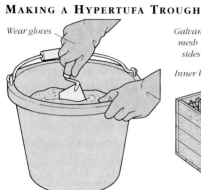

Wear gloves

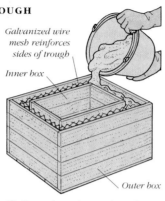

Galvanized wire mesh reinforces sides of trough

Inner box

Outer box

1 Mix 1 part cement, 1 part coarse sand, and 1–2 parts peat or peat substitute in a large, plastic bucket. Use a sturdy trowel to mix it into a thick consistency with water.

2 Pour the mixture into the cavity in a mould, which should be about 5-cm (2-in) wide. Cover the top with plastic sheeting, and leave to set for about one week.

MAKING A ROCK

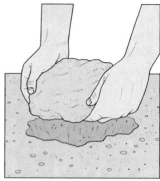

Making a hypertufa rock
Form a realistic-looking rock for your trough by digging a small, irregular hole in the ground. For each rock, fill the hole with hypertufa and leave to set.

PLANTING AN ALPINE TROUGH

Choose mound-forming plants, since these are less invasive than the sprawling types. For continuous seasonal interest, visit your local garden centre in all seasons to see what is in flower. The trough will need replanting when the available nutrients in the soil have been exhausted.

● **Drainage** Stand the trough on bricks. Place fine, galvanized mesh over the drainage holes, and add broken crocks, keeping the holes clear. Cover the base with a layer of coarse grit.

Slow-growing plants will not exhaust soil nutrients too quickly

Trailing plant hangs over edge

Take care not to damage roots

Hypertufa should be soaked in hot weather

Protecting roots
Wrap the delicate roots of small alpines in moist tissue before planting them into a crevice. This minimizes root damage and helps the plants to become established. The tissue is biodegradable.

Rosette-forming succulent

Gravel mulch

Maintaining an alpine trough
To prevent plant leaves from deteriorating in wet conditions, apply a layer of gravel as a mulch. In hot, dry weather, soak the hypertufa regularly. Remove dead leaves, and trim plants after flowering.

WINDOWBOXES

Planted up carefully, windowboxes can look stunning from both inside and outside a house. Use a selection of upright, trailing, and gap-filling plants, and include some scented plants for when the windows are open.

TYPES OF WINDOWBOX

Windowboxes are available in terracotta, wood, galvanized steel, plastic, and stone, and in a vast array of styles and sizes. Consider the colour and style of your house or flat before choosing windowboxes.

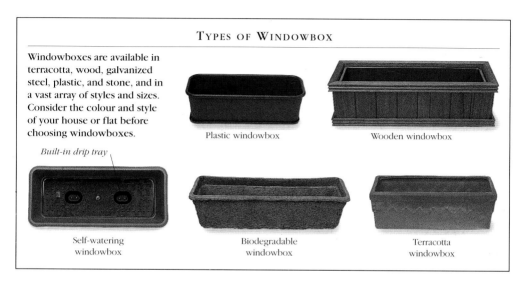

Built-in drip tray

Plastic windowbox

Wooden windowbox

Self-watering windowbox

Biodegradable windowbox

Terracotta windowbox

PLANNING WINDOWBOXES

Unless you have a sturdy window-ledge to support the box, it is best to plant using lightweight peat, or peat-substitute, compost.

Before finalizing your planting scheme, check that you can open your window, and that you have proper access to the box for maintenance.

USING FOLIAGE
● **Shape and colour** Foliage plants will add shape and colour to your planting throughout the entire year. They will form a framework to which you can add flowering plants for each season.

CHOOSING PLANTS
● **Tender plants** Consider including slightly tender plants in your planting, since these will thrive better in the shelter of a wall than in open ground.
● **Tall plants** Avoid using very tall plants unless the box is in a sheltered position. Tall plants may make the windowbox top-heavy and therefore unstable. Look for compact forms of your chosen plants.

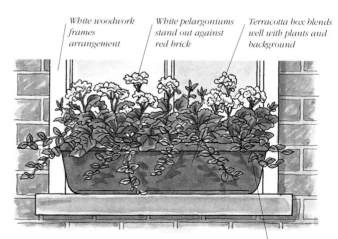

White woodwork frames arrangement

White pelargoniums stand out against red brick

Terracotta box blends well with plants and background

Trailing silver foliage blends well with pelargoniums

Blending and matching colours
Consider the background colour of your house or flat when selecting your plants and choosing or decorating your windowbox. You should also ensure that your box is in proportion to the window-ledge.

USING WINDOWBOXES

Windowboxes can be invaluable when it comes to brightening up a vista of grey, uninspiring buildings. They can also be used very successfully in many other places. The bleakest of surroundings can be brought to life with an imaginatively planted windowbox.

DISPLAYING WINDOWBOXES

Fixing to railings
You need a sturdy windowbox with a strong base for hanging on railings, since there is little, if any, support from below. Use strong metal hooks or brackets to attach the windowbox to the horizontal top rail. A lightweight compost will be essential.

Tumbling down walls
Used like an elongated planter on top of a wall, a windowbox like this should include trailing plants to tumble down the wall. Make sure it is firmly attached with brackets or galvanized screws, and that your neighbour is happy with the idea, too.

SITING WINDOWBOXES

● **Balconies** To conserve valuable space, attach windowboxes to a balcony balustrade, or place them on a balcony floor so that the plants are able to cascade through the railings.
● **Sunny spots** A sunny window-ledge is the ideal place for a windowbox planted up with herbs. Tumbling tomatoes also grow well in a windowbox.
● **High rises** If you live in a high-rise flat, choose only low-growing plants for your windowboxes, and plant them firmly to protect them from the wind. Be sure to stake any fragile plants.

MAINTAINING WINDOWBOXES

Wooden windowboxes may need treating with a water-based preservative every few years. Painted boxes may sometimes need stripping and repainting. Remember that it is not just the box itself that needs attention. The fittings may also need repairing or replacing.

PRESERVING WOOD

Apply at least one coat

Applying preservative
Ensure that the surface is clean, dry, and free from any flaky material before applying paint or preservative. Remove the windowbox from its position so that you can paint the base and sides as well as the front.

PAINTING WINDOWBOXES
● **Renovating** Brighten up a dull windowbox by painting the visible surfaces. Use gloss paint or a water-based wood preservative for wooden boxes, and a special plastic paint for discoloured, shabby plastic boxes. Ensure that the painted surface is completely dry before planting up.

INSURING WINDOWBOXES
● **Damage** Check that your insurance-policy cover extends to your windowboxes, as well as to any damage they might do to people or property should they fall. If you do not own the house or flat you live in, make sure that you are allowed to use windowboxes.

SECURING BOXES

● **Supported box** Screw galvanized, L-shaped brackets into wall plugs in the wall. Screw two brackets to each side of the windowbox.
● **Hanging box** If a box hangs below a window, support it with brackets fixed to the wall and base of the box.

HANGING BASKETS

O NE OF THE MOST POPULAR TYPES of container, hanging baskets can be used to great effect in the smallest areas. Choose as large a basket as possible, and use a good-quality liner to ensure that the plants do not dry out quickly.

TYPES OF HANGING BASKET

Hanging baskets are available in enough different styles and sizes to enable you to choose exactly what you want. A good-quality basket will last well and look attractive for many years.

BASIC EQUIPMENT

Pliers for removing basket chain

Knife for making cuts in basket liner

Built-in drip tray

Plastic basket

Plastic-coated wall basket

Terracotta wall pot

Plastic-coated wire hanging basket

Self-watering basket

PLANTING HANGING BASKETS

F or a really full effect, pack as many plants as you can into a hanging basket, and plant up the sides as much as possible to hide the liner (see p. 76). When planting trailing plants, alternate one trailing with one upright plant to prevent the basket from looking straggly.

PLANTING TRAILING PLANTS

Wrap from leafy end

Cover roots with wide end of cone

Ease plant through slit

1 Wrap any trailing plants in small pieces of polythene shaped into narrow cones. This protects the rootballs when they are pulled through the sides of the basket.

2 Use a sharp knife to cut a slit in the lining, and ease a plant through. Remove the polythene immediately. Always plant up in the shade to minimize stress to the plants.

BRIGHT IDEA

Disguising chains
Hide ugly basket chains by training trailing plants to cover them. Wind the stems around the chains gently, and tie them in loosely with garden twine or plastic ties.

TYPES OF HANGING-BASKET LINING

TRADITIONAL LININGS
● **Felt and foam** These basket liners are inexpensive, and unobtrusive if green.
● **Coconut fibre** These bulky liners provide winter insulation.
● **Recycled wool** Woollen liners are backed with polythene.
● **Sphagnum moss** This is a popular lining material but is not always considered to be environmentally acceptable.
● **Compacted card** These liners are designed to fit a basket but can be difficult to fit properly.

ALTERNATIVE LININGS
● **Newspaper** Cut several sheets of newspaper into circles to use as a liner. However, if visible it is not very attractive.
● **Knitwear** An old jumper or scarf can be cut up and used as a liner. Although not very attractive, knitwear is efficient.
● **Blanket weed** Try using a dense layer of blanket weed as a moss substitute.

Felt liner

Foam liner

Coconut-fibre liner

Pre-marked holes for trailing plants

Recycled-wool liner

Sphagnum moss

Compacted-card liner

Newspaper

Knitwear

Blanket weed

USING HANGING BASKETS

Most hanging baskets are suspended from brackets attached to buildings. However, they lend themselves to far more exciting uses. A porch, sun-room, conservatory, and outside garage are all suitable sites for hanging baskets, as are arches, pergolas, and garden walls.

DISPLAYING HANGING BASKETS

Hanging on a pergola
Brighten up a wooden pergola or arch with a few hanging baskets. Choose shade-tolerant plants such as *Impatiens*, *Begonia*, and *Fuchsia* if the pergola is covered with dense, well-established foliage.

Hanging on a wall
Half-baskets are especially well suited to garden walls, and the protection from the wall may prolong their growing season. Winter baskets attached directly to a building wall benefit from the extra warmth.

MAKING BALLS
● **Hanging ball** Create a sphere of colour using two baskets planted up with bushy plants through the sides only. When the plants have settled, tie the baskets together – flat surface to flat surface – to form a ball.

PROTECTING IN WINTER
● **Extra warmth** Winter baskets benefit from a dense lining to protect their roots from freezing. Use an attractive but thin liner that is lined with an additional, inexpensive material for additional insulation. A recycled circle of knitwear or a few sheets of newspaper are both suitable.

SUSPENDING HANGING BASKETS

Hang your planted basket at a height where maintenance will be possible. If it is too high up, it may be difficult to feed and water easily. Before hanging, check that the bracket is firmly in place, and position the basket so that its most attractive sides are showing.

USING A PULLEY SYSTEM

Basket can be lowered for watering and feeding

Lowering a basket
To make watering a high basket easy, buy a special bracket and basket hanger that incorporates a pulley system, enabling you to lower and raise the basket.

POSITIONING BASKETS

● **Checking brackets** Use wall plugs and galvanized screws to attach a bracket to a wall. Check that the bracket is long enough to hold the basket away from the wall.
● **Suitable position** In sunny gardens, avoid siting baskets on the sunniest walls. Plants benefit from some shade.
● **Leaving bare areas** If you run short of plants, leave one side of your basket more sparsely planted than the others, and ensure that you hang the basket in a corner where the sparsely planted side is hidden.
● **Recordkeeping** Photograph any baskets that you are particularly pleased with so that you have a permanent record of your successes.

USING WATER PRESSURE

Bracket must take weight of watered basket

Direct jet close to plant roots

Pumping water
Use a long tube attached to a pump-action container for regularly watering and feeding hanging baskets that are too high to reach easily.

MAINTAINING HANGING BASKETS

Of all containers, hanging baskets are the most difficult to keep looking good. Often positioned in windy, sunny, and exposed areas, they need watering at least once a day in summer. Once a basket has dried out, it can be very difficult to revive the plants fully.

CONSERVING MOISTURE

Chain removed before planting

Making a water reservoir
When planting up, place an old saucer or an aluminium pie dish in the base of the basket before adding the compost. This will act as a water reservoir.

REWETTING COMPOST

Add one or two drops of washing-up liquid

Using a wetting agent
If a compost becomes so dry that water runs off it, add a couple of drops of mild washing-up liquid to the water. This will allow the water to penetrate the surface.

RESCUING A BASKET

Taking emergency action
Lower a very dry basket into a bowl of water, and leave until the compost looks moist. Remove the basket, and stand it in the shade until the plants perk up.

RECYCLING CONTAINERS

W ITH A LITTLE IMAGINATION, you can transform something quite ordinary into an attractive planter. If you reuse household items imaginatively, you can have plenty of pots at a fraction of the cost of traditional containers.

CONVERTING CONTAINERS

A lmost any vaguely suitable item can be used as a plant container. To be really successful, the item must be large enough to hold sufficient compost for proper root growth, and to prevent the compost from drying out too rapidly. Drainage is also essential.

USING ALTERNATIVE CONTAINERS

Sides of colander disguised with trailing plants

Converting a colander
A colander comes complete with drainage holes. All you need to do is attach a set of basket chains. You could also use a large sieve, as long as it is lined first.

● **Catering containers** Catering food containers can often be obtained inexpensively. Made from plastic or metal, they are not very attractive, but – if carefully planted with plenty of trailing plants – the sides of a container can be completely hidden.
● **Car tyres** For a container that you can make as deep or as shallow as you like, try stacking a few old car tyres on top of each other.
● **Old bath** Use an old bath as a planter. Its depth is ideal for large plants that require a sizeable growing area.

Tall plant is supported by cane

Planting a chamber pot
An old chamber pot can make an ornamental pot suitable for seasonal displays of annuals. Create drainage by making a hole in the bottom.

BRIGHT IDEA

Keeping insects out
Put a piece of net curtain or fine-gauge wire mesh under a bottomless container to keep pests out.

MAKING DRAINAGE HOLES

Proper drainage is absolutely essential. Without it, water will accumulate and kill the plant roots. Use any suitable safe method to make drainage holes, and always wear goggles.

High-speed, steel drill bit

Metal container
Use a high-speed drill bit to make several drainage holes in the bottom of a metal container.

Push point through carefully

Plastic container
A metal awl should pierce plastic. You may need to heat the tool first to penetrate thick surfaces.

DECORATING CONTAINERS

Ugly, shabby, or boring containers can be transformed instantly with a coat of paint or wood stain. New terracotta, hypertufa, or stone can be artificially aged, too. Well-weathered containers look softer than new ones, and fit in better with their surroundings.

USING WOOD STAIN
● **Colours** Subdued colours are usually best because they do not detract from the beauty and style of the plants.

An old vegetable crate makes an inexpensive windowbox

Staining wood
Change the look of a wooden container by painting it with a wood preservative or stain. These come in a wide range of colours.

PAINTING CONTAINERS
● **Matching** Try linking your containers with your garden furniture by painting them with matching colours.

Paint rim in contrasting colour

Painting terracotta
Create a subtle but effective look by painting just the rim or raised pattern of a container, leaving the rest in the original colour.

WEATHERING EFFECTS

Apply yoghurt with paint brush

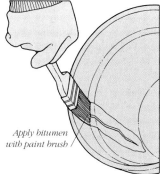

Ageing a container
Apply yoghurt to encourage surface growths of algae and mosses, which make stone, concrete, and terracotta containers appear older, or use a liquid-manure solution. Rubbing with fresh parsley gives an instant result, but takes much longer to apply.

LOOKING AFTER CONTAINERS

It is sometimes possible to repair a cracked, chipped, or slightly broken container. You should, however, mend any cracks as soon as they appear. A neglected crack can fill with water, which then expands as it freezes during the winter, causing even more damage.

SEALING SHALLOW CRACKS IN POTS

Apply mixture with spatula

Apply bitumen with paint brush

Filling external cracks
Shallow, exterior cracks may develop if a pot is knocked over or as a result of a sharp frost. Apply a mixture of PVA adhesive and sand to fill cracks in concrete or stone containers.

Covering internal cracks
Cracks on the inside can be repaired simply by using bitumen applied with a paint brush. This rather obvious mending cannot be seen from the outside of the pot.

PREVENTING DAMAGE
● **Frost-resistant pots** Choose frost-resistant containers. A pot that is not frost tolerant may be reduced to a crumbling mass.
● **Barrel-shaped pots** Never put a potentially large plant in an urn-shaped pot. It will be impossible to remove it without breaking the pot.
● **Repotting** Woody plants may outgrow small containers. Repot them regularly to prevent pots from shattering.

USING DAMAGED POTS
● **Damaged pots** Use damaged pots for temporary, seasonal planting of herbaceous or annual plants. These exert little, if any, pressure on containers.

PLANT CARE

QUICK REFERENCE

Protecting Plants, p. 82

Feeding Plants, p. 84

Watering Plants, p. 89

Weeding, p. 94

Pruning Plants, p. 100

ONCE YOU HAVE CHOSEN and planted the ideal plants for your garden, you must continue to look after them according to their needs. Regular maintenance and aftercare, especially during the first year, are vital to their long-term success. Plants that are well cared for will perform well, look attractive, and resist attack from pests and diseases.

AVOIDING PROBLEMS

Most problems in the garden can be avoided, or at least their impact can be kept to a minimum, by good aftercare. A plant should thrive if it is kept well watered, fed, and pruned. Some tasks, such as feeding, watering, and mulching, should be carried out as and when required throughout the year. Others, such as pruning and deadheading, may need to be done at specific times. Even problems with pests and diseases can be kept to a minimum by looking after plants well; a vigorous, healthy plant is well equipped to fight off a problem and to compensate for any damage.

LEAVES

Protect young foliage from late frosts; once damaged, dieback may occur. Check foliage for pests and diseases, and take prompt action to eradicate problems (see p. 108). Apply foliar feeds during the growing period to stimulate growth.

FLOWERS

Adequate sunlight and warmth are essential in order for flower buds to form. A regular supply of moisture is necessary for the continuing development of healthy buds. Use a high-potash fertilizer (see p. 86) to encourage flowering.

ROOTS

Keep roots well fed and watered. Avoid drought and waterlogging, since both can prevent roots from taking up nutrients in the soil. Do not restrict roots by poor planting, planting in a cramped position, or planting in compacted soil.

STEMS

Check plant stems for diseases and pests. Prune out if necessary, or apply other control measures. Prune to encourage flowering and to keep an open structure. This will allow air to circulate, making the plant resistant to attack from disease.

FRUIT

To ensure good fruit size and quality, supply adequate moisture throughout fruit development. Regular watering prevents fruit from cracking and developing disorders. Feed with a high-potash feed (see p. 85) to encourage good fruiting.

BASIC EQUIPMENT

Looking after your garden with good-quality tools will help you to perform tasks efficiently, and will prove cost-effective. The tools you need will depend on the size and type of your garden.

● **Comfort** Check that tools, including small tools such as secateurs, hand forks, and hand trowels are comfortable to hold, and that they are easy to grip. A moulded plastic handle is pleasant to hold, even in cold weather, and is easy to clean.

● **Weight** You may prefer to use lightweight tools. Many tools traditionally made of metal are available in plastic, including wheelbarrows and watering cans.

● **Length** It is important to use spades, forks, hoes, and rakes with the correct shaft length.

● **Tread** Choose a spade with a tread at the top of the blade; this will relieve pressure on your instep and improve grip.

● **Reach** Choose a hose that reaches all parts of the garden.

● **Small areas** Use a hand sprayer to apply pesticides to plants in a small area.

● **Protection** Protect your hands with gardening gloves.

Tread

Spade

Fork

Watering can

Dutch hoe

Garden rake

Hose-end attachment

Secateurs

Wheelbarrow

Hand sprayer

Hand fork

Hand trowel

Gardening gloves

Hose

PROTECTING PLANTS

WEATHER CONDITIONS VARY not only from season to season, but also from day to day. Many plants are able to withstand changing temperatures, but some will need special care and attention during extreme weather conditions.

PROTECTING FROM FROST

Frost is potentially very damaging. Its arrival may be unexpected, and it often follows or precedes fairly mild weather, when plants are particularly vulnerable. Early winter frosts, and the late frosts that occur once plants have started growing again in spring, are the most damaging.

PROVIDING INSULATION

Protecting plant and pot
Protect the rootball of a container plant, and the pot itself, by wrapping the container in hessian, newspaper, or bubble plastic. Tie in place with string.

PROTECTING ROSES

Mounding soil
Mound up soil around rose stems during very cold weather. Remove the soil when the weather warms up. If the soil is very heavy or wet, use garden compost instead.

FIGHTING FROST

● **Insulation** Protect the crowns of herbaceous plants and shrubs by surrounding them loosely with chicken wire. Anchor the wire to the ground, and pack it with dry leaves, bracken, or straw.
● **Air circulation** Make sure that air can circulate around insulated plants. Stagnant air allows moisture to accumulate, which can lead to rotting.
● **Fertilizers** Soft growth is prone to frost damage, so do not use high-nitrogen fertilizers late in the season (see p. 84–85). Feed with potash to encourage strong growth.

COVERING OVERNIGHT

● **Fleeces and films** Drape plants with horticultural fleece or film, or old net curtains, to protect flower buds and soft, new growth. Remove as soon as frost is no longer a danger.

Using newspaper
For simple and inexpensive overnight frost protection, cover vulnerable plants with a layer or two of newspaper held in place with bricks or large stones.

PROTECTING FROM SNOW

A covering of snow on hedges, shrubs, and trees is potentially damaging, since snow will weigh down stems. The greatest danger is from snow that has partly thawed and then frozen again.

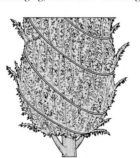

Protecting trees
Protect trees such as conifers, which have dense branch structures, by tying the branches together with galvanized wire.

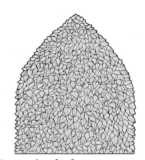

Protecting hedges
Clip hedges so that their upper surfaces slope. This will prevent snow from settling on them and causing them to lose their shape.

PROTECTING FROM HEAT

Excessive heat can be damaging to plants at all stages of growth. High temperatures can cause too much moisture loss, scorching, poor nutrient uptake, and wilting. Temperatures that fluctuate are potentially more damaging than those that are consistently too high.

PREVENTING WILTING

● **Vulnerability** Protect young plants and any that have been transplanted recently. These are particularly prone to damage from wilting.

Using a flowerpot

Protect a small, vulnerable plant with a temporary sun shield such as a flowerpot. Position the pot early in the day, before temperatures start to rise. Choose as large a pot as possible so that air can circulate inside it.

KEEPING TEMPERATURES DOWN IN A GREENHOUSE

Paving slabs absorb heat during daytime

Water away from plants

Damping down
Reduce greenhouse temperatures in very hot weather by wetting the floor with water several times a day. This will increase the humidity and lower the overall temperature. Avoid splashing the plants, since this may cause scorching.

CONTROLLING PESTS

● **Maintaining humidity** Red spider mites thrive in hot, dry environments, so damp a greenhouse down regularly to maintain high humidity and deter these pests (see above).

KEEPING AIR FRESH

● **Ventilation** Ensure that there is adequate ventilation in a greenhouse. Fit blinds or use paint-on greenhouse shading to reduce temperatures and the scorching effect of bright light.

PROTECTING FROM WIND AND POLLUTION

Within any garden there is a wide range of potential problems against which plants need protection. Some occur naturally, such as strong winds. Others, such as pollution, result from motor traffic and industrial activity. Take steps to minimize the effects of some of these.

PREVENTING DAMAGE

● **Exposed areas** Permeable windbreaks are suitable for large, exposed areas. Erect them around the affected area, and secure them with stakes.
● **Wind tunnels** Wind rushes through gaps between buildings. When siting a new shed or greenhouse, do not create a wind tunnel by putting it too close to another building.
● **Suitable plants** Choose plants that suit the conditions. Those that have small, thick, waxy leaves are more resistant to wind than plants with thin, delicate, or large leaves.

MAKING A WINDBREAK

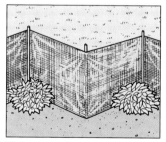

Using netting

Young plants are especially prone to damage from strong winds. Protect susceptible plants with a temporary windbreak made from flexible double netting secured with canes.

BUILDING A BARRIER

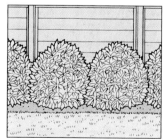

Using a hedge

A garden near a busy road will receive high levels of pollution. Help to keep excessive lead out by erecting a barrier of panel fencing. Plant up with a pollution-tolerant hedge such as laurel.

FEEDING PLANTS

To perform properly, plants will almost always need additional feeding. In any garden, and especially if plants are packed together, use either a complete fertilizer or specific nutrients. For more details, consult the chart opposite.

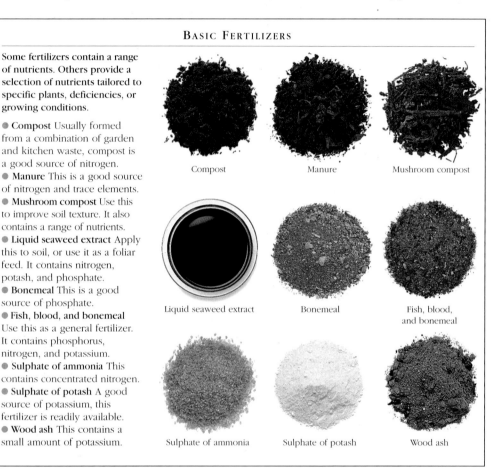

BASIC FERTILIZERS

Some fertilizers contain a range of nutrients. Others provide a selection of nutrients tailored to specific plants, deficiencies, or growing conditions.

● **Compost** Usually formed from a combination of garden and kitchen waste, compost is a good source of nitrogen.
● **Manure** This is a good source of nitrogen and trace elements.
● **Mushroom compost** Use this to improve soil texture. It also contains a range of nutrients.
● **Liquid seaweed extract** Apply this to soil, or use it as a foliar feed. It contains nitrogen, potash, and phosphate.
● **Bonemeal** This is a good source of phosphate.
● **Fish, blood, and bonemeal** Use this as a general fertilizer. It contains phosphorus, nitrogen, and potassium.
● **Sulphate of ammonia** This contains concentrated nitrogen.
● **Sulphate of potash** A good source of potassium, this fertilizer is readily available.
● **Wood ash** This contains a small amount of potassium.

Compost

Manure

Mushroom compost

Liquid seaweed extract

Bonemeal

Fish, blood, and bonemeal

Sulphate of ammonia

Sulphate of potash

Wood ash

SAFETY

● **Protecting skin and lungs** Always wear gloves when using fertilizer, and do not breathe in vapour or dust. Read the instructions, and use the recommended quantities.
● **Storage** Store fertilizers in a cool, dry, and preferably dark place. Ensure that all containers are tightly closed, and that they are out of the reach of children and animals.

USING FERTILIZERS

● **When to use** Correct timing of application is essential. Feeding late in the season may promote soft growth, which will be vulnerable to early frosts. Late feeding may also cause bud failure on ornamental shrubs such as camellias.
● **Avoiding scorching** Keep all fertilizers – except for foliar feeds – off leaves, flowers, and stems (see p. 86).

● **Appropriate choice** Choose a fertilizer that is formulated for the specific needs of the plant you are feeding, and for the time of year you are planning to apply the fertilizer.
● **Watering in fertilizers** Always keep a separate watering can specifically for applying liquid and foliar feeds. Never use this can for watering or for applying chemical pesticides to plants.

FORMS OF FERTILIZER

Fertilizers are available in different forms. The type you choose depends on the requirements of your plants and on how frequently you apply fertilizer.

● **Granular fertilizers** These usually contain balanced amounts of major nutrients.
● **Slow-release fertilizers** Nutrients are released into soil in response to temperature changes.
● **Liquid and soluble fertilizers** Diluted with water, most are applied to roots, but some can be applied to the leaves as a foliar feed (see p. 86).
● **Sticks and tablets** Push these fertilizers into soil or compost after planting has taken place.

Granular fertilizer

Slow-release pellets

Liquid fertilizer

Fertilizer sticks

Fertilizer tablets

Soluble, all-purpose fertilizer

PLANT NUTRIENTS

NUTRIENT	PLANTS MOST IN NEED	SOILS MOST IN NEED	SIGNS OF SHORTAGE
NITROGEN	All plants, but especially those grown for their foliage.	Most soils following heavy cropping, but especially poor soils.	Pale leaves and generally unhealthy-looking growth.
PHOSPHATE	All plants; especially useful for root development and for newly planted plants and bulbs.	Most soils following heavy cropping, but especially sandy or poor soils.	Poor root development and establishment, which is indicated by stunted growth.
POTASH	All plants, especially those grown for their flowers or fruit; use to harden plants before a harsh winter.	All soils, especially those that have had lots of high-nitrogen fertilizer or manure incorporated.	Poor flowering, poor fruiting and berrying; plants may also be prone to frost or general winter damage.
MAGNESIUM	All plants, since this is a major constituent of chlorophyll.	Sandy, acid, wet soils, and those with a high potassium content.	Yellow or brown patches around edges and between leaf veins.
IRON	All plants, especially those intolerant of alkaline soils, e.g. *Rhododendron*.	All soils, but especially those with a high pH caused by chalk, limestone, and lime.	Yellowing between leaf veins, especially on younger growth.
OTHER NUTRIENTS	Various minor nutrients and trace elements are needed in small amounts by plants.	Most light soils, but also any soil that has been used heavily.	General poor growth; symptoms may indicate a deficiency of a particular nutrient.

APPLYING FERTILIZERS

Fertilizers can be applied using one of many different methods, depending largely on the type or formulation of the fertilizer you use. Choose the method most suitable for the size of your garden, the effect you wish to achieve, and the amount of time you have available.

DILUTING FERTILIZERS
● **Quick absorption** Use a liquid fertilizer for a rapid effect. This is usually applied with a watering can.
● **Large areas** If you are feeding a large area, use a hose-end applicator that automatically dilutes the fertilizer.

Watering in fertilizer
Apply liquid fertilizer directly to roots by getting as close to the base of the plant as possible. Any liquid that is not absorbed by the soil is wasted, or may even feed nearby weeds.

APPLYING A FOLIAR FEED

Spraying leaves
Apply a foliar feed with hose-end applicator, or use a watering can with a fine rose. Most of the fertilizer will be absorbed by the leaves; any excess will be taken up by the plant roots.

SCATTERING FERTILIZERS
● **Saving time** Scatter fertilizer granules over the whole soil surface to benefit the greatest area of soil, and to minimize the risk of overfeeding.
● **Individual feeding** Apply fertilizer granules around the bases of individual plants.

Forking in fertilizer
Take great care not to damage plant roots when forking granules into the soil around the base of a plant. Water the granules in well afterwards unless heavy rain is forecast.

TIMING FOLIAR FEEDS
● **When to apply** Dusk is the best time to apply foliar feed. Never use foliar feed in bright sunlight. This may lead to scorching of leaves and petals.
● **Late application** Foliar feeds can be used relatively late in the growing season because they will not continue to promote plant growth during the cold winter months.

USING POTASH FEEDS
● **High flower yield** Encourage flowers by applying a high-potash fertilizer – the type used on tomato plants. This is most effective when used on bedding plants (see p. 87).

USING FERTILIZERS
● **Watering in** Always water in a fertilizer thoroughly. Plants can absorb nutrients only if they are dissolved in liquid.
● **Adjusting soil pH** If your soil has a high pH, or if you are growing lime-hating plants, choose a fertilizer formulated especially for this kind of soil or these plants (see p. 85).
● **Applying lime** Do not apply lime at the same time as manure. Lime reacts with the nitrogen in the manure, releasing nitrogen in the form of ammonia. This may cause damage to plants and is a waste of the nitrogen.
● **Avoiding scorch** Do not let concentrated fertilizers come into direct contact with leaves, flowers, or young stems, or they may scorch.
● **Drastic action** Combine a quick-acting foliar feed with a long-lasting general fertilizer applied at the roots for a plant in urgent need of feeding.

MIXING FERTILIZERS

Avoiding scorching
When planting, mix the fertilizer with soil or compost before backfilling the hole. This ensures that the fertilizer is available to all parts of the root system and minimizes the risk of scorching.

TIMING THE APPLICATION OF FERTILIZERS

Feeding should take place during a period of active plant growth, but not at a time when it could promote new growth too late in the season. The precise timing of applications depends both on the type of fertilizer you use and on the requirements of the plant.

FEEDING SEEDLINGS
● **Seedling boost** If your seedlings look unhealthy, it is possible that the nutrients in the compost have been exhausted. Unless you are able to transplant the seedlings immediately, apply a combined foliar and root feed.

Be careful not to drench seedlings when applying fertilizer

Applying fertilizer
Use a small watering can or plant mister to apply a liquid fertilizer to seedlings that are waiting to be pricked out. Make sure that you dilute the fertilizer to half its normal strength.

FEEDING A SHRUB

Keep feed away from stem

Boosting a pruned shrub
Encourage new growth in an extensively pruned shrub by applying a complete fertilizer. Sprinkle the fertilizer around the base of the shrub, and fork it in without damaging the roots.

FEEDING BULBS
● **Promoting flowering** The flowering capacity of bulbs can be improved by applying a foliar feed to the leaves. This is especially beneficial to naturalized bulbs, and to bulbs that have been growing in the same place for some time.

Feeding after flowering
Once flowering is over, apply a foliar feed every 10–14 days. Continue doing this until the foliage starts to turn yellow and die back. Do not tie or cut down any leaves for at least six weeks.

FEEDING LAWNS
● **Dry weather** If your lawn needs feeding during a dry, hot summer, and it is not possible to water in a granular feed, use liquid fertilizer on the lawn instead. Inadequate feeding often encourages *Corticium* (red thread) disease.
● **Application** To feed a lawn, weigh out the correct amount of fertilizer, and divide it in half. Apply the first half in one direction, up and down the lawn, apply the second half across, at right angles to this.
● **Yellow grass** If grass begins to turn yellow and is generally lacking in vigour, apply a nitrogen-rich fertilizer.

REGULATING FEEDINGS
● **Dry weather** Do not feed plants if they are suffering from lack of water. They will not be able to absorb the fertilizer properly and may be damaged in the process.
● **Overfeeding** Late in the season, avoid using more high-nitrogen fertilizer than plants require. This may promote soft growth, which is particularly prone to frost damage (see p. 82).
● **Encouraging flowers** To increase flower yield, apply a dressing of sulphate of potash to flowerbeds in autumn and in early spring.
● **Vegetables** Leafy plants that are in the ground for a long time, such as spring cabbage, may need an extra feed of nitrogen at the end of winter.
● **Liquid seaweed** Tomatoes, marrows, and courgettes benefit from a feed of liquid seaweed applied fortnightly during the growing season.

BRIGHT IDEA

Converting weights
To calculate how many handfuls of fertilizer are needed for an area, weigh one handful and divide the total weight needed by this figure.

USING NATURAL FERTILIZERS

Some gardeners prefer to use fertilizers of a natural origin; others use only chemical fertilizers. The best effect is usually achieved by using a combination of both. Whichever you select, there are plenty from which to choose, including many natural products.

UTILIZING NITROGEN

Cut plants close to ground level

Nourishing the soil

Peas and beans have bacteria in their roots that allow them to convert nitrogen into a usable form. Cut the plants down to ground level when they have finished cropping, and leave the roots to nourish the soil.

ADDING NUTRIENTS

● **Peas and beans** Always include these, and other legumes, in a crop rotation (see p. 109). They will help to increase nitrogen levels in the soil – even if their roots are not left in the ground at the end of the season.

● **Compost** Start a compost heap immediately if you do not already have one (see p. 43). Garden compost contains many natural plant nutrients and helps to improve and condition the soil.

● **Wood ash** Collect wood ash from a cold bonfire after burning plant material, and use it as a fertilizer. Wood ash contains useful nutrients, particularly sulphate of potash.

GREEN TIP

Using eggshells

Add a layer of crushed eggshells to the base of a planting hole as a natural source of calcium, and to help drainage. Use for all plants except those that prefer an acid soil, because eggshells are alkaline.

MAKING YOUR OWN FERTILIZER

Make your own totally organic liquid fertilizer from plants such as stinging nettles (or comfrey). The process is very simple and, provided that you have somewhere to store a quantity of fertilizer, is a cheap and satisfying way of providing your plants with good-quality, effective nutrients.

Pour water over nettles in bowl

1 Collect freshly picked stinging nettles, and press them into a large bowl or bucket. Start with as large a quantity of nettles as you can, since they decrease in volume once they start to rot down. Add water, allowing roughly 10 litres (18 pints) of water to 1 kg (about 2 lb) of nettles.

Use wooden spoon to stir nettles

Clingfilm

2 Mix the stinging nettles and water thoroughly, making sure that all the nettles are covered with water. Cover with clingfilm or a tight-fitting lid. Stir several times with a wooden spoon over a period of several weeks. Always replace the clingfilm or lid.

Strain liquid into plastic bucket

Leftover nettles can be used on compost heap

3 After a few weeks, when the mixture is rotted down, strain it into a bucket. Before using the liquid fertilizer, dilute it with water about ten times. The solid matter left behind can be incorporated into a compost heap for future use.

WATERING PLANTS

A REGULAR SUPPLY OF WATER IS ESSENTIAL for your plants. Without it, plants suffer moisture stress and may wilt and die. Established shrubs and trees can last without water longer than plants with shallow roots, such as annuals.

KEEPING GARDENS WATERED

Water is often in short supply, particularly during long, dry spells in summer, and is a precious resource we should try not to waste.

The watering technique you use, and precisely how, when, and where the water is applied, is important if you are to avoid wastage.

WATERING CORRECTLY

Directing water
To ensure that water is able to penetrate right down to a plant's roots, position the hose or watering can spout at the base of a plant, and water gently.

WATERING INCORRECTLY

Watering too strongly
Never direct a jet of water at the base of a plant. This washes away the soil from the roots and prevents the water from seeping down into the soil.

ASSESSING CONDITIONS

● **When not to water** Avoid watering during the heat of the day. Watering in bright light can cause scorching, especially on flowers, buds, and petals. The resulting humidity may also encourage fungal diseases, such as powdery mildew, scab, and grey mould, to develop.
● **Watering twice** Water the surface of very dry soil lightly to prevent water from running off the surface. Water again once the initial water has been absorbed into the soil.
● **Pot watering** To water a large plant, sink a pot that has a drainage hole into the soil near the plant, and fill with water.

PLANT-WATERING CHECKLIST

There are some situations in which soil is particularly prone to drying out. Use drought-resistant plants for these areas. Some plants and planting situations always need plenty of water.

SITUATIONS THAT ARE DROUGHT-PRONE
● Free-draining, light, sandy soil.
● Soil overlying chalk.
● Soil adjacent to a wall – walls absorb soil moisture.
● Plants growing against a house wall – rainfall on the soil is restricted by overhanging roof tiles and guttering.
● Plants on steep slopes, especially if they face the sun.
● Plants in windy situations.

PLANTS THAT ARE RESISTANT TO DROUGHT
● Silver foliage plants such as *Helichrysum* and *Stachys lanata*.
● Shrubs such as *Abelia* x *grandiflora, Azara, Ceanothus, Cistus, Cotinus coggygria, Genista, Hibiscus syriacus, Olearia, Potentilla fruticosa, Senecio,* and *Weigela*.
● Perennials such as *Alyssum, Armeria, Aubrieta, Coreopsis verticillata, Crassula, Dianthus, Oenothera, Phlox douglasii, Sempervivum,* and *Thymus*.

PLANTS THAT NEED PLENTY OF WATER
● Newly planted trees, shrubs, climbers, and perennials.
● Seedlings and transplants.
● Young trees, shrubs, and perennials.
● Leafy vegetables, which may flower and seed early if deprived of water.
● Peas, beans and other legumes, and sweetcorn – particularly during and just after the flowering period.
● Fruiting crops such as marrow, courgette, and tomato, particularly during and just after flowering, and when fruiting.
● Tree, bush, and cane fruit, from flowering until harvest.
● Shrubs such as *Camellia* and *Rhododendron*, the buds of which form at the end of the summer for flowering in spring.

CONSERVING AND SAVING WATER

Water may be in short supply at any time of the year. However, a long, hot summer is most likely to put plants at risk, and this is just the time when restrictions on garden watering are often in force. It therefore makes good sense to conserve water in any way you can.

IMPROVING MOISTURE RETENTION IN SOIL

● Organic matter Improve the water retention of soil by incorporating plenty of organic matter (see p. 42). This is especially important on sandy or light soils that drain very quickly.

● Mulch Apply a layer of mulch to the soil to retain moisture. An organic mulch should be applied in a 5–7.5 cm (2–3 in) deep layer. Keep the stem area free of organic mulch, since it can cause rotting.

Digging in humus
In all but the heaviest of soils, dig humus into the soil in large quantities before developing a bed. When planting, incorporate humus into each planting hole and the soil used to backfill them.

Using polythene
Black polythene is a useful and inexpensive moisture-retaining material. Once it is in place, cover it over with a layer of garden soil or a traditional and attractive mulching material.

USING CONTAINERS

● Water-retaining granules These are especially useful for plants in any type of container. You can either mix them together with the compost and water thoroughly, or mix them with water and allow them to swell thoroughly before incorporating them into the compost (see p. 66).
● Positioning Containers are usually displayed in the sunniest part of the garden, since this is where most plants flower best. During very hot weather, move them to an area that is sometimes in shade.
● Avoiding waste Check outdoor containers daily during very hot weather. They may need watering once or even twice a day.
● Self-watering Use planters that are designed to supply water on demand. They are particularly suitable for balconies and verandahs.

CONTROLLING WEEDS

Use hand fork to remove weeds

Removing competition
Lift weeds from around plants regularly. Weeds grow rapidly and take up a surprising amount of water from the soil in the process. As you weed, try to minimize disturbance to the soil.

WEEDING IN DROUGHT

● Cutting weeds In extremely dry conditions, cut off weeds at soil level as an alternative to lifting them. This method avoids disturbance of the surface and prevents further moisture loss from the soil.
● Wilting weeds In very hot weather, leave uprooted or decapitated annual weeds on the soil surface to die, forming a mini mulch layer.

MULCHING LAWNS

● Using grass clippings In drought conditions, do not rake up or collect grass clippings. Leave them as a mulch on the surface of the lawn after mowing.

TRADITIONAL TIP

Making a windbreak
Wind, especially wind from the sea, has a drying effect on plants and soil. Create a windbreak of trees and shrubs in an exposed garden.

COLLECTING AND RECYCLING WATER

Inside any house, a huge quantity of water is used every day. Much of it could be recycled for use in a garden with little effort. Not all water is suitable, however, so it is important to be selective. Use containers to collect and store as much water for recycling as you can.

COLLECTING WATER FOR GARDEN USE

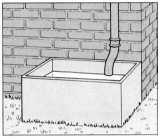

Using a container
Position any clean, watertight container under a downpipe to collect and store water for a garden. Make sure that you will be able to lift it when it is full. If it is too heavy, siphon off the water with a section of hosepipe.

Diverting water
The downpipe that carries water from a bathroom is an excellent source of water throughout the year. To collect the water, attach a section of pipe to divert it from the downpipe into a suitable container.

USING RECYCLED WATER
● **Safe water** Use water from the bath (it must not contain very much bubble bath) and from the hand basin for recycling. Suction pumps are available to drain bath water through a hose to the garden.
● **Unsafe water** Do not use excess water from a washing machine or from a dishwasher. Some of the chemicals contained in detergents could be damaging to plants and to the soil in the long term. The water from water-softening units can also be very damaging to garden plants because it contains salts.

USING WATER BUTTS

A water butt is ideal for collecting and storing rain and suitable waste water. If possible, install several water butts in different places around a house and garden. Position them to collect rainwater from a greenhouse or shed, and from gutters on a house and garage.

RAISING ON BRICKS

Adjusting height
If the tap on your water butt is difficult to operate because it is too close to the ground, raise the water butt by supporting it on several building bricks. The extra height will also make it easy to fill a watering can.

MAINTAINING HYGIENE
● **Preventing algae** Clean a water butt regularly to prevent a build up of algae and debris. Scrub the interior with a stiff brush and soapy water, and rinse thoroughly. Use a long-handled broom to reach inside.
● **Keeping water clean** Add some crystals of potassium permanganate to the water at regular intervals. These help to keep the water "sweet" and have no adverse effect on young or established plants.

USING THE WATER
● **Preventing disease** Use water collected from gutters on open ground only. It may contain harmful organisms that cause fungal diseases in seedlings, young plants, or those in containers.

BRIGHT IDEA

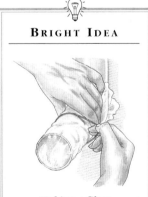

Making a filter
Prevent leaves, twigs, and other debris from entering a water butt by using a filter. Put a section of old tights over the end of the downpipe, and secure with a rubber band. Clear out this filter regularly, especially after heavy rain.

WATERING BEDS AND BORDERS

Successful flowering and fruiting, as well as healthy vegetable growth and development, are dependent upon a regular and adequate supply of water. Applying the right amount of water at the right time, in the right way, and with as little wastage as possible is important.

WATERING EFFICIENTLY

● **Frequency** Water plants throroughly from time to time rather than applying too little water too frequently.

Making a basin
To make sure that water goes down to the roots instead of lying on top of the soil, scoop out soil from around the base of a plant. Fill the hollow with water so that it can soak down slowly.

SAVING WATER

● **Dry areas** Select drought-resistant plants, such as those from Mediterranean countries (see p. 89), for dry, sunny spots.
● **Grouping plants** Keep plants that need a lot of water together so that, when watering, you will not waste water on nearby plants that do not need as much.
● **Directing a hose** Always point the end of a hose beneath the foliage when watering beds and borders. This will prevent water from being wasted, and will reduce the risk of leaf scorch.
● **Positioning plants** Do not put plants that prefer shade in a sunny spot. They will wilt very quickly, and copious amounts of water will be needed to revive them.

WATERING VEGETABLES IN BEDS AND BORDERS

● **Cloches** The soil in a cloche dries out faster than open ground, so use a leaky hose to water vegetables in a cloche.

● **When to water** Water vegetables regularly, preferably in the evening. If crops are wilting, water immediately.

● **Helping pollination** Apply plenty of water to the roots of runner beans at flowering time to encourage pollination.

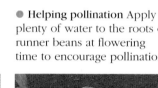

Use bradawl to puncture hose

Making a leaky hose
Take a length of hose – preferably one that is already leaky, and make small holes along it. Tightly tie up or block one end. Lay the hose along a row of plants, attach the open end to a tap, and turn on the tap very gently.

Making trenches
Use a hoe to make shallow trenches between rows of vegetables. Take care to leave plenty of room for normal root development. Water into the trench, thus allowing the water to seep down to the roots.

Watering long rows
To water long, inaccessible rows, first make small holes along a length of plastic guttering. Lay this between two rows, and pour water into one end. The water will run along the guttering so that each plant receives water.

WATERING LAWNS

During a dry summer, the grass in a lawn turns brown and growth slows down. An established lawn generally resists drought well. If there are no drought restrictions in force, water a lawn as soon as you notice that the grass does not spring back after it has been walked on.

IMPROVING DRAINAGE

Spiking a dry lawn
Before watering a dry lawn, use a garden fork to spike the soil. Drive the prongs in to make drainage channels. In this way, water is encouraged to penetrate down through the soil, rather than run off the top of it.

LOOKING AFTER LAWNS

● **Watering** After watering, the soil should be moist to a depth of 10–15 cm (4–6 in). Dig a small hole to see whether or not the soil is damp to the required depth. If it is, note how long it took to water.
● **Feeding** Never use a granular fertilizer on a lawn during drought conditions, since grass needs thorough watering both before and after the application of feed. Use a specially formulated liquid lawn fertilizer instead.
● **Dry weather** Allow grass to grow slightly longer than usual in very dry weather. Moisture is retained in the blades, and excessive cutting will deplete a lawn's store of moisture.

BRIGHT IDEA

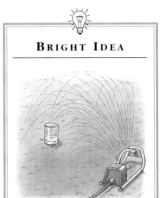

Using a sprinkler
Determine how long to water an area with a sprinkler by putting a straight-sided jar by the sprinkler. When the jar has collected 2.5 cm (1 in) of water, move the sprinkler.

WATERING GREENHOUSE PLANTS

However good the shading on a greenhouse is, the plants inside will be more vulnerable to heat or drought stress than those growing outside. Plants in pots will be in particular need of attention. Always choose a greenhouse that has adequate vents, windows, and doors.

USING CAPILLARY MATTING

Matting soaks up water

Plant positioned above water so that it can draw water as needed

Watering constantly
To ensure that plants are well watered, place them on one end of a piece of capillary matting. Submerge the other end in a water trough or other reservoir of water.

WATERING A GROW BAG

Bottle tied to plant support with string

Using a plastic bottle
Cut off the bottom from a plastic bottle, take the cap off, and insert this end into the growing bag compost. Water through the bottle so that the water does not run straight off the top of the compost.

WATERING EFFICIENTLY WITH CAPILLARY MATTING

● **Rapid action** It can take a long time for water to be drawn up dry capillary matting. To speed the process, wet the matting thoroughly before use.
● **Wick** To help a plant in a large pot take up water, insert a wick of matting through a drainage hole so that it protudes on to the wet matting below.

WEEDING

As WEEDS GROW, they compete with other plants for water, light, and nutrients. Weeds are invasive and soon set seed if you do not act promptly. The first and most important step in eradicating weeds is to identify them (see opposite).

BASIC EQUIPMENT

Weeds can be controlled by a variety of different methods and equipment. A combination of cultivation and chemical methods is usually effective.

● **Suppressing weeds** Use a 2.5–5 cm (1–2 in) deep layer of gravel or grass clippings to prevent weeds from growing. Black polythene, though less attractive, has the same effect.
● **Hoeing weeds** Use a Dutch hoe to cut through weeds without damaging plant roots. A draw hoe is good for chopping weeds in half. Use an onion hoe for weeding between onions and other closely grown plants.
● **Weeding by hand** For narrow crevices in a hard surface, use a patio weeder. Use a daisy grubber or an old kitchen knife for removing large weeds such as dandelions, docks, and daisies from lawns.
● **Applying weedkiller** Prevent spray from drifting on to nearby plants by using a dribble bar attached to a watering can. This will also help you to apply weedkiller accurately.

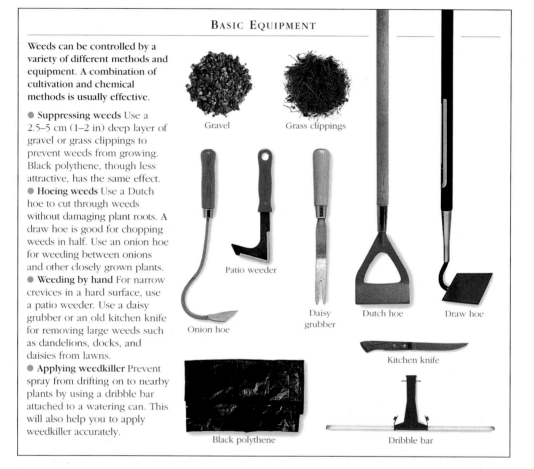

Gravel

Grass clippings

Patio weeder

Onion hoe

Daisy grubber

Dutch hoe

Draw hoe

Kitchen knife

Black polythene

Dribble bar

USING WEEDKILLERS SAFELY

● **Clothing** Wear protective clothing such as rubber gloves and old clothes when mixing and applying weedkillers.
● **Using chemicals** Never eat, drink, or smoke while mixing or applying chemicals. Wash hands thoroughly after use.
● **Dilution** Dilute soluble weedkillers according to the manufacturer's instructions given on the label.

● **Correct use** Always use each product only for the purpose recommended on the label.
● **Amount** Apply weedkiller at the rate stated on the label.
● **Weather** Never use weedkillers in windy weather, when spray can blow on to nearby plants.
● **Storage** To keep them safely out of reach of children and animals, lock weedkillers away in a cupboard or garden shed.

● **Watering cans** Do not use the same watering can for watering and applying liquid weedkillers. Keep one watering can and dribble bar, or sprayer, solely for applying weedkillers.
● **Containers** Store weedkillers in their original containers. Make sure they are clearly labelled.
● **Disposal** Always dispose of left-over diluted weedkiller. Never store and reuse it.

COMMON WEEDS

ANNUAL	TREATMENT	PERENNIAL	TREATMENT
HAIRY BITTERCRESS	This is a common annual weed that develops quickly. It often grows on the compost of pot plants; check new purchases before planting. Hoe regularly before it sets seed. Handweed, or cover with mulch.	HORSETAIL	Underground stems of horsetail can penetrate 3 m (10 ft) below the soil surface, so digging out is rarely successful in the long term. Instead, use repeated spot treatments with glyphosate or other systemic weedkillers.
ANNUAL MEADOW GRASS	Usually found in lawns, this may also appear in poorly maintained borders. It can be prevented by good cultivation of lawns, including regular mowing, appropriate feeding, watering, and aerating.	BINDWEED	Bindweed regenerates from sections of underground stem or root, which can be spread by digging and caught up in new plants. Repeated digging out is always necessary. Apply glyphosate to leaves.
ANNUAL NETTLE	Annual nettle grows in beds, borders, and any vacant spaces between plants. Handweed or spot-treat it with a suitable weedkiller such as glyphosate or glyphosate trimesium.	COUCH GRASS	Couch grass is common in beds, borders, vacant ground, and lawns. It spreads by creeping roots. Try forking it out from light soils, or smother it with black polythene. Treat with glyphosate, and mow the lawn regularly.
GROUNDSEL	This annual is found in borders, beds, and in the vacant spaces between plants. Hoe or handweed regularly before it can set seed. Cover affected ground with a deep mulch.	DOCK	Dock grows in lawns and in beds and paths. It regenerates from small root sections and spreads by seed. For docks in lawns, use a weedkiller containing 2,4-D or MCPA. On vacant ground, use a glyphosate weedkiller.
COMMON CHICKWEED	Common chickweed grows in borders, beds, and in the vacant spaces between plants. Hoe or handweed regularly before weeds set seed. Cover in deep mulch.	PERENNIAL NETTLE	This regenerates from a creeping root system and spreads by seed. Clear before mid summer when plants set seed. In light soils, dig roots out. Use glyphosate spray in uncultivated areas.

PREVENTING WEEDS

Try to prevent weeds from colonizing your garden whenever possible. Once weeds are established and have started to set seed, they can be extremely difficult to eradicate. Depriving weeds of light is one of the best organic ways of suppressing weed growth, and it is easy to do.

DEPRIVING WEEDS OF LIGHT TO INHIBIT GROWTH

● **Weeds in crops** Use black polythene as an inexpensive way of inhibiting the growth of weeds in a vegetable plot.

● **Uncultivated ground** Cover the ground with black polythene or old carpet to suppress perennial weeds.

● **Mulch** Before applying a weed-suppressing mulch, make sure that the ground is moist, and apply a fertilizer.

Using groundcover
Plant dense-growing plants close together to suppress weed growth attractively. Use a suitable mulch until the plants become sufficiently established to do the job on their own.

Using matting
Fruit bushes, and many other plants, cannot be planted very close together. If regular hoeing is impossible, deprive weeds of light by placing polypropylene matting around the plants.

Using grass clippings
Use a mulch of fresh grass clippings around plants. Do not use composted grass, since it may form an impenetrable barrier through which water and air cannot pass.

USING GRAVEL
● **Gravel mulch** Use a 5-cm (2-in) layer of coarse gravel around ornamental plants to suppress weed growth.

Preventing weeds and rot
Gravel is a particularly suitable mulch for alpines. It keeps weeds at bay and prevents rot caused by moisture build up around the crowns of the plants.

STOPPING THE SPREAD
● **Before mulching** Remove all annual and perennial weeds from the soil before putting down weed-suppressing mulch or matting. Weed seeds in the soil will still germinate once the mulch is in place, but these seedlings will be far easier to deal with than large, well-established weeds.
● **New plants** Before planting new purchases, remove any seedlings that are growing on the compost surface.
● **Weed regeneration** Never compost pernicious weeds, since many of them can regenerate from underground roots or stems – even if they have been chopped up. Do not put weeds that have set seed on a compost heap; some seeds may survive the composting process.

BRIGHT IDEA

Polythene lines one side of trench

Trench needs to be 30 cm (12 in) deep

Making a weed barrier
Prevent the creeping roots of weeds in a neighbour's garden from finding their way under a fence. Dig a 30-cm (12-in) deep trench, line one side with heavy-duty polythene, then replace the soil.

USING CHEMICAL WEEDKILLERS

Used with care, chemical weedkillers are a useful and labour-saving way of dealing with weeds. They offer a means of eradicating weeds when cultivation methods may not be feasible. You can combine chemicals with other control methods, or use them on their own.

TYPES OF CHEMICAL WEEDKILLER

Weedkillers are available in several forms, including powders, gels, liquids, and ready-to-use formulations, such as sprays.

WARNING!
Wear rubber gloves and old clothes when mixing and applying weedkillers. Always follow the instructions carefully.

Soluble powder   Gel   Liquid   Spray

WEEDING IN BORDERS

Using paint-on gel
Paint a gel-formulation weedkiller on to weeds that are growing where handweeding or spraying would be difficult without damaging nearby plants.

APPLYING WEEDKILLERS
● **Effective timing** Apply weedkillers when weeds are growing actively; this is usually when they are most effective.
● **Dry weather** Check the weather forecast before using weedkillers. Rain can ruin the effect of many weedkillers.
● **Nettles** When treating nettles, apply the weedkiller just before the foliage starts to die back at the end of the growing season.

WEEDING IN PATHS

Using a liquid
Use a liquid weedkiller on surfaces such as paths, patios, and drives. A dribble bar is an efficient, low-cost way of applying a liquid weedkiller.

BRIGHT IDEA

Using a shield
Protect garden plants with a sheet of cardboard when applying a weedkiller. Cover plants with cardboard boxes or polythene bin liners.

AIDING ABSORBTION OF WEEDKILLERS

Some weeds absorb weedkillers more easily than others. Increase the penetration of weedkiller into stubborn weeds such as ground elder and docks by crushing their foliage before application. The chemicals are more easily absorbed by bruised leaves. Use your foot or the back of a rake, but take care not to sever the foliage completely.

WEEDING BY HAND

Many weeds can be dealt with successfully using just a few hand tools. Like many other gardening jobs, the key to success when weeding by hand is timing and frequency. Weeds must be removed before they set seed, and before they begin to compete with garden plants.

KILLING ANNUAL WEEDS

Hoeing around plants
Use a Dutch hoe to control annual weeds. If you hoe during dry, sunny weather, preferably in the morning or middle of the day, do not gather the weeds, but leave them lying on the soil. They will soon shrivel under the sun.

PROTECTING KNEES
● **Knee protection** Knees can become very uncomfortable during prolonged spells of handweeding. Buy a kneeling pad from your garden centre.

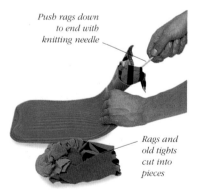

Push rags down to end with knitting needle

Rags and old tights cut into pieces

Making a kneeling pad
Stuff an old hot-water bottle with rags and old tights to make an inexpensive kneeling pad. Do not stuff the hot-water bottle so full that it becomes too rigid. Use just enough stuffing to create a cushion effect.

PREVENTING THE SPREAD OF WEEDS
● **When to weed** Start weeding in early spring to prevent the development and spread of weeds. Weeds can grow during mild winters and relatively warm spells, so watch for out-of-season growth, and remove it.
● **Flowering weeds** Always remove flowering weeds before they have set seed – preferably before they flower.
● **Large areas** If tackling a large expanse of weeds, start by cutting off all the flowerheads and seedheads rather than removing whole weeds in a small area. In this way, you will prevent most of the seeds from escaping into the soil.

WEEDING LAWNS
● **Handweeding** If you have a small lawn, or one with only a few weeds, you will not need to use chemical weedkillers. Handweed instead.

Removing a dandelion
Use an old kitchen knife to remove a dandelion. Keep the blade as vertical as possible, and cut downwards in a circle all around the weed. Lever the knife back and forth, then pull out the weed with its root intact.

● **Lifting weed roots** Many pernicious weeds can regenerate from tiny portions of root or underground stem left in the ground. Always lift as much of the root out of the ground as possible.
● **Weed disposal** Do not put weeds that have set seed on a compost heap. Place them straight into a polythene bag for disposal elsewhere.

> ### WARNING!
> Cover the tops of canes with upturned flower pots or yoghurt cartons to protect your eyes when you are weeding in a border.

LOOKING AFTER LAWNS
● **Control by mowing** Regular mowing to the correct height will kill many lawn weeds. Rosette-forming weeds, such as daisies, and those that form creeping stems, such as speedwell and buttercup, will escape the blades most easily. These will require more drastic action (see p. 129).
● **Blade height** Never mow a lawn with the blades set very low. This weakens the grasses considerably, making them vulnerable to invasion by unwanted weeds and moss.
● **Weeding and feeding** Apply a lawn weedkiller shortly after, or at the same time as, applying a lawn fertilizer. Fertilizer stimulates the rate at which the weeds take up the chemicals that kill them. Fertilizer also encourages the grass to grow over any bare areas left in the lawn after the weeds have died.

CLEARING NEGLECTED SITES

Without regular maintenance, a garden can soon turn into a jungle of unwelcome weeds, particularly during the summer months. On an uncultivated area, tackle the problem by combining cultivation and chemical techniques. For heavy weed infestations, use a weedkiller.

FORKING OUT WEEDS

Clearing woody weeds
Fork out large, woody weeds such as brambles. Remove the top–growth, and dig out as many of the roots as possible. Treat any subsequent growth with a brushwood killer, or dig out the remaining pieces of root.

SUPPRESSING WEEDS

Using black polythene
To protect a cleared area from new weed growth, cover it with heavy-duty black polythene. Make slits in the soil, and push the edges of the polythene into them. On an exposed site, secure with a few bricks as well.

USING WEEDKILLERS

● **Contact weedkillers** Consider using a total weedkiller on a site that needs clearing of weeds. Use one that contains glyphosate, which will kill most weeds. It is deactivated on contact with the soil, which allows you to replant the area as soon as the weeds are dead.
● **Second application** A really heavily weed-infested site will probably need more than one application of weedkiller. Wait until there is a good covering of foliage before reapplying.

IMPROVING THE LOOK

● **Covering up** Disguise black polythene with a layer of chipped bark or garden soil.

DEALING WITH PERSISTENT WEEDS

Weeds with roots that break off into pieces underground, such as oxalis, or those with deep, creeping roots, such as bindweed, are particularly difficult to eradicate from a garden. If left unattended, these weeds will take over a garden in next to no time.

REMOVING BINDWEED

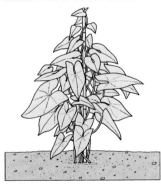

Using a cane
The twining nature of bindwind makes it difficult to treat without putting garden plants at risk. Train bindweed stems up a cane. You will then be able to apply weedkiller to the weed without damaging other garden plants.

WEEDING EFFECTIVELY

● **Disposing of roots** Never leave pieces of weed roots lying on the ground, in case any reroot. Collect them up, and either put them in a dustbin for disposal, or add them to your next bonfire.
● **Systemic weedkillers** Choose a systemic weedkiller (which is carried from the leaves right through to the roots) for persistent weeds, and for those with deep roots.
● **Correct dose** Never attempt to apply a weedkiller in a more concentrated form than that recommended by the manufacturer. This may scorch the foliage, limiting the amount of weedkiller that the weed is able to absorb.

DEALING WITH OXALIS

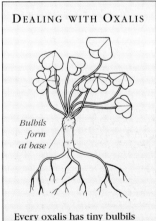

Bulbils form at base

Every oxalis has tiny bulbils around its base, each of which can form a new plant. These bulbils drop off and disperse in summer. Always dig out oxalis in spring before the bulbils spread the weed.

PRUNING PLANTS

P RUNING SERVES MANY PURPOSES. It can keep a plant's size in check, encourage flowering or fruiting, remove or deter potential pest and disease problems, and help to improve the overall appearance of a plant by changing its shape.

BASIC EQUIPMENT

Good-quality, well-maintained pruning tools are essential. Do not buy poor-quality tools.

● **Pruning saw** Choose a saw that has heat-treated hardpoint teeth. Use it to prune branches over 2.5 cm (1 in) in diameter.
● **Garden knife** Use a garden knife for light pruning tasks.
● **Secateurs** Use secateurs to prune soft and woody stems up to 1 cm (⅜ in) thick.
● **Pruners** Use long-handled pruners for pruning out-of-reach woody stems and branches.
● **Shears** Use shears to trim hedges and some woody plants.
● **Gardening gloves** Wear sturdy gloves to protect your hands.

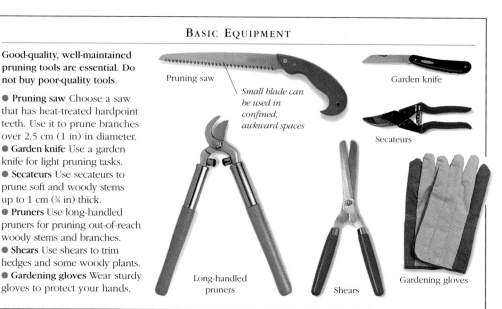

Pruning saw

Small blade can be used in confined, awkward spaces

Garden knife

Secateurs

Long-handled pruners

Shears

Gardening gloves

DEADHEADING AND DISBUDDING

D eadheading is the most basic pruning job of all. Regularly remove faded flowers in order to encourage new flowers throughout summer and possibly into autumn. Disbudding is the removal of small flower buds around the main bud so that it can develop without competition.

DEADHEADING PLANTS
● **Using hands** Deadhead soft-stemmed plants by hand. Using secateurs is inefficient and time-consuming, and does not allow proper access to small flowerheads.
● **Preventing disease** Remove faded flowers as soon as possible to prevent them from becoming colonized by pathogens such as *Botrytis cinerea* (see p. 106).
● **Geraniums** To encourage a second flush of flowers on herbaceous geraniums, use shears to cut back about one-quarter to one-third of the top-growth when flowering is over.

DEADHEADING ROSES

Encouraging new flowers
Use sharp secateurs to remove rose blooms as soon as they start to fade. Cut back the stem to a strong shoot or to an outward-facing bud lower down the stem.

DISBUDDING DAHLIAS

Use forefinger and thumb to remove buds

Removing competition
Disbud dahlias by pinching out surplus buds with your forefinger and thumb. This will allow the remaining buds to develop into full-sized flowers.

PRUNING ROSES

Roses need regular pruning in order to produce lots of good-sized flowers year after year. A rose that is not pruned will soon lose shape, and its flowering capacity will be diminished. Old, faded flowers and buds will also be vulnerable to attack from disease.

LOOKING AFTER ROSES

● **Inspecting stems** Always examine rose stems carefully. Black spot disease (see p. 121) may overwinter on the stems.
● **Avoiding disease** Prune out diseased stems. Prune cracked or injured stems, which are vulnerable to infection.
● **Neglected roses** Sudden, excessive pruning can sometimes cause dieback and may prove fatal. Over a period of time, gradually prune any roses that have been left unpruned.
● **Protecting hands** Always wear a pair of sturdy gardening gloves to protect your hands from rose thorns. It is impossible to prune properly without them.

PRUNING POOR GROWTH

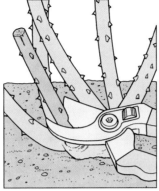

Cutting out weak growth
Use sharp secateurs to prune out any diseased, damaged, dead, or weak, spindly stems. Make a sloping cut just above an outward-facing, vigorous bud towards the base of the stem.

PRUNING STEMS

Improving air circulation
Crossing stems congest a plant and can encourage diseases such as black spot, rust, and powdery mildew. Prune any crossing, overcrowded stems back to a sturdy, outward-facing bud.

CUTTING AT THE CORRECT ANGLE

Plants vary in their pruning requirements, and some may require no routine pruning at all. Whatever the plant, however, there are some pruning techniques that always apply. One of the most important of these is making the pruning cut at the correct angle.

ALTERNATE SHOOTS

Make angled cut above outward-facing shoot

Making an angled cut
Use an angled cut to prune stems with alternate shoots or buds. This will prevent any shoots or buds from being damaged by the secateurs.

OPPOSITE SHOOTS

Making a straight cut
Use a straight cut to prune stems with opposite shoots or buds. Always use sharp secateurs, and take care to make a precise, swift cutting movement.

CUTTING AND SEALING

● **Where to cut** Never cut too close to a bud, since this may damage it and cause the bud to produce a weak shoot. Do not prune too far away from a bud, since this leaves a "snag" of stem. This dies back and may also cause more of the stem to deteriorate.
● **Sealing wounds** Apply a sealing paint to large pruning wounds on trees that are prone to fresh-wound diseases such as silver leaf.

CARING FOR TOOLS

● **Blades** Keep secateurs sharp. Blunt blades may crush a stem, leaving it vulnerable to infection from disease.

RENOVATING CLIMBERS

Most climbers produce vigorous growth. Sometimes this may be just what you need, but if a climber outgrows its position it will need cutting back. Some climbers require pruning to encourage them to flower. Other, established climbers need thinning from time to time.

REMOVING OLD WOOD

Cutting back old stems
Old stems that become woody rarely flower properly. Prune old, unproductive stems back to ground level with long-handled pruners, secateurs, or a saw – depending on their thickness.

PRUNING HONEYSUCKLE

Removing congestion
Many honeysuckles grow rapidly, and become congested and too heavy or extensive for their supports. Prune them by cutting away dead and damaged stems from beneath the new growth.

PRUNING CLIMBERS
● **Preserving foliage** Try to minimize damage to foliage when pruning a climber. This will prevent the plant from looking too stark immediately after it has been pruned.
● **Checking supports** When pruning, take the opportunity to check the condition of walls, pointing, trellis, and other structures or supports. They may be in need of renovation or repair (see p. 52).
● **Looking after birds** Climbers make perfect nesting sites for a variety of birds. To keep disturbance to a minimum, try to delay pruning and major renovation work until after any fledglings have flown the nest.

PRUNING HEDGES

A well-pruned and properly maintained hedge looks attractive and can provide a functional divider or boundary within or around a garden. Proper pruning should be carried out right from the very beginning if you want to keep your hedge in the best possible shape.

BRIGHT IDEA

Adding colour
Brighten up a straggly or thin hedge by growing a flowering climber through it. As well as helping to mask a hedge's condition, the flowers can provide both colour and scent.

SHAPING CONIFERS

Hedge cut into wedge shape

Maintaining shape
Leyland cypress and other hedging conifers need regular clipping if they are to look good. Once a hedge has reached the desired height, cut it back into a wedge shape at least once a year.

RENOVATING A HEDGE

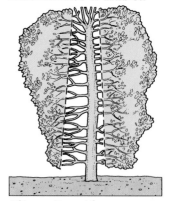

Alternating sides
Avoid cutting back all shoots severely in one season. In the first year, cut one side right back to encourage new shoots. The next year, trim the new shoots lightly, and cut back the other side hard.

PRUNING SHRUBS

Many shrubs need regular, annual pruning in order to stimulate the production of stems that bear flower buds, and to keep them to a compact and manageable shape and size. If you are in doubt about your shrub's flowering habit, consult a specialist book on pruning.

PRUNING DEAD WOOD

Spotting dead wood

Dead wood can be removed at any time of year, but, to make it easier to spot the dead wood, prune it out when the shrub is in leaf. Use sharp secateurs to cut stems back into perfectly sound, healthy wood.

PRUNING OLD WOOD

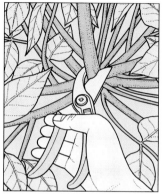

Cutting out old wood

Remove up to one-fifth of a shrub's old wood, cutting back to within 5–8 cm (2–3 in) of ground level. To maintain a well-balanced, even shape to the shrub, remove the stems evenly over the whole plant.

PRUNING WEAK GROWTH

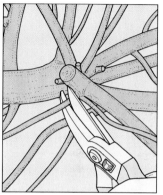

Promoting healthy growth

Prune out any spindly and crossing stems to just above ground level. Removing these unwanted stems ensures that all the nutrients go directly into the productive, healthy growth. If possible, prune back to an outward-facing bud.

WHEN TO PRUNE SHRUBS

As a general rule, if a shrub flowers after mid summer, it should be pruned in early spring. If it flowers earlier in the year, pruning should be carried out immediately after flowering.

EXAMPLES OF SHRUBS THAT NEED PRUNING IN SPRING

Abutilon (some),
Buddleia davidii,
Caryopteris,
Ceanothus,
Ceratostigma,
Cotinus,
Forsythia,
Fuchsia (hardy types),
Hibiscus syriacus,
Hydrangea,
Lavatera (shrubby forms),
Prunus triloba,
Spiraea douglasii,
Spiraea japonica,
Tamarix.

EXAMPLES OF SHRUBS THAT NEED PRUNING IN SUMMER

Buddleia alternifolia,
Chaenomeles,
Cotoneaster,
Deutzia,
Forsythia,
Magnolia stellata,
Magnolia soulangeana,
Philadelphus,
Syringa,
Weigela.

Fuchsia

TRADITIONAL TIP

Encouraging berries

To ensure that a Pyracantha is covered with berries in autumn, prune it in stages. Prune some stems in early spring, then leave them for the rest of the year. The flowers they produce will turn into berries. Cut back some of the other stems immediately after flowering.

PESTS & DISEASES

EVERY GARDENER *will encounter many different garden pests and diseases, some of which can have a devastating effect. As long as you can recognize them and take the appropriate action early on, many pests and diseases need not cause too much damage to your garden plants.*

IDENTIFYING PESTS AND DISEASES

Some pests and diseases are potentially very harmful. Others may cause serious problems only if a plant is badly stressed or already under attack from something else. Use the following charts to identify the major problems and to discover how best to deal with them effectively.

PESTS/DISEASES	SYMPTOMS AND CAUSES	METHODS OF CONTROL
SLUGS AND SNAILS Slug Snail	Both these pests feed mainly at night and after rain. Smooth-edged holes appear on foliage, stems, and petals. Both pests may tunnel into corms, bulbs, and tubers, making large holes. Silvery slime trails are often found nearby.	Use the slug nematode biological control (see p. 115). Cultivate soil to expose eggs, and clear up debris. Reduce the use of organic mulches. Use methiocarb or metaldehyde-based pellets or drenches. Collect up pests.
CATERPILLARS	Many garden plants are attacked by caterpillars, the larvae of butterflies and moths. Leaves, soft stems, and occasionally flowers develop holes as they are eaten. Some caterpillars bind up leaves with silken webbing.	Pick off the caterpillars. Prune out damaged stems and heavily webbed areas. Spray with the biological control *Bacillus thuringiensis* or with a pesticide such as pyrethrum, permethrin, or pirimiphos-methyl.
GLASSHOUSE WHITEFLY	Glasshouse whitefly is most common in greenhouses but may also be found outside in hot weather. Leaves discolour and distort, and may be covered with sticky excreta, which attracts black, sooty mould growth.	Introduce the parasitic wasp *Encarsia formosa* (see p. 115) into greenhouses and conservatories. Alternatively, spray with bifenthrin, pyrethrum, insecticidal soaps, permethrin, or pirimiphos-methyl.
VINE WEEVILS	Adult beetles cause notching around leaf edges. Their white grubs attack many plants below ground, particularly those in containers. They eat and tunnel into roots, tubers, and corms.	Use biological control drenches of nematodes (*Steinernema* and *Heterorhabditis* spp.). Collect up and destroy adult beetles and grubs. Try drenching containers with pirimiphos-methyl or HCH.

PESTS/DISEASES	SYMPTOMS AND CAUSES	METHODS OF CONTROL
RUST	Various fungi are responsible for rust infections. They are most severe in damp or moist weather and on soft, lush growth. Orange, buff, or brown pustules appear on leaves, mostly on the lower surfaces. The upper surfaces may have yellow blotches.	Pick off affected leaves promptly. Improve air circulation within and around the plants. To decrease humidity, avoid wetting the foliage. Spray with a suitable fungicide, such as one containing penconazole, mancozeb, or bupirimate with triforine.
LEAF SPOTS	Various bacteria and fungi cause leaf spots. If this is caused by bacteria, spots may be angular, with a yellow edge. Fungal spots have concentric zones and an area of tiny fungal fruiting bodies. Black, brown, or grey spots may cover the leaves.	Most leaf spots do not cause serious problems and may develop only on plants that are in poor condition. Remove badly infected leaves, and improve the plant's growing conditions. Spray with a suitable fungicide for fungal leaf spots.
POWDERY MILDEWS	These mildews cause a white, powdery layer of fungal growth to appear – usually in distinct patches or spots, which may then coalesce. A few mildews are pale brown and felty. Leaves, stems, and flowers may be attacked, and may wither and fall.	Powdery mildews thrive in humid air. Prune to improve air circulation, and keep plants well watered and mulched. Avoid wetting leaves. Spray with a suitable fungicide, such as one containing carbendazim, or triforine with bupirimate.
EARWIGS	Many plants are attacked by these pests, particularly dahlias, chrysanthemums, clematis, peaches, and certain annuals. Young leaves and petals are eaten, especially during the summer. In extreme cases, a plant can be severely damaged.	Make traps with rolled-up corrugated cardboard or flowerpots stuffed with straw (see p. 118). Collect up and destroy the pests. Alternatively, spray at dusk with an insecticide containing HCH, permethrin, or pirimiphos-methyl.
TOADSTOOLS	Toadstools are usually seen in lawns in the autumn, especially during mild, damp spells. Toadstools are usually short-lived and rarely survive the first frosts. They may form "fairy rings", which cause grass to discolour and die.	If the grass is unharmed, simply brush off the toadstools as soon as they appear, preferably before their caps open (see p. 121). If they reappear, they may be growing on buried organic debris, such as old tree roots. These should be dug out.
SPIDER MITES	Several species of spider mite occur on garden and greenhouse plants. The most common and troublesome species is the glasshouse red spider mite. In severe cases, leaves may die and turn brown. Fine webbing may appear on affected plants.	Control glasshouse red spider mites with the predatory mite *Phytoseiulus* (see p. 115). Allow adequate ventilation, and damp down frequently (see p. 83). Spray with an insecticidal soap or dimethoate, bifenthrin, pirimiphos-methyl, or malathion.

PESTS/DISEASES	SYMPTOMS AND CAUSES	METHODS OF CONTROL
BOTRYTIS	Most plants are susceptible to this fungus, particularly those with soft growth. Fuzzy, grey patches develop on infected areas. Plant tissue discolours and deteriorates, and there may be extensive dieback. White or yellow circles appear on tomato skins.	Clear up all plant debris. Remove infected tissue promptly, and dispose of it. Avoid injury to plants, and improve air circulation around them by pruning. If necessary, spray with a suitable fungicide, such as one containing carbendazim.
APHIDS	Aphids feed by sucking sap and may cause plant parts to discolour and distort. Their sticky excreta may encourage the growth of black, sooty moulds. Aphids can be green, black, yellow, pink, grey, or brown; some are covered in white, waxy wool.	Natural or introduced predators and parasites may help to reduce numbers (see p. 110). Spray with malathion, fenitrothion, pirimiphos-methyl, pyrethrum, derris, or an insecticidal soap. If possible, use pirimicarb, which is aphid-specific.
VIRUSES	Many viruses have a wide and diverse host range. Symptoms can vary. Stunting, poor growth, leaf yellowing (usually as flecks, ring-spots, streaks, or mosaic patterns), distortion, and flower-colour changes are the most common symptoms.	Viruses are spread by handling or other mechanical injuries, and by pests such as aphids, thrips, and nematodes. Some are seedborne. Avoid damaging plants, and disinfect pruning tools frequently. Control virus-carrying pests, and remove infected plants promptly.
CLUB ROOT	Club root affects many brassicas, including Brussels sprouts, calabrese, cabbages, swedes, and radishes, as well as some ornamentals. Symptoms include distorted and swollen roots and poorly developed, often discoloured, stunted foliage.	Improve soil drainage, and add lime, since this should discourage the slime mould responsible for club root. Raise plants in individual pots, and plant out when they have a strong root system (see p. 120). If possible, choose resistant varieties.
FOOT AND ROOT ROTS	Bedding plants, seedlings, beans, cucumbers, tomatoes, and peas are particularly susceptible. Soil- or waterborne fungi cause discolouration of stem bases, which shrink inwards. Plants show poor growth and ultimately wilt, wither, and die.	Observe strict hygiene: use sterilized, proprietary compost, clean trays and pots, and mains water. Do not overwater or overcrowd plants. Water seeds and seedlings with a copper-based fungicide. Remove affected plants immediately.
FUNGAL SCABS	These are most common on apples, pears, and *Pyracantha*. Grey or black, scabby patches develop on affected plants. Leaves and fruit are commonly affected, but stems may be attacked, too. Leaf puckering and fruit distortion often occur.	Avoid overhead watering. Rake up and dispose of affected leaves, and prune out infected shoots. Keep plants open-centred by careful pruning. Spray with a suitable fungicide, such as one containing carbendazim, or triforine with bupirimate.

PESTS/DISEASES	SYMPTOMS AND CAUSES	METHODS OF CONTROL
CODLING MOTHS	Apples and pears may be attacked by the larvae of codling moths. Holes, often surrounded by brown, powder-like droppings, appear on ripe fruit. The codling moth larvae feed in the core of the fruit, tunnelling out when mature.	Hang pheromone traps in trees from late spring to mid summer to catch male moths (see p. 119). This will reduce the number of codling moth eggs that will be fertilized. Spray against hatching larvae. Use pirimiphos-methyl, permethrin, or fenitrothion.
CABBAGE ROOT FLIES	Many brassicas, including swedes, cauliflowers, Brussels sprouts, cabbages, turnips, and radishes, may be attacked by this pest. Plants may wilt and discolour. Seedlings die, and roots are tunnelled into by larvae that measure up to 9 mm (½ in) long.	Place collars of carpet underlay, roofing felt, or cardboard around the base of each plant when it is transplanted (see p. 119). Alternatively, dust transplanted brassicas and seed rows with a suitable soil insecticide such as pirimiphos-methyl.
CARROT FLIES	Carrots are the most common host to this pest, but other plants may also be attacked, including celery and parsley. Carrot fly larvae tunnel into roots, causing rust-brown lesions on roots and plants. Plants may develop discoloured foliage.	Erect a polythene barrier around crops to keep out female flies (see p. 119), or cover a whole crop with horticultural fleece. Avoid handling crops, since the smell of the leaves may attract adult flies. Treat seed rows with pirimiphos-methyl.
FLEA BEETLES	Seedlings of brassicas, leafy vegetables, radishes, stocks, nasturtiums, and wallflowers are particularly vulnerable. The tiny beetles feed on leaves, making numerous holes on the upper surfaces. Hot, dry summers encourage this pest.	Flea beetles overwinter in plant debris, so clear up debris thoroughly. Use sticky traps (see p. 118). Warm soil before sowing seeds, and water regularly to encourage rapid, strong growth. Use HCH, pyrethrum, derris, or pirimiphos-methyl.
WIREWORMS	Many plants may be attacked, particularly potatoes and other root crops. Perennials, annuals, seedlings, and bulbous plants may also be damaged. Young plants may wilt, wither, and die as their roots are tunnelled into by wireworms.	Recently cultivated soil, or an area recently converted from grassland, is most likely to harbour these pests. Bury carrot and potato pieces as bait (see p. 120). Lift root crops as early as possible. Water infested soil with pirimiphos-methyl.
PEACH-LEAF CURL	Peaches, nectarines, and ornamental and edible almonds may be attacked by this fungus. Affected leaves pucker and become blistered and swollen, then turn red or purple. As spore layers develop on the leaf surfaces, the leaves turn white.	Erect a polythene shelter over susceptible trees to prevent the air- or waterborne spores from landing (see p. 121). Pick off affected leaves. Spray with a copper fungicide in mid winter, and again two weeks later. Spray again when the leaves fall.

PREVENTING PROBLEMS

MOST PEST AND DISEASE PROBLEMS can be avoided to a large extent by careful planting, good hygiene, the use of disease-resistant plant varieties, and good cultivation practices. Should problems occur, prompt action is vital.

ESTABLISHING HEALTHY GARDENS

Plants that are encouraged to grow strongly and healthily are less prone to disease and better able to compensate for damage done by pests or diseases than weak plants. Encouraging natural predators into a garden will also help to keep the pest population under control.

MAKING A GOOD START
● **Positioning plants** Always choose the best site and position. Plants grown in a spot that suits them, and which are correctly and carefully maintained, are unlikely to suffer serious or significant damage if attacked by pests or disease-causing organisms.
● **Spacing plants** Space plants correctly when planting. Congested plants are prone to disease because of poor air circulation. The build up of muggy conditions encourages a variety of diseases. Fungal spores and pests can also spread easily if plants are positioned close together.

INSPECTING PLANTS

Removing pests
Pick off pests or diseased leaves regularly. Prompt action should prevent a problem from spreading to healthy parts of a plant. Dispose of pests and diseased leaves carefully.

USING GREENHOUSES
● **Watering** Water seeds, seedlings, young plants, and container plants with tap water. Water taken from butts often harbours soil or water-borne pathogens that attack and damage these plants.
● **Canes** Always check that the ends of canes and stakes are completely clean. They can contain soil that harbours fungal spores or pests.
● **Rubbish** Always clear away deteriorating or dead plant material and debris that is lying around the greenhouse; it may be infected.
● **Ventilation** Always provide good ventilation in a greenhouse or cold frame.

CULTIVATING PLANTS
● **Encouraging growth** Always use correct levels of watering and feeding (see p. 86) in order to encourage sturdy, vigorous growth. Certain nutrients, such as potassium, toughen plant growth slightly and improve a plant's resistance to attack by many pathogens.
● **Pruning plants** Pruning is a useful way of limiting certain pests and diseases. Create an open-centred crown or branch structure to reduce humidity, and so prevent the onset of various diseases. Some pest and disease infestations can be eradicated simply by removing infected stems.

STERILIZING CONTAINERS

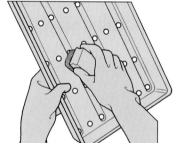

Scrubbing trays and pots
Healthy growth must be encouraged from the beginning. Before sowing seeds, use a stiff scrubbing brush and very hot water to clean plastic seed trays and pots. As an extra precaution, add a little garden disinfectant, soap, or detergent.

TRADITIONAL TIP

Using plastic containers
Use plastic trays and pots for young plants, because they are much easier to clean properly than those made from terracotta or wood. Wooden trays and clay pots are porous, so are likely to harbour pests.

PRACTISING CROP ROTATION

By rotating crops around a number of distinct plots, you can prevent the build up of many serious pests and pathogens. This traditional method of crop cultivation encourages healthy plants and high yields with relatively little effort. Leave one plot free for permanent crops.

USING MANURE
● **Quality soil** Whenever possible, treat vegetable plots with well-rotted manure. This results in a water- and nutrient-retentive soil that will give your crops the best possible start.

USING LIME
● **Brassicas** Liming the soil is advisable for growing brassicas, but take care if the next crop is to include potatoes. Lime will encourage scab disease on the skins of the potato tubers.

ROTATING BORDERS
● **Bedding plants** Although rotation is used mainly for vegetable crops, try rotating bedding plants in flower borders from year to year. It can have a beneficial effect.

THREE-YEAR CROP-ROTATION PLAN

Whatever size your plots, you can use a system based on this three-year plan. Divide the area, and your crops, into four groups. Each year, prepare the soil as indicated, and move three of the groups to another plot (see bottom), ensuring a two-year gap before these crops return to their original sites.

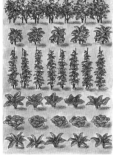

Plot A
Plant cauliflower, Brussels sprouts, swede, turnip, calabrese, cabbage, radish, kale, Chinese cabbage, and broccoli. Before planting, dig over the soil, and apply lime to raise the soil pH to 6.5–7.0. Incorporate blood, fish, and bonemeal or other general fertilizer. Additional feeding during the growing period is beneficial to the vegetable crop.

Plot B
Plant peas, French or dwarf beans, runner beans, spinach, lettuce, broad beans, Swiss chard, globe artichokes, and chicory. Two to three weeks before sowing takes place, dig over the soil, and apply blood, fish, and bonemeal or other general fertilizer. Maintain a regular watering programme to ensure a good set of leguminous crops such as peas and beans.

Plot C
Plant potatoes, carrots, onions, tomatoes, leeks, parsnips, beetroot, shallots, marrows, salsify, celery, scorzonera, aubergines, and Florence fennel. Before planting, double dig the plot, and incorporate well-rotted manure into both levels of ground, adding a small amount of blood, fish, and bonemeal or other general fertilizer. Some crops may need additional feeding.

Plot D
Keep a plot free for permanent crops that do not move within the rotation plan. Leave space for some tender or half-hardy herbs. Plant rosemary, chives, parsley, mint, basil, globe artichokes, Jerusalem artichokes, rhubarb, and asparagus. In a small garden, grow some permanent crops in the flower border, ensuring soil fertility is adequate for the crop.

YEAR ONE				YEAR TWO				YEAR THREE			
A	B	C	D	B	C	A	D	C	A	B	D

ENCOURAGING USEFUL WILDLIFE

All too often, any small creature that walks, flies, or crawls in a garden is squashed, just in case it could damage the plants. The vast majority of insects, however, are completely harmless to plants. Many are actually beneficial and should be encouraged and preserved.

BENEFICIAL GARDEN CREATURES

Many insects – either in their adult or juvenile stage, and sometimes both – are active predators. They help to reduce the numbers of plant pests by eating them. In some cases, this may mean pesticides are unnecessary.

Centipede
Centipedes feed on many different soil pests. Do not confuse them with harmful millipedes.

Ladybird
Both the adult beetles and their larvae feed on pests, aphids in particular.

Lacewing
Lacewings lay their eggs on leaves. When they hatch, the larvae eat vast quantities of aphids.

Garden spider
Spiders feed on a range of insects, including many pests, which they trap in their webs.

Hoverfly
Hoverflies and their larvae, which look like caterpillars, feed on aphids. The flies also pollinate flowers.

LOOKING AFTER ALLIES
● **Garden allies** There are many beneficial garden creatures. These include anthocorids, ground beetles, rove beetles, many birds, certain midge larvae, parasitic wasp larvae, and even commonly found wasps and ants.
● **Providing shelter** Although you should aim to have a clean, tidy garden in order to prevent as many pest and disease outbreaks as possible, try to leave a few dead leaves and stems as shelter for beneficial garden creatures.
● **Using chemicals** Use chemical sprays (see p. 117) only if they are absolutely necessary. Select the spray carefully, and choose one that is as specific as possible in order to reduce the risk to harmless insects.

ATTRACTING PREDATORY BIRDS

Some birds can cause damage in gardens, but this can be kept to a minimum by using nets or other barriers (see p. 113). Many birds are useful predators of garden pests, such as slugs, caterpillars, and aphids, and should be actively encouraged into the garden.

FEEDING BIRDS
● **Providing food** Hang suitable food directly from tree branches. Nuts and fat will help to keep many bird species alive during a cold winter. Do not feed them with highly spiced or salted food.
● **Providing water** Always make sure that garden birds have a source of water so that they can drink and bathe throughout the year. Replace the water regularly in winter so that it does not freeze over.
● **Lurking cats** Make sure you place bird food and water out of the way of lurking cats.

SUPPLYING FOOD

Using a bird table
Erect a bird table so that you can supply suitable food in a safe place. Use it to hang up peanut feeders and halved coconuts.

TENDING CLIMBERS

Protecting birds
Climbers are ideal nesting sites. Remember this when cutting back climbers, and try to avoid pruning during the nesting season.

MAKING A WILDLIFE POND

A pond never fails to add extra interest to a garden, but if constructed to encourage and attract wildlife it can be a special feature all year long. Birds, toads, frogs, and a huge range of beneficial insects and other small animals will visit to feed and drink.

ATTRACTING WILDLIFE TO A POND

Shallow, sloping sides allow animals to leave easily

Deep water provides safe hiding and overwintering sites

Plants around pond edge provide shelter, hiding, and mating places

Marginal plants provide sites for creatures that prefer moist environments

The ideal wildlife pond
A well-constructed wildlife pond is beautiful to look at and can include a wide range of native plants. It provides food, water, and an attractive environment for a vast array of animals throughout the year.

Stones and rocks provide spots for sunbathing and drinking

Floating plants create shade and help to prevent water from becoming too warm

PLANTING TO ATTRACT INSECTS

Insects not only add interest to a garden, but many species also help to keep down pest populations and pollinate flowers. Any garden will attract some insects, but – to make sure you encourage the ones you want – provide as varied a collection of plant life as possible.

ATTRACTING INSECTS

Growing varieties
Grow a wide range of plants to create food sources for insects. *Helianthus, Nicotiana, Stachys, Gazania,* and fennel – and others with open, daisy-like blooms – are particularly useful.

PLANTING FOR INSECTS
● **Single flowers** Always try to include some single-flowered varieties in your planting. These are far more attractive to bees and other pollinating insects than double-flowered plants.
● **Nettles** Include a patch of nettles in a garden. These provide a useful source of aphids early in the year, which will attract many predatory insects. Cut back the nettles in early or mid spring so that the predators move on to other garden plants, where they will help to control any pests.

SUITABLE PLANTS

Include as wide a variety of plants as possible in your garden. Daisy-like flowers are particularly accessible and attractive to insects.

Alyssum, Anchusa azurea, Anemone x hybrida, Arabis, Campanula, Erigeron, Eryngium spp., *Geranium* spp., *Geum* spp., *Gypsophila paniculata, Liatris spicata, Papaver* spp., *Polemonium caeruleum, Rudbeckia, Salvia x superba, Scabiosa* spp., *Veronica longifolia.*

GROWING COMPANION PLANTS

Companion planting involves the growing of a combination of plants that benefit one or more of the plants in their particular area. Not all gardeners believe in companion planting, and attempts at proving how successful it is are often inconclusive. It is, however, worth a try.

GROWING CROPS

● **Onions and carrots** Plant onions and carrots as a combination to minimize attacks by both onion fly and carrot fly. For maximum effect, plant four rows of onions to every row of carrots.
● **Cabbages and beans** To reduce levels of mealy cabbage aphid and cabbage root fly, plant one row of a compact form of cabbage with one row of dwarf beans.
● **Marigolds and cabbages** Try planting French marigolds between rows of cabbage plants. This may help to deter attack from brassica whitefly.
● **Mixing crops** Avoid growing a large area with a single crop. This acts like an illuminated sign advertising a restaurant, and it will attract plenty of hungry pests.

GREEN TIP

Planting marigolds
Marigolds are thought to attract hoverflies, control pests, and deter whitefly and eelworm. Whether they do all of this or not is debatable, but it is worth experimenting. Plant them with crops such as tomatoes, either in a growbag or in open ground.

PLANTING PEPPERS

● **Sweet peppers** These plants are prone to aphids. Grow them with basil, which seems to grow well with peppers, and okra. All these plants need warmth and shelter.

Deterring fungi
Try planting *Capsicum* peppers among plants that are prone to *Fusarium* foot or root rots or wilts. The secretion from the peppers' roots is believed to deter attack from these fungi.

PROTECTING POTATOES

● **Companion plants** *Tagetes* marigold, celery, flax, *Lamium*, savory, and nasturtium may all help to protect potatoes from pests. Peas are also thought to be beneficial when grown with potatoes.
● **Eelworms** Try growing French marigolds in soils that are infested with eelworms, which attack potatoes in particular. The secretion from the marigold roots is said to kill these destructive pests.

GROWING COURGETTES

● **Mutual benefit** Try growing courgettes with peas, beans, or sweetcorn. The peas and beans turn the nitrogen in soil into a usable form, the courgettes shade the soil, and the corn provides support.

HELPING ROSES

● **Roses** To prevent roses from being attacked by aphids, try planting them with alliums and catmint. Parsley, thyme, and *Limnanthes douglasii* may also be beneficial to roses.

Combining plants
There is some evidence that foxgloves, rhododendrons, and azaleas thrive when growing together. Foxgloves help to keep the shrubs healthy and seem to grow particularly well themselves.

DISGUISING CROPS

● **Visibility** Large areas of a crop are easily visible to pests. Grow small areas, and disguise the crop by interplanting with unrelated vegetables.

Hiding vegetables
Grow ornamental plants and vegetables together. This makes the crop less obvious to those pests that see their host plants rather than smell them.

CONTROLLING ANIMALS

MANY ANIMALS ARE LIKELY to come into a garden, including wild birds and other wildlife, as well as domestic animals such as cats and dogs. These are often harmless but may need to be deterred if they cause any damage.

CONTROLLING BIRDS

Most birds are welcomed by gardeners, but some, such as bullfinches, eat fruit tree buds and the buds of ornamental shrubs and trees during late autumn and winter. Others, such as blackbirds and thrushes, eat ripening fruits, while pigeons eat brassicas.

PROTECTING MARROWS

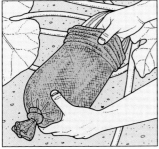

Using tights
Use an old pair of tights or stockings to protect ripening marrows from birds and other pests. Pull a leg section over each marrow, and tie at each end.

MAKING A SNAKE

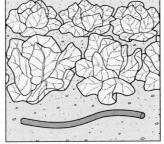

Using hose pipe
Use a piece of old hose pipe to deter large pests such as birds and cats. Lay it in a bed, and bend the hose in a couple of places so that it resembles a snake.

DETERRING BIRDS
● **Humming tape** Keep birds away from crops by using thin strips of proprietary buzzing or humming tape stretched between posts. As the wind blows, the vibrating tape produces a sound that deters many birds. The tape from the inside of a broken music cassette is a useful alternative.
● **Netting** Drape netting over crops, but check regularly to ensure that no birds or other animals are trapped in it.
● **Pretend cats** Make cut-out cats, using marbles for eyes. Hang these in vegetable plots.

CONTROLLING MOLES

Moles create unsightly mounds of loose soil in flowerbeds and on lawns. Their underground activity loosens the soil. This can cause plants to suffer from drought stress, because their roots need to be surrounded by firm soil in order for them to take up water.

USING SMELLS
● **Smoke** Consider using proprietary mole smokes that are placed inside, or at the entrance to, a mole run. Although often effective, the mole may return once the smell has dispersed.
● **Strong smells** Put household items such as strongly smelling scents, mothballs, and orange peel inside a mole run.
● **Plant smells** Although often considered a weed, try planting caper spurge, the smell of which seems to be intensely disliked by moles.

MAKING VIBRATIONS

Planting bottles
Dig several holes, and push an empty bottle into each one. As the wind blows across the top of each bottle, it will produce a noise that drives away moles.

CREATING SOUNDS
● **Windmills** Push plastic toy windmills into the ground at regular intervals. The noise they make as they spin around in the wind can often deter any nearby moles.
● **Using ultrasound** Try using electronic devices that emit ultrasonic waves. These seem to work in some cases.

USING PROFESSIONALS
● **Last resort** If all else fails, employ the services of a reputable, reliable mole-catcher to sort out the problem for you.

CONTROLLING RABBITS AND MICE

Both rabbits and mice can cause considerable damage in gardens and greenhouses. Rabbits particularly enjoy vegetables, fruit, and tender young shoot growth, while mice are particularly fond of fruit, vegetables, and seeds – especially when other food supplies are in short supply.

PROTECTING CROPS AND TREES FROM RABBITS

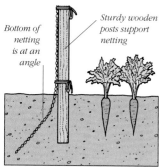

Bottom of netting is at an angle

Sturdy wooden posts support netting

Making a rabbit fence
Make a rabbit-proof barrier with galvanized wire netting that is at least 90 cm (3 ft) high. Bury about 30 cm (1 ft) below the soil. Angle the bottom 15 cm (6 in) outwards so that rabbits cannot tunnel underneath it.

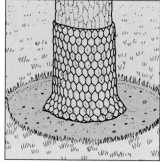

Making a tree guard
Rabbits may gnaw at tree bark, particularly on young trees. Wrap a collar of chicken wire around a trunk to prevent this. Check it at least once a year to make sure that the wire is not restricting trunk expansion.

CURBING MICE
● **Conventional traps** Use mousetraps in greenhouses, polytunnels, and cloches if mice are a serious problem. This is also the most effective way of controlling mice that are raiding seeds stored inside a shed or garage.
● **Humane traps** These trap mice, but do not kill them, which means that you can dispose of the mice humanely. If released several miles from your garden, they are unlikely to trouble you again.
● **Feline solution** If you do not mind dead mice being brought into the house from time to time, a cat may help to control this pest.

CONTROLLING CATS AND DOGS

Domestic animals can sometimes prove to be some of the worst pests in the garden. If at all possible, try to deter them from coming into the garden in the first place. If this fails, there are a number of solutions to some of the problems that cats and dogs can cause.

DETERRING CATS

Lay bottle on ground among plants

Positioning bottles
Cats seem to strongly dislike the reflections from clear plastic bottles half-filled with water. To keep cats away from areas that they use as a litter tray, position these bottles among plants. This can look unsightly but may force cats to look for another litter area.

USING OTHER METHODS
● **Moist soil** Keep soil moist to deter cats. Water regularly, and use a moisture-retentive soil mulch wherever possible.
● **Netting and wire** Buried netting or chicken wire may prevent a cat from digging up soil where seeds have been recently sown. Lay the netting or wire on the ground surface, and cover it lightly with soil.
● **Buried prickles** Buried prickly stems, such as holly, are often enough to deter a cat as soon as it begins to scratch up the soil.
● **Electronic devices** Use these to deter cats and dogs; they emit a high-frequency sound that humans cannot hear, but which cats and dogs dislike.

BRIGHT IDEA

Keeping dogs out
Stop a neighbour's dog from crawling under a fence or through a gap into your garden by planting a prickly hedge. Shrubs such as *Pyracantha* work well. Plant them so that they will grow to form an impenetrable barrier.

USING PEST CONTROLS

WHENEVER GARDEN PESTS ARE A PROBLEM, there is usually a remedy that can be achieved by cultivation or chemical methods. In many cases, it is a combination of the two methods that proves to be the most effective solution.

BIOLOGICAL CONTROLS

The use of biological control agents has become increasingly popular over recent years, and the range of predators and parasites available to gardeners has increased dramatically. Many biological controls are most effective when used in a greenhouse or conservatory.

IN THE GARDEN
● **Helping out** Try to remove some pests by hand to help predators or parasites. Make sure that enough pests are left behind to allow the population of the biological control agent to build up.
● **Chemicals** Before using chemicals to control pests, check that they will not harm any biological control agents.
● **Caterpillars** Use a biological control for caterpillars. Mix *Bacillus thuringiensis* with water, and spray it on caterpillar-infested plants. Eating the sprayed foliage poisons the caterpillars.

CONTROLLING SLUGS AND VINE WEEVILS

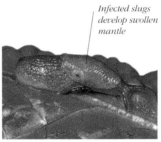

Infected slugs develop swollen mantle

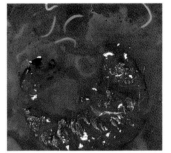

Infecting slugs
Use a nematode parasite to control slugs. Infected slugs develop a swollen mantle, stop feeding rapidly, and die within a few days. The soil must be moist and warm for this to work.

Eliminating vine weevils
Control vine weevil grubs with nematodes, tiny, white worms that kill and then feed on the remains of the grub's body. This method is most effective on plants grown in containers.

GREENHOUSE CONTROLS

Biological controls are generally most successful in the controlled environment of a greenhouse or conservatory. Make sure that you introduce enough predators or parasites to deal with the pests.

Parasites are supplied as eggs inside a plastic tube

Mottling caused by red spider mites

Controlling whiteflies
Use the wasp *Encarsia formosa*, which parasitizes young whiteflies. The flies are killed as wasps develop inside them.

Controlling red spider mite
The predatory mite *Phytoseiulus persimilis* moves rapidly and eats all stages of the red spider mite, including the eggs.

IN THE GREENHOUSE
● **Suitable pests** Try using biological controls for aphids, slugs, vine weevils, thrips, caterpillars, mealybugs, and scale insects.
● **Temperature** Always check that the temperature in a greenhouse is suitable before introducing biological controls.
● **Timing** Introduce biological controls when pests are present, but do not wait until the infestation is too heavy; the biological controls may not be able to multiply rapidly enough to cope with the situation.
● **Ventilation** Ventilate a greenhouse when necessary. Predators and parasites will not escape – they usually stay where the pest population is.

ORGANIC CONTROLS

Organic controls are derived mostly from plants. Although they can be effective, the range of problems they can control is limited, and none are systemic (carried to the roots). Many organic remedies are unselective and may kill a variety of insects, including beneficial ones.

USING DERRIS
● **Uses** Derris is derived from *Derris* and *Lonchocarpus* roots. It controls flea beetles, thrips, caterpillars, raspberry beetles, sawflies, and red spider mites.

Applying powder
For effective control, apply derris powder regularly and thoroughly, following the manufacturer's instructions. Derris is not selective, so target only the pests you wish to control.

USING PYRETHRUM
● **Uses** Pyrethrum is derived from the flowers of *Pyrethrum cinerariifolium*. Use it to treat thrips, leafhoppers, whitefly, caterpillars, ants, and aphids.

Spraying liquid
Pyrethrum is a non-selective but quick-acting pesticide, so aim at target pests only. Spray leaves on both surfaces to ensure that most of the pests are killed. Pyrethrum is harmless to mammals.

APPLYING CONTROLS
● **Non-persistent controls** Many organic treatments remain active for no more than a day, so you may therefore need to apply them more frequently than their chemical counterparts.
● **Spraying** Always use a good-quality sprayer to apply a control, and be sure to wash it out thoroughly between applications. Never keep leftover solution for future use.
● **Looking after bees** Never allow spray to drift on to open flowers, especially blossoms, in case you harm visiting bees.
● **Harvesting crops** It is usually safe to eat most crop plants fairly soon after an organic control has been applied, but always check the product label carefully for preparation details.

GREEN TIP

Making a barrier
To lay her eggs, a vine weevil must crawl or climb to her destination, since weevils cannot fly. To prevent a weevil from laying her eggs in pot-plant compost, apply a circle of non-setting glue around pots. Remove any debris that accumulates on the glue.

USING OTHER ORGANIC TREATMENTS

There are several different types of organic treatment available to gardeners, but availability may change since, like chemical controls, they are constantly subject to legislation. Because some organic treatments are unselective, find out all you can about each one before deciding which product is suitable for your purposes.

● **Insecticidal soaps** Use these for effective control of aphids, red spider mites, thrips, leafhoppers, scale insects, mealybugs, and whiteflies. Insecticidal soaps are based on fatty acids produced by animal or plant sources. The soaps are unselective in their action, however, and last only for approximately one day.

● **Copper-based sprays** Copper-based fungicides are suitable for use on edible crops. They control a range of plant diseases, including potato blight, celery-leaf spot, apple canker, bacterial canker, and leaf spots on fruits.
● **Sulphur** Use sulphur to control diseases such as storage rots and powdery mildew on ornamental plants and fruits.

SAFETY POINTS
● **Storage** Keep all organic concentrates out of reach of children and inquisitive pets.
● **Checking the label** Read the manufacturer's instructions and follow them very carefully.
● **When to use** Spray on a windless day and in the evening.

CHEMICAL CONTROLS

There are many different chemicals available to gardeners for use against a large number of pests and diseases on a wide range of plants. Provided that they are used safely, carefully, and never indiscriminately, chemical controls are a useful aid to trouble-free gardening.

USING CHEMICAL CONTROLS SAFELY

● **Combining methods** Use chemicals only if they are absolutely necessary. Whenever possible, combine chemical controls with cultivation methods.

● **Accurate choice** Choose the chemical that is most appropriate for a particular problem, and follow the instructions carefully. Not all products are suitable for every type of plant.

● **Checking the label** Always observe stated limitations, precautions, and restrictions.

● **Protecting hands** Always use gloves when handling or mixing chemical concentrates.

● **Avoiding contamination** Never eat, drink, or smoke when working with pesticides. Always wash your hands thoroughly after using them.

● **Using chemicals safely** Avoid contact with the skin, and wash off any splashes immediately. Do not inhale any dusts or sprays.

● **Treated areas** Keep children and animals away from the area being treated. Most chemicals are considered safe once the foliage in the treated area is dry.

● **Conditions for use** Do not spray or treat with pesticides on windy, gusty, or very hot days.

● **Bee protection** If possible, spray at dusk to minimize risk to pollinating insects, such as bees.

● **Containers** Always wash out the apparatus used to apply chemicals thoroughly after use.

● **Labelling items clearly** Always label every piece of equipment used for applying pesticides. Never decant chemicals into other containers.

● **Storage** Store pesticides in their original containers, and ensure that these are tightly closed. Keep all pesticides in a safe place well out of the reach of animals and children.

AVOIDING DAMAGE

● **Following instructions** All pesticides carry detailed instructions. Always apply the product at the precise rate and frequency stated. If used incorrectly, pesticides can damage both the plant and the environment.

Covering a plant
Many pests and diseases, such as rose rust, lurk on the undersides of leaves. To ensure efficient coverage and control of the pest or pathogen, use a curved nozzle to enable you to spray the undersides of the leaves as well as the upper surfaces.

APPLYING CHEMICALS

● **Suitability** If you are uncertain about whether a particular chemical will cause an adverse reaction in a plant, test it first on a small area before treating the whole plant.

● **Size of spray** Choose a fine-droplet spray for controlling insects, since they are most likely to be killed by small droplets. Large droplets are more suitable for weed control.

● **Ready-mixed chemicals** If you have only a minor problem to control or a small garden, buy ready-to-use proprietary pesticides and fungicides with attached spray.

● **Minimizing stress** Do not apply chemicals to young plants or plants under stress, which can be easily damaged.

● **Shiny leaves** If you need to treat a plant that has shiny leaves, choose a product that contains a wetting agent. Without this, the chemicals will not adhere to the leaf surfaces and will not be effective.

DISCARDING CHEMICALS

● **Leftover solution** Always dispose of chemicals that are old or that are surplus to requirements. Apply any excess to a similar plant, or pour it on to waste ground. Never pour unwanted chemicals down a lavatory or drain.

RESISTANCE TO CHEMICALS

More and more pests and pathogens are becoming resistant to chemicals – red spider mite and greenhouse whitefly, for example. Some thrips and aphids are also now resistant to common pesticides.

● **Changing products** Reduce the likelihood of resistance developing by using pesticides only when really necessary, and by changing the product from time to time.

● **Avoiding carbendazim** Some fungi, such as grey mould, are resistant to this fungicide. Choose an alternative product.

CONTROLLING SPECIFIC PROBLEMS

ALTHOUGH THEY CAN BE CONTROLLED by currently available pesticides, certain pests and diseases are often most easily kept at bay by cultivation or organic methods. You can use these as an alternative to, or in conjunction with, pesticides.

SLUGS, SNAILS, AND EARWIGS

Slugs and snails can strip plants of their leaves. They feed mostly at night and in wet weather, attacking seedlings, annuals, shrubs, herbaceous perennials, climbers, bulbs, vegetables, and fruit. Earwigs are particularly fond of chrysanthemum, dahlia, and clematis leaves and petals.

SLUGS AND SNAILS

Making a barrier
Slugs and snails dislike crawling over rough surfaces. Use this to your advantage; create a barrier around susceptible plants with coarsely crushed eggshells.

EARWIGS

Creating a hiding place
Make a shelter in which earwigs will collect by using rolled-up, corrugated cardboard. Tie a roll on to a cane near earwig-prone plants. Burn or crush the earwigs.

METHODS OF CONTROL
● **Snail search** Hunt for slugs and snails after rain, and with a torch at night. Collect up and dispose of the pests.
● **Beer traps** Pour a little beer into a small container, and submerge it so that the lip protrudes just above the soil. Slugs and snails will drink the beer, fall in, and drown – but, unfortunately, so will other species that are not pests.
● **Flowerpot traps** Trap earwigs by placing an inverted flowerpot filled with hay on a cane near susceptible plants.

FLEA BEETLES

Although small, these black, metallic blue, or striped jumping beetles are capable of causing a lot of damage, since they can make hundreds of small holes in plant leaves. Young plants are particularly prone to attack and are likely to be seriously damaged or killed.

METHODS OF CONTROL
● **Sticky card** Try using a yellow card coated in non-setting glue for catching flea beetles. These and other flying or jumping pests are attracted by the colour yellow and will fly or jump on to the card.
● **Clearing debris** Flea beetle grubs may cause slight damage by nibbling roots of seedlings. Clear up plant debris to remove the grubs' usual overwintering sites.
● **Using chemicals** If an infestation is severe, dust the soil surface, as well as plant leaves, with an insecticide.

TRAPPING FLEA BEETLES ON INFECTED PLANTS

1 Coat the surface of a piece of board measuring about 15 x 7.5 cm (6 x 3 in) with heavy grease or non-setting glue. Take care not to disturb the foliage of infected plants.

2 Run the sticky side of the board over the plants, about 2.5–5 cm (1–2 in) above them. Many of the flea beetles will jump or fly up and stick to the grease or glue.

CABBAGE ROOT FLIES AND CODLING MOTHS

These pests are not related to one another, but the damage that both cause can be limited by anticipating and interrupting their reproductive cycles, and by setting traps. Cabbage root flies devastate brassica crops, while codling moths lay their eggs on apples.

CABBAGE ROOT FLIES

Surrounding stems
To prevent female flies from laying eggs close to host plants, cut out circles of carpet underlay, felt, or cardboard. Make slits in the circles, and place the circles around the bases of young brassica plants.

CODLING MOTHS

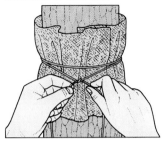

Wrapping a trunk
Scrape off loose bark on an apple-tree trunk in mid summer, and wrap a small area of the trunk in hessian. As the moth caterpillars crawl up the trunk to pupate, they will hide in the hessian. Remove and burn the hessian.

METHODS OF CONTROL
● **Moth traps** In late spring, try hanging pheromone traps in apple trees. These triangular, plastic boxes contain sticky paper, and in the middle of each is a capsule containing the pheromone that a female moth excretes to attract a mate. The male moths are attracted by the smell and become trapped on the sticky paper. The female's eggs remain unfertilized.
● **Last resort** If all else fails, protect transplanted cabbages and seedlings with chlorpyrifos plus diazinon or pirimiphos-methyl dust.

CARROT FLIES AND POLLEN BEETLES

Carrot flies can kill young carrots and other susceptible crops, including parsley, celery, and parsnips. Although pollen beetles do not cause much direct damage, they are present in large numbers on flowers and can be very irritating when cut flowers are brought indoors.

CARROT FLIES
● **Resistant plants** Select relatively resistant carrot varieties to grow. These include 'Sytan', 'Fly Away', 'Nandor', and 'Nantucket'.

Obstructing flies
Protect young carrot plants by making a polythene barrier 60 cm (24 in) high. The carrot fly is a low-flying pest and will not be able to reach the crop.

METHODS OF CONTROL
● **Timing** To avoid much of the damage caused by carrot flies, sow carrots after late spring, or ensure that the crop is lifted before mid summer.
● **Killing larvae** When sowing carrot seed, treat the seed drill with a soil insecticide to kill off any fly larvae in the soil that have not yet hatched.
● **Avoiding smells** Avoid bruising the carrot crop, or excessive thinning, since the smell of carrots attracts carrot flies. Use pelleted carrot seed, which is easier to sow thinly and will reduce or eliminate the need for thinning.
● **Covering with fleece** Lay horticultural fleece over carrot crops. Make sure that there are no gaps through which the flies can enter.

BRIGHT IDEA

Removing pollen beetles
Shake any cut flowers infested with pollen beetles, and leave them overnight in a dark shed or garage with a single light source. Most of the beetles will fly towards the light, leaving the flowers beetle free.

WIREWORMS

Wireworms are the larvae of click beetles. Although they are common, especially in recently cultivated soils, wireworms are mainly a vegetable pest. They bore into potato tubers and attack other root crops – and sometimes perennials, annuals, and bulbs, as well.

METHODS OF CONTROL

● **Exposing pests** If you are developing a new garden or plot that was previously grassland, dig over the ground regularly. This will expose both the eggs and hatched wireworms to predators.

● **Planting wheat** In the first year or two of cultivating new ground, try growing a row of wheat between crops. The wireworms will be attracted to the wheat, which you can then dig up and burn.

● **Chemical control** As a last resort, use chlorpyrifos as an effective wireworm control.

MAKING WIREWORM TRAPS

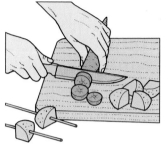

1 Make wireworm traps by cutting unwanted potatoes and carrots into chunks. Spear each piece with a wooden skewer, which will act as a marker for each trap.

2 Bury the chunks among crops to entice the wireworms away from the vegetables. When infested, remove each trap, and dispose of the wireworm larvae.

CLUB ROOT

Club root is a vegetable grower's nightmare. The fungus attacks several members of the cabbage family, as well as swedes. It can also attack stocks and wallflowers. The symptoms of this disease are distortion and swelling of the roots, and affected plants fail to develop.

AVOIDING CLUB ROOT INFECTION

● **Growing from seed** Raise your plants from seed. Club root is often introduced into gardens via soil adhering to roots of infested plants.

● **Strong roots** Help your plants to resist attack by establishing strong roots before planting out. This can work for kale, cabbages, and Brussels sprouts.

1 Check seed catalogues, and choose disease-resistant varieties whenever possible. Sow the seed in a tray. When the seedlings are about 4 cm (1½ in) tall, transfer each one to a pot that is at least 5 cm (2 in) in diameter.

2 Water the pots regularly, and grow the plants on for about six weeks – until the roots fill the pot. Plant them in open ground, and water well. The plants should be strong and healthy enough to cope with any club root.

METHODS OF CONTROL

● **Adding lime** The slime mould responsible for club root thrives in heavy, acidic soils. Improve drainage and add lime to decrease the mould's chances of thriving.

● **Limiting spread** Do not move soil from areas infected with club root to other areas. Clean all tools and boots thoroughly after use.

● **Regular weeding** Keep the vegetable plot free of weeds, which can harbour infection.

● **Checking roots** Inspect the roots of all vulnerable plants very carefully before planting out. Discard any vegetables with roots that appear to be swollen or distorted.

● **Disposing of plants** Do not compost infected plants. Burn them, or dispose of them with the household rubbish.

PEACH-LEAF CURL AND BLACK SPOT

Peach-leaf curl is caused by a fungus that attacks ornamental and edible nectarines, peaches, and almonds. An unrelated fungus causes rose black spot, and affects only roses. These leaf infections cause leaves to fall early from a plant, progressively weakening it.

PEACH-LEAF CURL

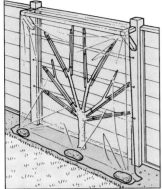

Making a shelter
The fungal spores of peach-leaf curl are carried in rain and on air currents. Protect plants by erecting an open-sided shelter with wooden battens and clear polythene. Put in place by late winter, and remove in mid spring.

BLACK SPOT

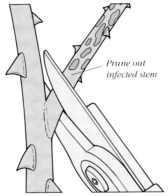

Prune out infected stem

Removing infected stems
Black spot fungus is able to overwinter on fallen leaves and rose stems. When pruning in early spring, cut out any stems bearing the tiny, purple-black lesions that are typical of this disfiguring fungal disease.

METHODS OF CONTROL
● **Using fungicide** Spray trees infected by peach-leaf curl with a copper-based fungicide such as Bordeaux mixture. This must be applied in mid winter and again two weeks later. This mixture will kill many overwintering spores and will protect the new leaves as they open.
● **Early treatment** Straight after pruning roses in spring, spray the whole of each plant with a suitable fungicide.
● **Fallen leaves** Rake up and dispose of fallen leaves infected with black spot; the fungus may overwinter on them. Do not put them on the compost heap or leave them lying around the garden. Burning them is the safest option.

LAWN PROBLEMS

A lawn may occasionally suffer from unsightly brown or yellow patches, which can be caused by drought, fungal diseases, or pests. Sometimes a lawn is disfigured by heaps of fine soil – molehills. Dealing with moles can be difficult, but there are remedies (see p. 113).

CONTROLLING PROBLEMS
● **Lawn maintenance** Keep to a regular programme of lawn maintenance (see p. 128–129). A well-fed and properly watered lawn – which is also aerated, spiked, and scarified – will be less vulnerable to pests, diseases, and weeds.
● **Late feeding** Do not feed a lawn with a high-nitrogen fertilizer very late in the year, since this will encourage the development of *Fusarium* patch (snow mould).
● **Nitrogen deficiency** Feed a lawn throughout the season to avoid nitrogen deficiency, which can lead to the onset of red thread disease.

REMOVING TOADSTOOLS

Sweeping toadstools
Most lawn toadstools are short-lived and have little detrimental effect. Use a stiff yard broom to break the fungi before the caps open to release their spores. Collect and dispose of the fungi.

ANIMAL URINE

Large brown patches on a lawn may be caused by dog (especially bitch), fox, or cat urine. Prompt action can alleviate the problem considerably. If you catch an animal in the act, wash down the area immediately with plenty of water. This will noticeably reduce the scorching effect on the grass. If you reseed an area, make sure you remove all the urine-soaked soil first, otherwise the grass seed will not germinate. Prevent animals from urinating on small areas of lawn by using plastic netting.

LAWNS

A GREEN, GRASSY CARPET can be the perfect setting and foil for the colours of an ornamental garden. Providing that a lawn is sown or laid properly, looking after it will not be difficult. Mowing and watering need to be done regularly in the summer, but other routine tasks need be done only occasionally.

SELECTING THE RIGHT SURFACE

Choosing the right type of lawn is essential to its future success. Standard lawn grass mixtures (see below) are not always ideal in certain situations. There are grasses to meet all kinds of needs, so do take the time to research the various possibilities, and choose carefully.

USING ALTERNATIVES
● **Moist, small areas** *Cotula squalida* has soft, fern-like, bronzy-green foliage and forms a closely knit carpet of creeping stems. It is suitable for light shade or sun but prefers a moist site, although it will tolerate direct sun. *Cotula squalida* is best reserved for small areas.
● **Sunny banks** *Acaena novae-zelandiae* is a semi-evergreen subshrub that forms a dense, 2.5–5-cm (1–2-in) carpet of soft, feathery foliage. It is especially useful in areas where mowing is difficult, and on sunny banks near paths and driveways.

CREATING NON-GRASS LAWNS

Chamomile lawn
Chamomile makes a good alternative to grass, but it requires weeding by hand. The fine leaves are strongly aromatic when crushed underfoot. Chamomile grows best in an open, sunny site.

Thyme lawn
Thyme has tiny, green, aromatic foliage and produces small purple-pink flowers in summer. It is best-suited to a well-drained, sunny site and works very well on uneven or stony ground.

CHOOSING A SEED TYPE

Use a standard seed mixture for most situations, except those mentioned below. You can buy mixtures that establish rapidly or that do not need much mowing because they grow slowly.

● **Family lawns** Mixtures with a high proportion of rye grasses are best for play areas.

● **Shady sites** Choose a special shady lawn seed mixture for growing under trees, or if your garden is not very sunny.
● **Fine lawns** To create a formal, high-quality lawn with even colour and texture, choose a special seed mixture that contains a high proportion of fine-leaved bents and fescues.

PREPARING A SITE
● **Measuring up** Always measure the area to be sown before buying grass seed, and remember to subtract areas such as island beds and paths.
● **Eradicating weeds** Eliminate perennial weeds that have deep tap roots or underground rhizomes before sowing seed. Spray the weeds with a suitable weedkiller (see p. 124).

BASIC LAWN EQUIPMENT

The equipment you need to look after your lawn depends both on its size and on your budget. Most of the necessary items are readily available.

● **Cutting and trimming** Lawnmowers are essential items for cutting. The most common are rotary and cylinder types. A rotary mower is always powered and performs well on long, uneven grass. A cylinder mower may be manual or powered and gives a neat cut on a good-quality lawn. A half-moon edger is useful for neatening lawn edges and cutting and shaping turves. Long-handled edging shears allow you to neaten up the edges of an established lawn quickly and easily, and without danger of back strain.

● **Maintenance** A garden fork can be used to prepare the ground before a lawn is sown or laid. A fork also comes in handy for aerating small, compacted areas in autumn. A spring-tined rake can be used for raking up leaves and small twigs. It is also ideal for removing moss once the moss has been killed, and for scarifying an established lawn to remove dead grass, leaves, and other debris.

● **Sowing seed** Small items such as canes, string, and plastic sheeting are useful for helping to shape your lawn.

● **Watering** Unless you have a tiny garden, a garden hose is essential. An oscillating sprinkler, which delivers water evenly over a rectangular area, or a rotating sprinkler, which covers a circular area, makes watering your garden an almost effortless task.

Rotating sprinkler

Oscillating sprinkler

Garden hose

Spring-tined rake

Long-handled edging shears

Half-moon edger

Garden fork

Cane

Plastic sheeting

Powered cylinder lawnmower

String

Powered rotary lawnmower

WARNING!

Fit a circuit breaker when using electrical tools in the garden. It could save your life. Do not use electric mowers on wet grass.

CREATING LAWNS

W HETHER YOU DECIDE TO SOW A LAWN or lay turves, creating the lawn does not take too long. It is the preparation that is the most time-consuming and the most important contributory factor to the ultimate success of the lawn.

SOWING LAWNS

Sowing seed may not produce the instant effect that you can achieve with turf, but it is much more economical. Unless you have access to a wide range of turf types, sowing seed also allows you the greatest choice. Select the most appropriate seed mixture for your garden.

MAKING STRAIGHT EDGES AND CURVES

Using a plastic sheet
Lay a piece of heavy-duty plastic so that its edge is placed where you need to make a straight line. Sow the grass seed over the area. The ground under the sheet will be kept free from seed.

Using canes and string
Mark out a curve using two canes and some string. Tie the string to one cane, and drive this into the ground. Tie another cane to the free end of the string, pull it taut, and draw a curve into the soil.

SOWING GRASS SEED
● **Before sowing** Thorough preparation is essential. Remove all large stones and other debris. Then apply a complete or balanced fertilizer to the whole area to encourage strong, healthy growth.
● **Using a mask** Grass seed can be very dusty. To avoid breathing in this dust, wear a DIY dust mask when sowing.
● **Where to start** Start sowing at the far end of the designated area so that you do not need to walk on the newly sown seed.
● **Raking** After sowing, lightly rake a thin layer of soil over the seed. This improves germination and helps to protect the seed from birds.

AVOIDING PROBLEMS
● **Weeds** Kill off all old grass and weeds before you start to sow any seed. Choose a non-selective weedkiller such as glyphosate. This is deactivated on contact with the soil, so that once the weeds are dead you can start to work safely.
● **Sowing thinly** Sowing grass seed very sparsely is false economy in the long term. Thin grass is readily colonized by weed grasses, broadleaved weeds, and moss.
● **Sowing densely** This can lead to problems, since the poor air circulation that dense sowing causes encourages a variety of fungal infections.

BRIGHT IDEA

Keeping birds off
To protect a small, newly sown area from birds, push canes into the ground, and put flowerpots on top of them. Drape lightweight fruit netting over this, and weight the edges down with stones.

APPLYING SEED

To help you distribute grass seed evenly, use a plastic flowerpot with several holes in the base as a shaker. Once you know the area a potful of grass seed covers, this method will help you to sow at a consistent rate.

LAYING TURVES

Making a lawn from turves must be one of the most instantly satisfying garden jobs. Once you have prepared the site, the next step is easy, and the effect instant. Always buy good-quality turf from a reputable supplier. Cheap turf may be infested with weeds, pests, and diseases.

STORING TURVES
● **Rolls** Turf is often delivered in rolls. Order it for delivery on the day you need it; turves should not be left rolled up for more than a day or two.

Unrolling turves
If you cannot use the turf straight away, you must unroll it. If you do not, the grass will deteriorate rapidly. Once unrolled, water the turves, and keep them moist until you are ready to lay them.

USING TURVES
● **Best time** Turf can be laid most of the year, but late summer, early autumn, or early spring are the best times. Avoid very wet, dry, or cold weather.

Staggering rows
Lay the first row alongside a straight edge. To lay the next row, kneel on a plank to protect the turves. Stagger the joints to give an even finish, and brush top-dressing into any gaps.

TRADITIONAL TIP

Boxing turves
If you are using turf lifted from another area of your garden, it may be uneven. Trim the turves so they are the same depth by placing each turf upside down in a box of the correct depth. Scrape off excess soil with any suitable sharp implement. Re-lay the turves as soon as possible.

SHAPING TURVES

The edges of a newly laid lawn will be formed from the ends of the turves, which will need to be shaped. It is easiest to do this after laying the turf, rather than beforehand. The same technique can be used subsequently for reshaping the established lawn.

DEALING WITH EDGES
● **Sharp spade** Use a sharp spade to shape turf if you do not have a half-moon edger.
● **Straight edge** Use two pegs and some string to mark out a straight edge. Drive the pegs into the ground, then mark out the line by stretching the string taut between the two pegs. Cut just inside the line.
● **Watering** Do not water a new lawn until you have finished shaping the edges. Watering before cutting will make it hard to make a sharp cut, and will increase the amount of damage done as you stand on the turf.

MARKING OUT AND CUTTING A CURVE

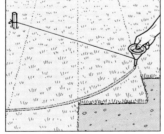

1 Drive a short piece of wood into the ground, and tie a length of string to it. Draw the string taut, and attach a funnel to the piece of string. Fill the funnel with sand, and use the funnel to mark out an accurate and even curve.

2 When you have finished marking out the curve, use a half-moon edger to cut along it. Try to cut with a straight, downwards motion. Standing directly above the edger is the best way to make an accurate, sharp cut.

PLANTING IN LAWNS

AN EXPANSE OF PURE GREEN can be ideal in some situations, but you may decide to break up and enliven the area. Whether you choose to plant bulbs, shrubs, or trees, or to introduce an island bed (see p. 12), the effect can be dramatic.

PLANTING BULBS

Many bulbs are suitable for growing in lawns, especially those that flower in the spring. Once they are established, most bulbs naturalize well and multiply each year. Cutting the grass as short as possible before planting bulbs helps you to do this task efficiently.

PLANTING SMALL BULBS

Cutting turf
Make a cut in the turf, and peel back the flaps. Fork the soil over lightly, and add fertilizer. Set the bulbs in position, replace the turf, and tamp it down by hand or with the back of a rake.

PLANTING LARGE BULBS

Scattering bulbs
To create a random, informal display, scatter the bulbs over the area you wish to plant. Check that none of the bulbs is touching another before planting them where they fall.

GROWING IN GRASS
● **Choosing** Choose bulbs with relatively small foliage. Dwarf cultivars of *Narcissus* work well. Small foliage is especially important if you are planting an area you need to mow around.
● **Planting preparation** Cut grass short before planting bulbs to make the job easy.
● **Planting hole** When using a bulb planter, make sure that the base of the bulb is firmly in contact with the soil.
● **Feeding** Feed naturalized bulbs once a year to ensure that they continue to grow and flower well (see p. 87).

NATURALIZING BULBS

Drifts of naturalized bulbs in a lawn can look stunning, but try to keep the extent of a drift in proportion to the size of the lawn. If you are planting a small area, it may be best to use dwarf bulb varieties. Always consider what the drift will look like once flowering is over.

LOOKING AFTER BULBS IN GRASS
● **Soil** Check that the soil is not too dry for the type of bulb you choose. The soil underneath trees and large shrubs is often very dry.
● **Flowering** When bulbs become overcrowded, they may flower poorly. Prevent this by dividing and replanting clumps regularly (see p. 156).
● **Foliage** Leave *Narcissus* foliage intact for at least six weeks after flowering. If tied up or cut back any earlier than this, flowering will be affected the following year.

● **Feeding** If bulbs in grass need feeding, use a high-potash fertilizer to encourage flowering (see p. 85). Do not use a nitrogen-rich fertilizer, since this will encourage the grass to grow at the expense of the growth of the bulbs.

SHAPING DRIFTS
● **Drifts** Plant bulbs in naturally shaped, uneven drifts with irregular edges. If planting more than one area, make each one a slightly different shape and size.

SUITABLE BULBS
● **Economical choice** Daffodils and other *Narcissi* are often naturalized. Purchased in large quantities, they are reasonably priced and can produce a great show over a number of years.
● *Galanthus* (snowdrops) These naturalize well and soon increase in number.
● **Crocuses** Select either a complete mixture of colours, or restrict your choice to just one or two. Choose crocuses that grow to the same height.

PLANTING A WILDFLOWER MEADOW

When surrounded by grass, wildflowers can transform an uninteresting or unkempt and infertile patch of land into a flower-rich area that attracts insects and other wildlife into the garden. Choose fine grasses, such as bents and fescues, that will not swamp the plants.

SOWING SEED

Add seed to sand in bucket

Sowing evenly

To ensure that the seeds are evenly distributed, mix grass seed, wildflower seed, and some horticultural sand together in a bucket before sowing. Do not fertilize the soil first.

USING AN EXISTING SITE

● **Soil** Wildflowers thrive on poor soils. If your grass is not growing well, consider turning it into a wildflower meadow.

Making planting holes

Use a trowel or bulb planter to make holes in existing grass. Plant up with pot-grown wildflowers. For the most natural effect, plant several of a single type in each group.

BUYING SEED

● **Conservation** Buy wildflower seed from a reputable source. Seeds of agricultural origin may carry diseases or pests. Make sure that you buy commercially cultivated wildflower seeds.

MAINTAINING A MEADOW

● **Cutting a meadow** Never cut the grass until the flowers have set seed, otherwise you will seriously limit the meadow's potential lifespan.
● **Infertile soil** Never feed a wildflower area, since wild flowers thrive in soil that is poor and infertile. Feeding invariably causes excessive growth of grass and weed at the expense of the wildflowers.

ADDING INTEREST

Take a good look at your lawn before you decide how to make it more interesting. A tree could create a visual break, for example, but what effect would a tree have on the rest of your garden? If your grass is not thriving, it may be best to abandon the idea of grass altogether.

PLANTING A TREE

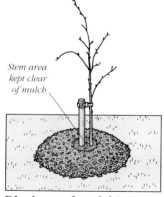

Stem area kept clear of mulch

Digging and mulching

When planting a tree in a lawn, dig the hole about three or four times the diameter of the tree's rootball to minimize competition from grass. Lay a mulch 5-7 cm (2-3 in) deep around the tree.

USING ALTERNATIVES

● **Maintenance** Areas of lawn that are difficult to maintain are perfect for changing into sites for shrubs, bulbs, or single trees. A thriving planted area looks much better, and is easier to maintain, than grass that grows poorly.
● **Island bed** Break up a large expanse of grass by creating an island bed. Plant this up with herbaceous plants or shrubs and bulbs so that it looks good throughout the year.
● **Damp areas** Grass in very damp areas is soon invaded by moss and other weeds. A site like this is ideal for planting up with moisture-loving plants, or for converting into a bog garden (see p. 133).

BRIGHT IDEA

Plants help to keep soil on slope in place

Planting a slope

The angle of a slope, especially if the slope itself is extensive, may make it extremely difficult to mow. Instead of grassing it, try planting it up with groundcover plants and scrambling climbers.

MAINTAINING LAWNS

IF YOU WANT A LAWN TO BE PROUD OF, you need to carry out a certain amount of routine maintenance. The effect you will achieve is almost entirely dependent on the amount of time and effort you put into looking after your lawn.

MOWING LAWNS

Regular mowing is essential if a lawn is to look good. Mowing must be done to the correct height for the time of year. If left too long, a lawn will become yellow and uneven when cut. Cutting too short can scalp a lawn. Both of these extremes encourage weak grass.

ESTABLISHING AND MAINTAINING NEAT EDGES

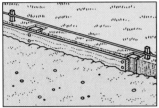

Using buried edging
Use a wooden batten, corrugated metal, or plastic lawn edging to create a buried edge. Fit it so that most of the material is buried in the soil, but the top is slightly higher than the grass roots.

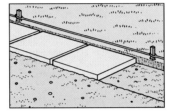

Using a mowing strip
A mowing strip made from bricks or narrow paving slabs prevents grass from spreading on to adjacent flowerbeds. Instead of using edging shears, simply mow over the edges.

CUTTING GRASS
● **Dry weather** Avoid mowing in dry weather. If you cannot, raise the mower blades so that the grass is not cut very short.
● **Wet weather** Do not mow if the ground is very wet. This will encourage compaction of the soil, and the wet clippings may clog the mower.
● **Lawn edging** Always set edging lower than the grass. It must be level with, or very slightly higher than, the roots of the grass. If set too high, it could damage your mower.

TRIMMING EDGES

Even if your lawn is growing well, it will still look untidy if the edges are left uncut, or if they are uneven. Once lawn edges start to collapse, it is better to recut them rather than to try to neaten them up. Even on neat lawns, it is worth doing this once or twice a year.

USING A PLANK

Making straight edges
Use a plank to guide you when cutting a lawn edge with a half-moon edger. This will ensure that you make a straight edge and will prevent you from crushing the edge when you step on it.

USING TOOLS
● **Tools** Use edging shears to trim or cut lawn edges regularly. Once or twice a year, use a half-moon edger to neaten up the edges. This cuts cleanly through soil, as well as through any grasses that have escaped into the borders.
● **Adjustable heads** Some lawn trimmers have an adjustable head that allows you to use them for edging a lawn as well as for cutting it. Check for this before you buy.
● **Cutting technique** Cut down through the roots, and keep the edger in the vertical position. Compost any trimmings.

TRADITIONAL TIP

Protecting frozen grass
Do not walk on frozen or frost-covered grass. This causes damage that makes the grass susceptible to diseases such as *Fusarium* patch.

FEEDING LAWNS

Your lawn will need feeding if it is to grow dense and lush. When it is mown regularly, grass responds by putting on more growth, which uses a lot of energy. There are different methods of feeding. Choose the one that best suits the type of your lawn and your budget.

APPLYING FERTILIZEERS

Estimating quantity
Use four flowerpots to mark out a test area measuring 1 sq m (1 sq yd). Weigh out the quantity of fertilizer recommended for this area, and apply it using another flowerpot. Use this as a guide for feeding the rest of the lawn.

USING FERTILIZERS
● **Selecting fertilizer** Choose the right fertilizer for the time of year. Some formulations are more suitable for spring application; others are more appropriate for the autumn.
● **Late feeding** Avoid feeding late in the year, since this can promote new growth, which is vulnerable to winter damage and fungal attack.
● **Avoiding scorch** Use a liquid lawn fertilizer if the weather is very dry, or if a dry spell is forecast. This minimizes the likelihood of scorch.
● **Excess fertilizer** Avoid over-application or double-dosing the lawn; this can scorch grass.

BRIGHT IDEA

Collecting up leatherjackets
Starlings feeding on a lawn may be a sign of leatherjackets. Water the lawn, and cover it with black polythene. The next morning you will be able to collect the grubs from beneath the polythene.

WEEDING LAWNS

However well you sow or lay your lawn, and subsequently maintain it, some weeds are bound to appear and will need to be dealt with. For small areas, handweeding is sufficient (see p. 98), but in most instances a chemical weedkiller is needed to rid the lawn of weeds.

USING A DRIBBLE BAR
● **Special attachment** Apply a selective weedkiller using a dribble bar. Keep one watering can just for weedkillers.

Applying weedkiller
Use a dribble bar for accurate application with the minimum risk of contamination to plants. More than one application may be necessary for stubborn weeds.

IMPROVING DRAINAGE
● **Aeration** Prevent moss growth on damp, compacted soil by aerating the lawn regularly (see p. 131).

Eliminating moss
Apply mosskiller, and wait for the specified time before raking any dead moss out. If it is not dead, you will spread the spores and make the problem worse.

USING WEEDKILLER
● **When to apply** Avoid risking accidental contamination of garden plants by choosing suitable weather and time of day before applying lawn weedkillers (see p. 94).
● **Saving time** Do two jobs at once by using a combined fertilizer and weedkiller.
● **Strength** Select a weedkiller with two or more active ingredients to maximize the chances of killing all weeds.

READING LABELS
● **Reading instructions** Most lawn weedkillers are safe for pets, wildlife, and humans. If using a liquid weedkiller, allow time for the treated area to dry before use. Always check the label for details (see p. 94).

DEALING WITH LAWN PROBLEMS

THE WEAR AND TEAR ON A LAWN can be quite considerable, especially if it is subjected to heavy use. The type of soil you have in your garden, and the weather, can affect the sorts of problem your lawn may develop.

REPAIRING DAMAGED EDGES

Neat edges are just as important as the lawn itself. However well maintained a lawn is, the overall effect will be spoiled if the edges are left untrimmed or damaged. Edges that have been damaged only in one or two small areas can be repaired very simply.

LIFTING AND TURNING TURF

1 To repair a damaged edge, use a half-moon edger to cut an accurate square of turf around the damage (see right). Carefully lift the turf, and turn it around so that the damaged area faces the lawn.

2 Re-lay the turf, checking the level, and reseed the damaged area with suitable grass seed mixed with a little topsoil. Water well. Away from the edge, the damaged area will be able to recover quickly.

CUTTING TURF
● **Accuracy** Always cut a section of turf into an accurate, regular square or oblong shape so that it fits into position when rotated through 180 degrees.

PROTECTING EDGES
● **Mowing strips** Consider fitting a mowing strip or brick edge. Both of these will protect an edge (see p. 128).
● **Using containers** Rest frequently damaged areas alongside a path by placing a stable container of flowers on the path by the damaged area.

REPAIRING DAMAGED PATCHES

Localized soil conditions, or frequent heavy use by children, may cause parts of an otherwise healthy, vigorous lawn to deteriorate. The resulting patches can spoil the appearance of the entire lawn. If ignored, the problem may become worse, so always take prompt action.

CARRYING OUT REPAIRS
● **Timing** The best time to carry out lawn repairs is when grass seed or turf is most likely to establish quickly and thoroughly. Spring and late summer or early autumn are generally the most favourable times of year for this task.
● **Starting again** If damage to a lawn is extensive, or if it recurs very often, this could suggest a fundamental problem. It may be best to resow or returf the whole area, but only after extremely thorough preparation.

REPLACING DAMAGED TURF

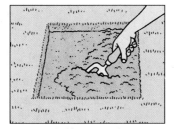

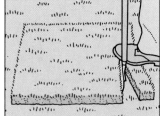

1 Use a half-moon edger to cut around the damaged area, and remove the turf with a spade. Lightly fork over the exposed soil, and incorporate a liquid or granular fertilizer. Firm the surface before returfing.

2 Try to use turf of the same type and quality as the original in order to achieve a good match. Place the new turf in the hole, and use a half-moon edger to cut it to size. Firm the turf in, and water.

CARING FOR HEAVY-USE AREAS

Some parts of a lawn are more likely than others to be subjected to heavy use: around a barbecue, in a children's play area, or on strips that are used as short cuts, for instance. These parts will inevitably be more likely than less-used areas to need extra attention.

IMPROVING DRAINAGE

● **Annual maintenance** Poor drainage is often the cause of poor grass growth. Improve drainage by aerating and top-dressing once a year in autumn. This improves root growth and rain penetration.

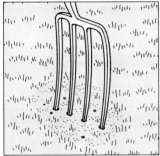

Spiking a lawn
Aerate a compacted area using a garden fork. Drive the fork into the lawn to a depth of at least 10 cm (4 in). Repeat this action every 15 cm (6 in) or so, easing the fork backwards and forwards to enlarge the holes.

MAINTAINING LAWNS

● **Top-dressing** After spiking a lawn (see left), use a brush to work a sandy top-dressing mixture into all the holes. Doing this will create long-lasting drainage channels.
● **Aerating large areas** If you need to aerate a large area, consider buying or hiring a hollow-tine aerator. This tool will remove cores of soil every time it is driven into the turf and is especially useful for use on a heavy soil.
● **Mowing height** Never cut grass very short in a heavily used area. A regular programme of feeding, watering, and maintenance (see p. 128–129) will help to encourage replacement grass to grow vigorously and healthily.
● **Making a path** An area that is subjected to heavy use may benefit from the installation of a path. Use stepping-stones to create a pathway (see p. 13).

PLAY AREAS

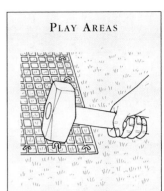

To help protect grass under a swing or other garden play equipment, secure sturdy netting to the ground with U-shaped staples. If this does not give enough protection, reseed the area with a specially formulated mixture of tough grasses (see p. 122), having first incorporated ground-up tyres in the soil (see p. 14). Alternatively, change the surface entirely. Use 5–7 cm (2–3 in) of finely chipped bark in areas prone to damage.

HOMEMADE PAVING

Making your own paving slabs allows you to design them to precisely the shape and size that you want, and for a fraction of the cost of manufactured slabs. If you want coloured slabs, buy concrete dye to mix in with the cement mixture. To make an irregular surface on your slabs, lay a crisscross of small twigs in the base of the mould, and pour the mix on carefully so that you do not dislodge them.

Use a flat, wooden board

Peel mould away from slab

1 Use semi-rigid, smooth plastic or metal to form the sides of the paving slab mould. Allow for expansion by using two pieces tied together with string or plastic tape.

2 Put the mould on a wooden base, ensuring that there are no gaps for the concrete mix to seep out. Carefully fill the mould with concrete. Wipe up any spillages with a damp cloth.

3 When the concrete has set properly (allow about 48 hours), untie and remove the mould. Protect the slab from frost until the concrete is completely dry.

WATER FEATURES

INTRODUCING WATER INTO A GARDEN instantly adds life. The sight or sound of water helps to give a feeling of calm and relaxation – whatever the size or style of the garden, and the water will soon attract all kinds of wildlife (see p. 111). If you do not have room for a pond, make a small water feature instead.

BASIC EQUIPMENT

● **Creating ponds** To convert an old half barrel into a miniature pond, a wire brush, scraper, paint brush, and wood preserver are useful. Wear rubber gloves to protect your hands. Heavy-duty polythene can be used to line a bog garden. Use a hose to fill a large pond.

● **Siting and maintaining plants** When positioning planted-up pond baskets, garden twine is useful for lowering down the plants. Gravel can be used for weighting the plants down and keeping them in position. Lining a basket with hessian trimmed with scissors helps to keep the soil around the plant's roots. You may need a sharp knife to trim pond plants. An old colander is an effective piece of equipment for removing unwanted algae and other pond weeds.

● **Protecting your pond** Plastic netting is useful for catching fallen leaves, which can cause the build up of toxic gases. A wooden log will help to protect your pond from ice damage.

Wire brush

Paint brush

Rubber gloves

Colander

Gravel

Scissors

Garden twine

Sharp knife

Wide gauge

Wooden log

Narrow gauge

Hose

Plastic netting

Scraper

Wood preserver

Hessian

Heavy-duty polythene

WARNING!
Always install electrical equipment properly. Make sure that it is inspected and serviced regularly. Use a professional if necessary.

INTRODUCING WATER

BEFORE CHOOSING A WATER FEATURE, take the time to look at the variety available in specialist catalogues and garden centres. Consider the style, shape, and size, and think about how the feature will fit in with the rest of your garden.

MAKING WATER SAFE

Always consider the potential danger of water in a garden used by children. If you feel a pond is unsuitable, there is a range of features that you can buy or make yourself that does not need deep water. Existing features can be made safe if they are filled with smooth pebbles.

TAKING PRECAUTIONS

- **Natural barrier** Block access to a pond by creating a rock garden or a dense, wide planting strip around it.
- **Pond covering** Fix heavy-duty mesh across the surface as protection for young children.
- **Shallow end** Make a shallow end, and line it with large stones to help children clamber out if they do fall in.
- **Water pots** Using a selection of pots and a pump is one of the safest way of introducing water to a garden (see p. 134). However, do not allow water to accumulate to any depth.

CREATING A BARRIER

Choosing a raised pond
A raised pond is less dangerous than a pond at ground level. A child would have to climb in, rather than fall in, which is how accidents usually occur.

USING A WATER FEATURE

Choosing a fountain
A bubble fountain is an attractive and safe alternative to a pond. Water is pumped up through the centre of an object, and trickles down over surrounding stones.

MAKING BOG GARDENS

Some of the most interesting plants can be grown around the edges of a pond in boggy or marginal areas. You may even prefer to drain the central area of water and have a larger area purely for marginal plants. It is possible to make a bog garden even if you do not have a pond.

DIGGING AND PREPARING A SITE

1 Dig out the allotted area, and line it with a sheet of heavy-duty polythene. Use a fork to make a few holes in the polythene to allow excess water to drain away.

2 Fill the hollow with garden soil, and firm gently. Water thoroughly, adding the water in stages so that it soaks right through. Leave overnight to settle before planting up.

PLANNING BOGS

- **Size** A large bog garden does not dry up as quickly as a very small one, so is easy to keep looking good.
- **Different depths** Slope the sides of a bog garden, or cut shelves into it to provide varying depths of soil. The wider the range of conditions, the more plants you will be able to grow successfully.
- **Attracting wildlife** Make a small depression in the bog garden, and line it with a tray or basin to make a mini-pool to provide water for wildlife.

USING CONTAINERS

Water in the garden does not have to be restricted to ponds or pools. Features such as freestanding ponds, bubble fountains, and spouts each provide the sight and sound of running water, and all are suitable for small areas – or even a conservatory.

CHOOSING CONTAINERS

● **Durability** All water containers must be frostproof, since they are especially vulnerable to extensive damage from frost.
● **Avoiding toxins** If you plan to add pond plants or fish to your container, check that it does not have any flaky paint.
● **Unique feature** Try a combination of pots piled on top of each other. Use a pond pump to circulate the water from one to another.

ELECTRICAL SAFETY

● **Cables** Make sure that any electrical cabling is buried underground in a conduit to protect it from damage.

USING TERRACOTTA

Bubbling water
Used singly, or in groups, pots make an attractive water feature. A bubbling spout of water coming from each one provides both movement and the relaxing sound of moving water. Pots such as these can be used in even the smallest garden.

SUITABLE PLANTS

Single dwarf water lilies such as *Nymphaea alba* 'Pygmaea' or water hyacinths (*Eichhornia crassipes*) work well in a small pond or in a container. Many normal pond plants can be used, but because of their potential size, they will need regular dividing and cutting back.

Nymphaea alba 'Pygmaea'

MAKING BARREL PONDS

A half-barrel miniature pond is particularly suitable for a small or overcrowded garden. It is also portable, which allows you take it with you if you move. In addition, you can move it out of a central spot into a secluded area when the plants begin to die back in winter.

PREPARING THE WOOD

Coat inside of barrel with sealant

Sealing the surface
Use a scraper and wire brush to scrape off all loose or rotted wood on the inside. Make sure that the wood is thoroughly dry before applying plenty of sealant (see right) with a paint brush. Allow this to dry thoroughly before applying a second coat.

PREPARING TO PLANT

● **Sealant** Make sure that the sealant you use is not toxic to plants and animals.
● **Suitable weather** Do not attempt to apply sealant in frosty or extremely cold weather. The sealant may not perform too well.
● **Drying** Allow the sealant to dry thoroughly out of direct, strong sunlight or frost. Fill it with water only once the sealant is completely dry.
● **Metal bands** Treat any rust, and repaint the metal bands.
● **Leaving to stand** Check that the barrel is watertight by allowing it to stand full of water for several hours. Discard this water, and refill before planting up.

SITING A HALF BARREL

Standing or burying
You can stand a barrel pond on almost any surface in the garden – on a gravel area, for instance, or on a paved patio or terrace. Alternatively, you can partially bury a barrel in soil in a suitable spot in the garden, or sink it to just beneath the level of its rim.

PLANTING IN WATER

I T IS PLANTS THAT BRING A POND TO LIFE, and the combination of plants and water that brings wildlife to a pond. There are plenty of pond plants to choose from; hardy plants are easier to maintain than those requiring special attention.

POSITIONING WATER PLANTS

D ifferent pond plants have different needs and preferences. Of these needs, planting depth is the most fundamental. If planted at an unsuitable depth, even a vigorous plant will fail to flourish. If you are building a pond, incorporate shelves to create different depths.

SITING POND PLANTS

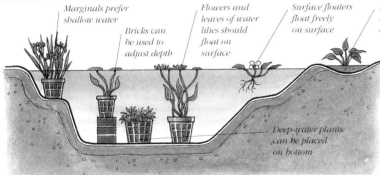

Marginals prefer shallow water

Bricks can be used to adjust depth

Flowers and leaves of water lilies should float on surface

Surface floaters float freely on surface

Bog plants thrive in constantly wet, but not submerged, soil at edges of ponds

Deep-water plants can be placed on bottom

Assessing depth
Make sure that you place plants at the correct depth for the species. Measure depth as the distance from the top of the soil in the pot to the surface of the water.

ADJUSTING DEPTH
● **Stacking bricks** Use bricks to make sure that a plant is at exactly the right depth. You can remove some of the bricks as the plant grows.

USING FLOATERS
● **Deterring algae** Use surface floaters to provide shade, which deters algae. Some surface floaters grow rapidly, so they may require thinning.

USING MARGINALS
● **Wildlife shelter** Include marginal plants in your planting scheme. Not only will they look good, they also provide shelter for wildlife.

OXYGENATING PLANTS

Oxygenating plants are essential for a healthy pond. The oxygen released from their leaves helps to deter algae, especially during the summer. Some oxygenators need to be planted; others should be left to float on the surface.

● **Planting oxygenators** Some oxygenators are planted as bunches of unrooted cuttings. Prepare a small container (see p. 136), then insert several bunches together.
● **Keeping plants wet** Keep oxygenating plants moist until they are ready to plant. Even during planting, they should not be exposed to the air longer than absolutely necessary.

SUITABLE PLANTS
Callitriche spp., *Ceratophyllum demersum*, *Elodea canadensis*, *Fontinalis antipyretica*, *Hottonia palustris*, *Lagarosiphon major*, *Potamogeton crispus*.

Potamogeton crispus

TIME-SAVING TIP

Eliminating duckweed
New pond plants often harbour tiny duckweed plants, which multiply rapidly. Save time and frustration by rinsing all new pond plants.

PLANTING UP

A newly planted pond takes time to become established, in the same way as any other new planting, but it will soon take shape. For the best results, choose plants for as many depths as possible, and include a few surface floaters. Choose plants with striking foliage.

LINING BASKETS
● **Hessian** Use basket linings to help keep soil around the roots of a plant without interfering with the flow of water. Hessian is the traditional material, but old sacking or coconut-fibre hanging-basket liners also work well.

KEEPING PLANTS MOIST
● **Avoiding damage** Pond plants are easily damaged by dry conditions, so make every attempt to minimize the risk of this by keeping them in water until you are ready to plant up. Always plant in the shade, never in direct sunlight.

USING AQUATIC GRAVEL
● **Preventing disturbance**
A 2.5-cm (1-in) thick layer of gravel on the soil surface helps to keep the soil and plant in position. It also prevents disturbance by fish or other pond creatures, as well as weighting the pot down.

PLANTING A WATER PLANT IN A BASKET

Trim excess hessian

Position plant centrally

Add gravel to just beneath rim of basket

1 Choose a basket large enough to hold the root system of the plant when the plant is fully grown. Line the basket with hessian, and half fill it with aquatic soil to hold the hessian in position.

2 Place the plant centrally in the basket. Add more soil as necessary, and firm gently. Top up the soil to within about 2.5 cm (1 in) of the basket rim. Water the plant gently, taking care not to flood the basket.

3 Gently top-dress the soil with a layer of horticultural gravel or tiny stones. Take great care not to bury any small leaves as you do this, or to damage the vulnerable young shoots and stems.

CHOOSING MATERIALS
● **Soil** Use aquatic soil, not garden soil. Aquatic soil contains the correct level of nutrients for healthy growth.
● **Gravel** Use horticultural, or special aquatic gravel. Avoid builders' gravel, which may contain several contaminants.
● **Alternative containers** Use plastic "tidy crates", which you can buy in most supermarkets at a fraction of the cost of special pond baskets.
● **Taking notes** To make the maintenance and purchase of replacement pond plants easy, always keep a record of which plants you use and where you plant them.

ADDING HANDLES

Thread string through holes in basket

Lowering a water plant
Position a planted basket easily and safely by attaching string handles to opposite sides of the basket's rim. Allow enough string to lower the basket to the correct depth, whether this is on a shelf or in the middle of a large pond.

ANCHORING A PLANT

Young plants, especially those with small root systems, are easily dislodged. Use several large stones, or an extra-deep layer of gravel, to help anchor a plant and keep its roots beneath the soil. The extra weight also helps to keep the container in position.

MAINTAINING WATER FEATURES

A LTHOUGH A POND or water feature requires a lot less maintenance than many other areas of a garden, it may deteriorate over a period of time if left entirely unattended. A little routine maintenance should keep everything in order.

REMOVING WEEDS

Weeds can very quickly build up in water, especially if a pond has not yet achieved a good, natural balance. Unwelcome pond weeds can be introduced in the soil of new plants (see p. 135), while other weeds may be introduced by visiting birds and other wildlife.

BLANKET WEED

Using a stick
Blanket weed is formed from a very dense, mat-like growth of algae. Left to grow unchecked, blanket weed will soon clog the water. Use a stick to remove it, turning the stick slowly in one direction to gather up the weed in large quantities.

DEALING WITH WEEDS
● **Natural balance** A new pond invariably turns bright green with algae soon after planting up. However, do not be tempted to clear it out and refill with fresh water, since this usually makes it worse. Be patient; the situation should improve once a natural balance is established.
● **Seasonal growth** Algal blooms and duckweed infestations are usually seasonal; depending on the temperatures, most die down in the late autumn or winter. Keep a close look out for any reappearance in spring, and remove growths promptly.

DUCKWEED

Using a colander
Duckweed floats on the surface of the water and can be scooped off a small pond with a large sieve or colander. Use a slow, skimming, scooping motion to gather it up. Remove as much of the weed as you possibly can; duckweed multiplies rapidly.

BURYING DUCKWEED

Preventing regeneration
Duckweed is a natural survivor and is very easily spread. Once you have removed it, never leave it lying around. Dispose of it safely by burying it in a deep hole, or by putting it on the compost heap or into a dustbin.

PREVENTING WEEDS
● **Surface floaters** Use surface floaters such as water lilies. Algae thrives in the sun, and the large leaves of lilies help to provide shade.
● **Fish** Over-stocking with fish can cause a sudden and dramatic increase in algal growth, due largely to the nitrogenous material in fish excreta. Combat this with oxygenating plants (see p. 135).

COLLECTING UP WEEDS
● **Removing duckweed** Hold a plank vertically, and draw it slowly across the surface of the water to collect up the duckweed. Remove with a colander or sieve.

GREEN TIP

Using barley straw
To stop algae from growing in water, stuff the leg of an old pair of tights with barley straw. Tie both ends securely, and attach a weight to the bundle before submerging it.

PROTECTING AGAINST WINTER DAMAGE

The approach of winter is the time when a water feature or a pond will need most maintenance. While many plants die back over winter, it is essential that the remaining plants, the water, and any living creatures are protected against the effects of plummeting temperatures.

TAKING PRECAUTIONS

● **Feeding fish** Fish do not eat much in the winter, since their metabolism slows down. Do not allow fish food to accumulate in the water.

● **Plywood cover** If very severe weather is forecast, cover a small pond or water feature with a sheet of plywood. Make sure that the water plants are not deprived of light for too long.

● **Heating the water** If you have a pond pump, consider replacing it with a water heater over the late autumn and winter months. Make sure to put the heater in place before the really cold weather arrives.

PROTECTING PLANTS

● **Using buckets** Protect tender plants by removing them from the water and placing them in a bucket of water. Leave the bucket in a sheltered, frost-free position until the spring.

BRIGHT IDEA

Melting ice
Fill a saucepan full of hot water, and rest it on the ice. Hold it there until it melts a hole in the ice, which will allow any potentially toxic gases to escape.

DIVIDING AND TRIMMING

● **Container plants** Divide any congested water plants in early autumn. Treat them like herbaceous border perennials, discarding any weak or damaged sections before replanting the rest (see p. 60).

Trimming leaves
In late autumn, trim back deteriorating and trailing foliage on all water plants, including marginals. Make sure not to let any leaves fall into the water. Collect them up, and put them on the compost heap.

DEALING WITH ICE

● **Removing ice** Never smash up any ice on a pond, since the vibrations this would cause could seriously damage any fish or other wildlife.

● **Creating an air space** If water freezes over, melt a hole in the ice. Carefully bale out water to lower the level by 2.5 cm (1 in). If the water freezes over again, any toxic gases will accumulate in the gap between the ice and the water.

● **Insulation** Lay planks over one-third to one-half of a pond's surface, and cover with hessian or bubble plastic. This will keep ice from forming on the covered part of the pond in all but the most severe weather.

PREVENTING GASES

● **Toxic gases** Prevent leaves from falling into the water. If the water freezes over, leaves can cause the build up of toxic gases, including methane, which are harmful to fish and other pond wildlife.

Catching falling leaves
Use plastic netting to prevent leaves from falling into the water. To make collecting the leaves easy, lay an old net curtain over the netting. When this is covered by leaves, remove the curtain, and shake it out before replacing it.

AVOIDING ICE DAMAGE

Floating a log
As water freezes and expands, it may cause substantial damage to a pond or water container. To prevent this, float a log or plastic ball on the water. The floating object will absorb some of the pressure, thus alleviating pressure on the container itself.

REPAIRING PONDS

HOWEVER CAREFULLY YOU INSTALL YOUR POND, it may start to leak at some stage, and repairs will be necessary to maintain the water level. The method you use will depend entirely on the material from which your pond is made.

EMPTYING PONDS

You will need to drain your pond before carrying out any repairs. Most ponds can be drained either with an electric pump or by siphoning off the water. Small ponds and individual water features can be emptied by bailing out the water with a bucket.

CLEARING A SMALL POND

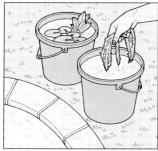

Removing contents
You may have to remove some or all of the pond life before carrying out any repairs. Put plants, fish, and any other aquatic life into plastic buckets. Handle everything as carefully and as gently as possible.

CLEARING A LARGE POND

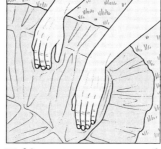

Making a temporary pond
Provide a home for the contents of a large pond by making a temporary pond. Dig a hole, and line it with heavy-duty polythene. Fill it with water from your pond, and gradually add the plants, together with any pond animals.

CHECKING PLANTS
● **Unhealthy plants** When removing plants from a pond, take the opportunity to dispose of any that show signs of disease or pest infestations.

STORING CONTENTS
● **Providing shade** Make sure that you store pond plants and creatures in the shade. Without their usual depth of water, they will be particularly susceptible to damage from high temperatures.
● **Providing protection** Place wire mesh over temporary containers to prevent cats and other animals from preying on any fish or frogs.

CONCRETE PONDS
● **New lining** If a concrete or rigid lined pond is leaking rapidly, you will probably need to reline it. Empty the pond, and simply lay a butyl liner over the old shell. Refill the pond with water.
● **Tiny cracks** Clean and dry the surface thoroughly, then paint the whole area with a proprietary pond sealant.
● **Large cracks** To prolong the effectiveness of a repair, undercut the crack (see p. 166) so that it is wider at the base than it is at the surface.
● **Ice** In very cold areas, you may need to empty a concrete pond entirely to prevent damage from freezing water.

REPAIRING CONCRETE

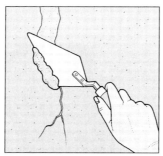

Filling a large crack
Concrete ponds are the most difficult to repair once they have sprung a leak. First, chisel out the crack with a chisel (see left). Then fill it with waterproof mastic cement, which should prevent further leakage. Follow this with a coat of pond sealant.

MENDING A POND LINER

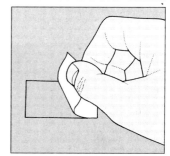

Patching a tear
Dry and clean the damaged area. Position double-sided adhesive sealing tape over the tear, and wait for it to become tacky. Cut out a patch from a spare piece of liner, and press it firmly on to the adhesive, making sure that all edges are stuck down flat.

PROPAGATING PLANTS

PROPAGATING YOUR OWN PLANTS *is immensely satisfying and exciting. Growing plants from seed is the most common method of propagation, but it is not the only one. Other methods include layering, dividing, and taking cuttings. Whether you collect propagating material in your own garden or from a friend, you can quickly build up your collection of plants without having to spend a lot of money.*

EQUIPMENT FOR SOWING SEEDS OUTDOORS

You can achieve brilliant results with minimum equipment by sowing seeds directly into the ground. This makes direct sowing extremely economic, even if you buy the seeds.

● **Surface preparation** The soil must be prepared properly before sowing. Use a rake to create a level and fine surface.
● **Warming the soil** Use black polythene, or horticultural fleece, to warm up the soil before sowing. Hold it in place with bricks or large stones.
● **Marking** Use canes and twine to mark out straight lines, which are particularly useful for sowing vegetable seeds in rows. A hand fork and hand trowel are useful for marking out straight lines for sowing annuals, and are also essential for moving or thinning seedlings and young plants. Use silver, or other horticultural grade, sand in a plastic bottle to mark out areas when creating a mixed border of hardy annuals. Do not use builders' sand, which may harm the seedlings. Mark each area with a label.
● **Watering** Use a watering can to water seeds. The jet from a hose may be too strong.

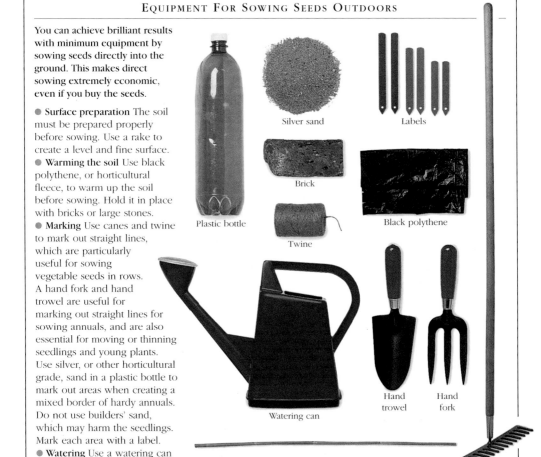

Silver sand

Labels

Brick

Black polythene

Plastic bottle

Twine

Watering can

Hand trowel

Hand fork

Canes

Rake

EQUIPMENT FOR SOWING SEEDS INDOORS

Although you need slightly more equipment for raising seeds indoors than outdoors, much of it need not be specially purchased. A propagator, preferably one that is heated, is a useful item but is not essential.

● **Sowing** Seed trays are available in either full or half sizes and are usually made from semi-rigid plastic. Invest in a selection of small plastic pots, and reuse any that come with plants you buy. Use a sieve to remove the large lumps and part-composted twigs often found in compost. A light dusting of sieved compost can also be used to cover fine seeds. A plant mister is useful for moistening the surface of compost with minimum disturbance to the seeds or seedlings.

● **Storing seed** Film canisters and envelopes make excellent containers for storing any seeds that you have collected, and for the remains of any opened packets (see p. 147). Use paper towels and newspaper to dry seeds before storage.

● **Aftercare** Use clingfilm to cover seed trays while the seeds germinate to prevent the compost from drying out. Clingfilm also protects the seedlings from cold draughts, which may damage them.

● **Transplanting** A plastic dibber and fork are invaluable for transplanting seedlings.

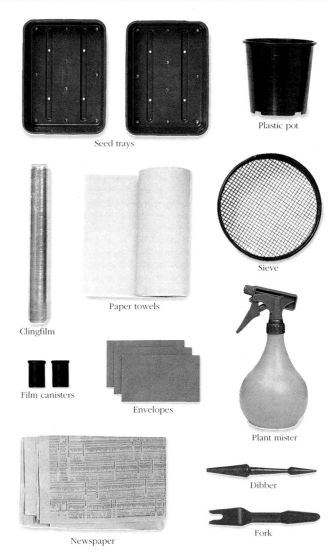

Seed trays

Plastic pot

Clingfilm

Paper towels

Sieve

Film canisters

Envelopes

Plant mister

Dibber

Newspaper

Fork

SEED POTTING MIXES

Most seeds can be raised in any multi-purpose or seed compost. The most important feature of these composts is that they have an open texture and a suitable nutrient content. For healthy seedling growth, a relatively low level of nutrients is required, otherwise the roots will be scorched and will die back.

Peat-free multi-purpose compost

Loam-based multi-purpose compost

Seed compost

SOWING SEEDS OUTDOORS

SOME SEEDS CAN BE SOWN directly into the ground, without the need for trays, compost, or a propagator. This works particularly well for seedlings that resent root disturbance. Check each seed packet for individual seed requirements.

SOWING VEGETABLE BEDS

Many vegetables can be raised successfully from seeds sown into the ground where they are to mature. To ensure success, prepare the soil by adding organic matter (see p. 38) and fertilizer (see p. 84) well before sowing. Keep all seeds and young plants well watered.

SOWING IN A STRAIGHT ROW

Base of cane is marked to indicate correct sowing depth

1 Push a cane into the ground at each end of the proposed row. Tie string tightly between the two canes to indicate the position of the row. Draw the end of another length of cane along the string to mark out a straight row.

2 Sprinkle some seeds into the row, and cover them with soil by running the back of a rake down the middle of the row. Use the back of the rake to gently tamp down the soil so that the seeds are in close contact with the soil.

EARLY SOWINGS

Warming up soil
Early sowings are possible if you warm up the soil first. A few days before sowing, cover the prepared seedbed with a sheet of black polythene or horticultural fleece. Weight down the edges with bricks or stones.

SOIL COMPACTION

Reduce soil compaction when you sow seeds in a vegetable plot by standing on a wooden plank. Do this whenever you work on the plot - use a brick and plank bridge if necessary - and you will need to dig over the soil only every five years.

SOWING SUCCESSFULLY

● **Capturing heat** If you are using black polythene (see above) or horticultural fleece, position it over the soil during the warmest part of the day.
● **Seed stations** For most direct-sown vegetable seeds, sow two seeds on each station to allow for poor germination. Thin if more than one seed germinates at any one station.
● **Intersowing** To save space, try sowing two different crops in a single row. Sow a slow-growing crop, such as parsnips or carrots, at well-spaced intervals, and a fast-growing crop, such as lettuces or radishes, in between.

AVOIDING DISEASE

● **Soil condition** Sowing in cold, damp conditions may cause the seeds to rot. If the soil is very wet or frozen, delay sowing until conditions are more suitable.
● **Preventing disease** Water rows with a copper-based fungicide to reduce the risk of damping off (a fungal disease). Guard against slugs and snails (see p. 118).
● **Crop rotation** Rotate all vegetable crops to minimize the risk of disease. Some crops, such as beans and peas, are especially prone to foot- and root-rotting diseases that build up in the soil (see p. 106).

SOWING FLOWERBEDS

Propagating by seed produces a wealth of new plants with little effort. A colourful summer border is easy to achieve with direct sowing, and the only cost is that of a few packets of seeds. It is an ideal way to raise many annuals, including many wildflowers.

MARKING OUT INDIVIDUAL AREAS FOR SOWING

1 Rake the soil level before defining individual areas to be sown. To mark out sowing areas, fill a plastic bottle with silver sand, and pour it out to mark out each separate area.

2 Rather than scattering the seeds, mark out straight rows for them within each area. You will then be able to distinguish between the seedlings and young weeds.

3 Cover the seeds with soil. Mark each area with a weather-resistant label. Push the labels firmly into the soil to prevent them from being dislodged by wind or animals.

SCATTERING SEEDS

Shake plant over soil to scatter seeds

Using self-seeding plants
Create new patches of flowers by lifting plants that have set seed. Shake the seedheads where you want new plants to grow.

USING SEEDS
● **Selecting colour** For an elegant effect, restrict yourself to a few colours when sowing a hardy annual border. Use a wider range of shades for an eye-catching display.
● **Good value** Save part-used seed packets from one year to the next (see p. 147).
● **Second choice** Transplant any seedlings you have thinned out from the main display into containers or into another patch of ground. They may be seconds, but most flowers will still look good if they are well watered and fed.

SOAKING SEEDS
● **Successful germination** Help seeds with hard coats to germinate by soaking them overnight in water. To assist water absorption, file very hard seeds with a nail file before soaking them.

TIME-SAVING TIP

Keeping weeds down
Scatter the seeds of hardy annuals into gaps and cracks between paving slabs to help prevent a patio from becoming colonized by unwelcome weeds.

SEEDS FOR DIRECT SOWING

*Adonis aestivalis,
Amaranthus caudatus,
Brachycome iberidifolia,
Calendula officinalis,
Centaurea cyanus,
Clarkia elegans, Consolida ajacis,
Convolvulus tricolor,
Dimorphotheca aurantiaca,
Echium lycopsis,*

*Eschscholzia californica,
Gilia lutea, Godetia grandiflora,
Gypsophila elegans,
Iberis umbellata, Linaria
maroccana, Lychnis viscaria,
Malcolmia maritima,
Nemophila menziesii,
Nigella damascena,
Papaver rhoeas, Reseda odorata.*

SOWING SEEDS INDOORS

SOWING SEEDS IN TRAYS OR POTS, either in a greenhouse or on an indoor window-ledge, gives you control over the growth of the seedlings. The extra warmth is especially suitable for seeds that do not germinate reliably outdoors.

SOWING IN TRAYS

Trays are ideal containers for sowing seeds; they already have drainage holes and are the correct depth for the early development of seedlings. If you want to grow only a small number of any one type of seedling, choose trays that are pre-divided into strips or cells.

SOWING SEEDS IN A PLASTIC TRAY

Place compost lumps on bottom of tray

Hold seed tray level

Cup your hand slightly

1 Large lumps of compost inhibit seed germination. If you do not have a sieve, remove large lumps from the compost bag, and place them in the bottom of the tray.

2 Use the bottom of an empty seed tray to level the compost. Holding the tray level, press it down firmly into the compost to create an ideal surface for sowing.

3 Dry your hands thoroughly, and place a small amount of seed in the palm of one hand. Gently tap your palm with the other hand to distribute the seeds evenly.

TRADITIONAL TIP

Sowing fine seeds

Sowing fine seeds evenly can be difficult. To facilitate distribution, fold a piece of cardboard or paper in half. Tip the seeds into the fold, and gently tap the card with your finger to scatter the seeds over the compost.

SOWING SMALL SEEDS

Gently shake sieve over seeds

Covering small seeds
Small seeds should not be covered with too much compost. To avoid dislodging the seeds when covering them, use a sieve to shake a fine layer of compost over them.

SOWING SUCCESSFULLY
● **Sticky hands** To stop seeds from sticking to your hands, sow seeds in a cool room, or run cold water over your wrist before you begin sowing.
● **Watering** Water the compost before you sow seeds to prevent them from being washed into a heap.
● **Tiny seeds** Settle tiny seeds into compost with a fine mist from a plant mister.
● **Light** If your seeds require light for germination, cover the tray with a sheet of glass or clingfilm to prevent the compost from drying out.
● **Heat control** Too much or too little heat can hinder germination. Invest in a propagating thermometer.

SOWING IN POTS

Some seeds, particularly large ones, are best sown in individual pots, since they need room to develop. This also minimizes root disturbance when the seedlings are transplanted. Using separate pots is ideal if you are sowing only a small quantity of each seed.

PLANTING IN POTS

Seeds sown thinly in each pot

SOWING SWEET PEAS

Put one sweet pea seed into each tube

SEEDLING CONTAINERS

Use empty household pots as seedling containers. Yoghurt and dessert containers make good pots, and margarine tubs can be used as seed trays. Make sure that you clean all containers thoroughly, and remember to make drainage holes in the bases.

Filling gaps

Use thinly sown seedlings in pots as temporary gap fillers to provide spots of colour in flowerbeds. You can plant out the whole pots and then remove them once the beds fill out.

Avoiding root disturbance

Roll newspaper strips into 3-cm (1½-in) diameter tubes. Fill each one with compost, and moisten before sowing the seeds. Plant out each tube – the roots will grow through the newspaper.

LOOKING AFTER SEEDLINGS

The correct conditions and proper care are essential for growth once seeds have been sown. Always consult each seed packet for details of temperature and light requirements. When the seeds have germinated, the seedlings usually require a lower temperature.

CARING FOR SEEDLINGS

● **Using fungicide** Prevent fungal diseases from developing by drenching compost with a copper-based fungicide before sowing seeds. Repeat once the seedlings have emerged.
● **Best conditions** Provide plenty of natural light, increase air circulation, and lower the temperature.
● **Sun scorch** Do not put developing seedlings in direct sunlight, since this may cause too great a rise in temperature.
● **Reflecting light** If light levels are low, stand trays or pots of seedlings on aluminium foil. Put foil behind the seedlings, too, to ensure that they receive plenty of reflected light.

USING CLINGFILM

● **Versatility** Clingfilm can be used to cover seedlings to conserve moisture, to exclude draughts, and to help to keep the temperature constant.

Remove clingfilm gently

Reducing condensation

Remove the clingfilm from time to time to prevent the build up of excessive condensation. Allow any water droplets to run back into the pot before replacing the clingfilm.

PROVIDING LIGHT

● **Lighting** Light is essential for the development of sturdy seedlings. Seedlings that do not receive enough light soon become pale and leggy.

Turn pots and trays regularly

Turning to the light

Seedlings grown by a window, or other one-sided light source, will grow towards the light. Prevent them from becoming lopsided and bent by turning the container regularly.

CREATING IDEAL GERMINATION CONDITIONS

Some seeds are capable of germinating under almost any conditions, but most have fairly specific requirements. Temperature is a major factor. Check the recommended temperature for sowing, and make sure that you provide it throughout the germination period.

PROVIDING HEAT IN GREENHOUSES

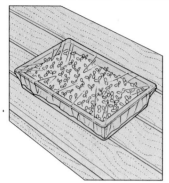

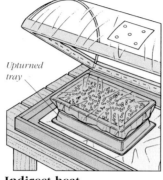
Upturned tray

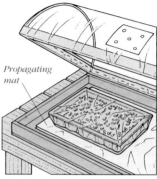
Propagating mat

Greenhouse bench
Seeds and seedlings that do not require much heat can be placed in a frame or on a greenhouse bench. Cover with clingfilm to help reduce temperature fluctuation and exposure to damaging draughts.

Indirect heat
Some seeds and seedlings can be damaged by high temperatures, but still require extra warmth. Place them on an upturned tray in a heated propagator, ensuring that they are not in direct contact with the heated propagating mat.

Direct heat
Seeds that require high temperatures for germination can be placed directly on a heated propagating mat in a propagator. This makes it possible for them to benefit from the highest temperatures.

PROPAGATORS

● **Condensation** Regularly wipe the inner surface of the lid to remove condensation, which can reduce the amount of light reaching the seedlings if it is allowed to build up.
● **Algae** Wiping the lid of the propagator will also prevent the build up of algae, which can form a thin, green layer. This not only looks unsightly, but also prevents light from reaching the seedlings.

USING PROPAGATORS
● **Uneven heat** The heating element in a propagator base may supply heat unevenly. Find the warmest and coolest areas, and use them for the appropriate plants.
● **Water supply** Always keep the capillary matting in the base of a propagator moist. This ensures a constant supply of water for the seedlings.
● **Cleaning** After each use, clean out the propagator thoroughly to limit the risk of disease build up. Take care not to wet the electrical apparatus.
● **Safety** If you are worried about its safety, have your electrically heated propagator checked by an electrician.
● **Bottle propagator** To make a basic propagator, cut off the bottom of a clear plastic bottle, remove the screw top, and place the top half of the bottle over a pot of seedlings.

MONEY-SAVING TIP

Using a linen cupboard
Use the warmth of a linen cupboard to propagate seeds that do not need light. Check the temperature on each shelf with a thermometer to gauge the most appropriate place for each tray. Cover the trays with clingfilm, and check them daily. Remove each tray as soon as the first seedlings emerge.

COLLECTING AND STORING SEEDS

Collecting seeds from your own plants is great fun and can be a very inexpensive and exciting way to fill your beds and borders with colour. Swap your seeds with those from friends and neighbours, too. Remember that home-saved seeds may not grow true to type.

CATCHING SEEDS
● **Paper bag** Most garden plants reliably set seed. Loosely tie a paper bag around ripe seedheads to catch the seeds as they are released.

COLLECTING SEEDS FROM VEGETABLES AND FRUIT
● **Anticipating variation** Many vegetable varieties will not produce plants exactly the same as the parent plant, so be prepared for variation.

● **Diseases** Some virus diseases are seedborne. Minimize the risk of producing unhealthy plants by collecting only from healthy looking plants.

On a dry day, shake seeds on to folded paper

Remove seeds from fleshy fruits with thumb

Leave seeds to dry on paper towel

Collecting seedheads
Cut ripe seedheads off plants, and shake them to release the seeds inside. Store these in an envelope or paper bag. Mark each one clearly with the plant name and date of collection.

Scooping out seeds
Choose ripe, healthy looking vegetables or fruit. Cut each one in half, and carefully scoop out the seeds. Examine them carefully, and discard any that do not look perfect.

Drying seeds
Dry home-saved seeds by spreading them out on a clean paper towel. Put this into a clean, dry seed tray, and allow the seeds to dry thoroughly. Store them in a cool, dry place.

STORING SEEDS
● **Suitable containers** Seeds are best stored in an airtight container. They must be completely free from moist plant material, otherwise they may rot or start to germinate.

STORING PODS
● **Seed pods** Seeds in pods should not be stored in airtight conditions. They require a flow of air to dry the pods. Once the seeds are ripe, they can be removed.

Use folded paper to pour out seeds

Pods spaced out to allow good air circulation

Excluding light
Black film canisters are good for storing seeds. Ensure that the seeds are thoroughly clean and dry before putting them in each canister, and remember to label each one clearly.

Drying seed pods
Store pods on newspaper in a seed tray until they are quite dry. Do not apply artificial heat. When the pods are completely dry, carefully remove the seeds, and store them in paper bags.

CYCLAMEN SEEDS

Ripe seed capsule

● **Seed capsules** Collect seeds from hardy cyclamen as soon as the capsules begin to split open. Tie a paper bag loosely around the capsules to ensure that no seeds are lost.
● **Soaking seeds** To improve germination, remove the seeds from each capsule, and soak them overnight. Sow them as soon as possible.

THINNING SEEDLINGS

ONCE SEEDLINGS HAVE EMERGED, they usually require thinning or transplanting. Although this is quite a fiddly job, it gives you the chance to select the best seedlings, which you can then provide with a fresh supply of nutrients.

THINNING IN OPEN GROUND

Seedlings raised in open ground are usually thinned as soon as they are large enough to handle. A few seeds, mainly for vegetables, are sown thinly and then transplanted. Thinning is best carried out in two stages, providing two chances to choose the most vigorous seedlings.

THINNING SEEDLINGS

Removing weak seedlings
Carefully remove any weak or diseased seedlings. Be careful not to disturb the roots of the remaining seedlings.

TRANSPLANTING PLANTS

Reducing moisture loss
Use a hand fork to lift young plants. Put them straight into a plastic bag to reduce moisture loss from the leaves.

MOVING SEEDLINGS
● **Before lifting** To reduce root damage, water the soil thoroughly before lifting plants for transplanting.
● **Cool temperatures** Thin or transplant seedlings and young plants during the coolest part of the day – preferably at dusk. This reduces both moisture loss and stress on the plants. The plants will also have sufficient time to recover before temperatures rise again.
● **Watering** To settle the soil around the roots, water well after thinning or transplanting.

THINNING IN TRAYS

Seedlings raised indoors will need thinning or transplanting. The controlled conditions make the timing less critical than if working outdoors, but you should still minimize stress by working out of direct sunlight. Water the seedlings well, both before and after transplanting.

TRANSPLANTING AND WATERING SEEDLINGS

Water will be absorbed by soil

1 Ease the roots of each seedling out of the compost, and support the seedling by gently holding it by the seed leaves. Do not hold it by the stem or by the true leaves.

2 Make a hole with a dibber, and carefully lower a seedling into the hole. Refirm the soil around each seedling to ensure that the roots are in close contact with the compost.

3 To avoid compost being washed away from the base of the seedlings, water them by standing the pot in water until the compost surface appears moist.

CARING FOR YOUNG PLANTS

Seedlings and young plants need special care and attention. Their stems and foliage are relatively soft, which makes them especially vulnerable. Young plants need to be weaned gradually so that they have time to adjust to their new conditions in the garden.

MAINTAINING PLANTS

● **Avoiding extremes** Young plants can suffer in extreme conditions. Do not subject them to very bright sunlight or very dull conditions. Avoid extremes of temperature, too.

● **Watering** A regular and adequate water supply is essential, since young root systems are easily damaged by erratic moisture levels.

● **Diseases** Reduce the risk of fungal diseases by watering with a copper-based fungicide after transplanting or thinning.

● **Scorching** Soft foliage is easily scorched, especially if it is exposed to sunlight when wet. Keep moisture off the leaf surfaces, particularly during bright light and when temperatures are low.

PROTECTING YOUNG PLANTS FROM DAMAGE

● **Plant care** Protect plants from pests and diseases (see p. 104) and adverse weather conditions (see p. 82–83).

Making a mini-cloche
Put half a clear plastic bottle over seedlings or young plants to make a mini-cloche. Harden off the plants gradually by making holes in the bottle.

● **Pest barriers** Prevent pests from ever reaching young plants by strategically placing a barrier. Some barriers can also insulate large areas of plants from the cold.

Covering with film
Perforated horticultural films and fleeces allow light and air to penetrate. They also protect against cold and pests. Weight down or tuck in the edges.

MAKING A POLYTUNNEL

Polytunnels are usually used to protect low-growing plants from extreme weather conditions (see p. 82-83). Make a polytunnel to cover a small area of your vegetable patch. For each supporting hoop, you need 2 m (6½ ft) of 12-mm (½-in) diameter flexible pipe and two 45-cm (18-in) lengths of dowel to fit inside the pipe. You will also need clear polythene, wooden battens, and drawing pins.

1 Mark out the base of the polytunnel with the battens. Push a piece of dowel into each end of the pipe. Make the hoops by pushing the dowels into the ground just inside the battens.

2 Place the hoops about 1.5 m (5 ft) apart along the length of the battens, and cover them with polythene. Wrap the polythene edges under the battens, and secure with drawing pins.

3 Secure the polythene at the ends of the polytunnel with bricks or large stones. Seal the polytunnel for maximum warmth, and open it up to provide ventilation during warm weather.

LAYERING PLANTS

Propagating plants by layering is not difficult. Plant stems are encouraged to produce roots, usually by bending them down to ground level and covering them with soil. Making a cut in the stems helps to stimulate the rooting process.

BASIC EQUIPMENT

Layering does not require much equipment. Some plants self-layer and need little more than a covering of soil where the stem touches the soil.

● **Rooting mediums** Hormone rooting powder stimulates the natural rooting process. Treating the cut stem area produces the best results. Good-quality, multi-purpose or cuttings compost also encourages rapid rooting. This can be used in a plunged plastic pot (see opposite), or it can be incorporated into the soil around the plant you are layering.

● **Other items** Canes, twine, a sharp knife, and some metal pegs are useful for many types of layering technique.

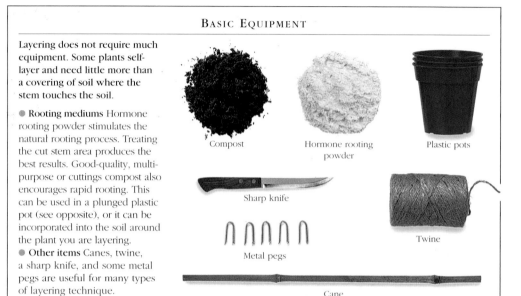

Compost

Hormone rooting powder

Plastic pots

Sharp knife

Metal pegs

Twine

Cane

SUITABLE PLANTS

Many commonly grown trees, shrubs, and climbers are propagated by layering. Those described as self-layering will root unaided when in contact with garden soil. Pot them up when well rooted.

Actinidia, Akebia, Andromeda, Aucuba, Carpenteria, Cassiope, Celastrus (S), *Chaenomeles, Chionanthus, Cissus, Corylopsis, Ercilla, Erica, Fothergilla, Hedera* (S), *Humulus, Hydrangea petiolaris* (S), *Kalmia, Laurus, Lonicera, Magnolia, Mandevilla, Osmanthus, Parthenocissus* (S), *Passiflora* (most), *Periploca* (S), *Pilostegia,*

Rhododendron, Rosa, Rubus, Scindapsus, Skimmia, Stachyurus, Strongylodon, Syringa, Trachelospermum (S), *Vaccinium corymbosum, Vitis amurensis, Vitis coignetiae, Wisteria.*

(S) – plants that are self-layering

Magnolia

BRIGHT IDEA

Applying a foliar feed
Invigorate a developing young plant by spraying the new leaves with a foliar feed. This method of feeding also helps to stimulate root development and growth, ensuring a layered plant with a well-developed and strong root system.

LAYERING TECHNIQUES

There are a number of layering techniques, all suited to different plants and to different purposes. Simple layering, as shown below using a clematis, is the most straightforward method. Propagating clematis in this way is best suited to the large-flowered hybrids.

CUTTING, ROOTING, AND SECURING A CLEMATIS

1 Sometime between autumn and spring, choose a vigorous, flexible stem that you can bend down to the ground. Make a slanting cut on the lower side of the stem, preferably just below a node joint. Cut about halfway into the stem to form a "tongue".

2 Plunge a pot of moist compost beneath the plant, close to the stem you are layering. Dip the cut stem into hormone rooting powder, and shake off any excess. Hold the cut open with a piece of wood to ensure that the powder gets right inside it.

3 Bury the cut area into the pot of compost. Secure it in position with a metal peg or a small piece of wire. Water the cut area well, and continue to water over the next few months. After six months test for roots by pulling gently on the end of the stem.

IMPROVING THE SOIL
● **Soil condition** If rooting directly into the soil, improve the soil's texture and fertility by incorporating compost. If the soil is heavy, dig in some grit as well. Good drainage is essential for healthy roots.

Use twine to tie shoot to cane

Avoiding moisture loss
Mound moist compost over a pegged area to prevent the soil from drying out and to help encourage rooting. Tie a shoot carefully to a cane to minimize any disturbance to the developing roots from wind.

SELECTING PLANTS
● **Healthy stems** Always choose healthy, flexible stems for layering. These are easy to bend down and most likely to produce good-quality plants.
● **Shoots** Prune a plant hard in the appropriate season to encourage shoots for layering.

CHOOSING A TECHNIQUE
● **Serpentine layering** This method is suitable for climbing plants such as clematis, *Celastrus, Campsis,* and *Schisandra.* Make a cut in a long, young stem close to each node. Peg the stem down with the buds exposed to produce several plants along one stem.
● **Air layering** Shrubs such as *Hamamelis, Kalmia, Magnolia,* and *Rhododendron* respond well to air layering. Make a cut in the stem, and wrap it in moist sphagnum moss tied into position with polythene. New roots will grow into the moss.

MONEY-SAVING TIP

Revitalizing heather
Instead of buying new heather plants, revitalize old, straggly heathers by mound layering. To do this, place a mound of cuttings compost in the centre of the plant, and firm around the shoots. Moisten the compost. New roots will form within the compost in about six months.

TAKING CUTTINGS

Taking cuttings is an economic way of increasing your stock. Remember, though, that cuttings have to survive until new roots have grown, so they need the best possible conditions and care throughout the rooting process.

BASIC EQUIPMENT

You probably already own most of what you need to raise cuttings. These items are all you need to produce plants from those already in your garden.

- **Cutting tools** Use a knife or secateurs to take cuttings.
- **Rooting mediums** Multi-purpose or special cuttings compost is suitable for rooting many cuttings. Some will root in garden soil, but this is not suitable for cuttings raised in pots. Hormone rooting powder helps to stimulate root formation. Choose a brand that contains a fungicide to deter fungal attack.
- **Identification tags** Labels are essential, since cuttings can look remarkably similar until they start to develop.
- **Containers** Plastic and terracotta pots are both suitable. Thoroughly cleaned glass jars and yoghurt pots can also be used (see p. 145).
- **Other items** Garden netting is useful for securing softwood cuttings in a jar. Use a rubber band and plastic bag for creating a mini-cloche.

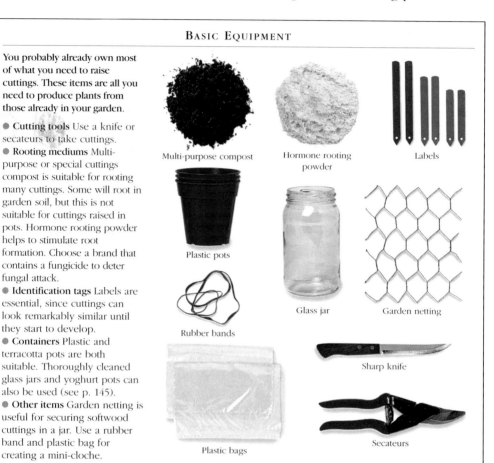

Multi-purpose compost

Hormone rooting powder

Labels

Plastic pots

Glass jar

Garden netting

Rubber bands

Plastic bags

Sharp knife

Secateurs

SUITABLE PLANTS FOR CUTTINGS

SOFTWOOD CUTTINGS
Abelia, Abutilon, Betula, Bignonia, Catalpa, Caryopteris, Ceratostigma, Clematis, Cotinus coggygria, Enkianthus, Eucryphia lucida, Forsythia, Fuchsia, Hydrangea, Koelreuteria paniculata, Kolkwitzia, Lonicera, Liquidambar styraciflua, Metasequoia glyptostroboides, Parthenocissus, Perovskia,
Philadelphus, Prunus, Potentilla, Solanum, Tropaeolum, Ulmus, Wisteria.

SEMI-RIPE CUTTINGS
Abutilon, Andromeda, Aucuba*, Berberis*, Camellia, Carpenteria*, Caryopteris, Ceanothus*, Chamaecyparis*, Clematis, Cotoneaster x Cupressocyparis*, Cupressus*, Cytisus*, Daphne, Deutzia, Elaeagnus*, Enkianthus,
Eucryphia lucida, Fallopia, Garrya*, Ilex, Juniperus*, Lavandula, Magnolia grandiflora*, Mahonia, Olearia*, Parthenocissus, Philadelphus, Photinia*, Pieris*, Prunus lusitanica, Rhododendron*, Skimmia*, Solanum, Thuja*, Tsuga*, Viburnum, Weigela.
* = take cutting with a heel (see opposite)

SOFTWOOD CUTTINGS

Take softwood cuttings in spring, when the new shoot growth should root readily. This type of cutting needs particular care because, although softwood cuttings root easily, they can also wilt and deteriorate quickly. Choose the strongest, healthiest, non-flowering side shoots.

TAKING A CUTTING

Removing lower leaves
Choose a shoot with three to five pairs of leaves. Use a sharp knife to take a 7–12-cm (3–5-in) cutting, making a straight cut just below a leaf node. Pinch off the lowest pair of leaves.

STANDING IN WATER

Place several cuttings in jar

Securing cuttings
To hold cuttings in place, bend a piece of garden netting over a jar of water, and secure it with a rubber band. Softwood cuttings can also be rooted successfully in cuttings compost.

COLLECTING CUTTINGS

Preventing moisture loss
Soft, young shoots lose moisture rapidly. Place cuttings in a plastic bag until you are ready to prepare them.

SEMI-RIPE CUTTINGS

Take semi-ripe cuttings from stems of the current year's growth during mid- to late summer or in the early autumn. Some cuttings, particularly evergreens, root best if taken with a "heel" of old wood at the base. Always choose a healthy looking, vigorous shoot.

MAINTAINING CUTTINGS

● **Woody stem base** Choose cuttings where the stem base is slightly woody but the tip is still soft. If in doubt, take several batches of cuttings at two-week intervals.
● **Cutting leaves** Reduce moisture loss from large-leaved shrub cuttings by cutting the leaves in half before inserting the cuttings in compost.
● **Rooting** Apply hormone rooting powder to stimulate growth of new roots and to deter fungal infections. Shake off any excess, since too much can damage the cutting base.
● **Labelling** Put pots of semi-ripe cuttings into a propagator or a cold frame. Label them with the date and plant name.

MAKING A HEEL

Slice away strip of bark 2.5–4 cm (1–1½ in) in length

Preparing healthy stems
Trim a healthy stem into several cuttings, each about 10–15 cm (4–6 in) long. Sever each one just below a node. Remove side shoots and the lowest pair of leaves. Stimulate root formation by removing a sliver of bark from one side of the base.

MAKING A MINI-CLOCHE

Bag secured with rubber band

Using a plastic bag
If you do not have a propagator, use a clear plastic bag as a mini-cloche instead. This will retain both moisture and warmth. Before removing the bag completely, harden off the cuttings gradually by cutting the corners of the bag.

HARDWOOD CUTTINGS

Hardwood cuttings are taken from fully ripened or hardened stem growth that is produced during the current season. Suitable stems can be selected from mid autumn to early winter. Wait until the leaves have fallen before taking cuttings from deciduous plants.

ANGLING A CUT

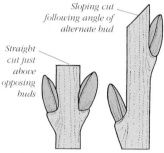
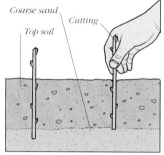

Sloping cut following angle of alternate bud

Straight cut just above opposing buds

Different cuts
Take cuttings large enough to trim to about 15 cm (6 in). Cut off any softwood at the tip of each cutting. Make a straight cut above opposing buds and a sloping cut above alternate buds.

PLANTING CUTTINGS

Coarse sand

Cutting

Top soil

Sandy trench
Insert cuttings 12–15 cm (5–6 in) deep into a well-prepared bed or trench with a 2.5–5-cm (1–2-in) layer of coarse sand in the base. Plant the cuttings against the side of the trench.

TAKING CUTTINGS
● **Suitable shrubs** *Forsythia, Philadelphus, Salix, Spiraea,* and *Tamarix* root easily from hardwood cuttings.
● **Soft fruits** Many soft fruits can be increased with hardwood cuttings. For gooseberries and redcurrants, prepare cuttings that are at least 37 cm (15 in) long. Remove the lower buds, leaving only the top three or four. Leave all the buds on blackcurrant cuttings.
● **Roses** Take rose cuttings from shoots that have flowered.
● **Saving space** If you need to root only a few cuttings, insert them at the back of a border.

ROOT CUTTINGS

Root cuttings should be taken in autumn or early spring. Lift a young plant, and tease the root system apart to expose the roots, then loosen the surrounding soil. Alternatively, cut out part of the root system of larger plants, leaving the rest of the roots in the ground.

ENSURING SUCCESS
● **Suitable plants** These include: *Acanthus, Aesculus parviflora, Anemone* x *hybrida, Aralia, Campanula, Clerodendron, Echinops, Erodium, Gypsophila, Papaver orientale, Phlox, Primula denticulata, Pulsatilla vulgaris, Rhus, Trollius,* and *Verbascum.*
● **Watering** Water cuttings after inserting. This may prove sufficient until the cuttings have rooted; excess moisture may lead to rotting.
● **Avoiding eelworm** Avoid attack by *Phlox* eelworm by taking root cuttings – the pest does not enter the roots.
● **Keeping moist** Keep root cuttings in a plastic bag until you prepare them. This will stop them from drying out.

TAKING AND INSERTING ROOT CUTTINGS
● **Minimum size** Choose roots from a healthy plant. The roots should be at least 5 mm (¼ in) in diameter and close to the base of the stem.

Preparing roots
Cut off any lateral roots. Make a straight cut at the end where the root has been removed from the plant. Make a slanting cut at the other end. Repeat this process along the length of the root.

● **Ideal length** The ideal length of the roots depends on the plant. After trimming, each root cutting should be 5–15 cm (2–6 in) long.

Cuttings spaced about 5 cm (2 in) apart

Inserting into compost
Firm compost into a tray, and insert the cuttings with the slanted cut downwards. Top up the compost so that the tips of the cuttings are just showing. Cover with 3 mm (⅛ in) of grit.

DIVIDING PLANTS

ANY HERBACEOUS PLANTS respond well to division, especially those that produce lots of basal shoots, and those with a wide-spreading root system. The best time for dividing most plants is between late autumn and early spring.

BASIC EQUIPMENT

The few items of equipment shown here are all you need for the successful division of plants.

● **Cutting tools** A sharp knife is essential to ensure neat cuts and divisions. A smoothly cut surface is an important factor in preventing attacks by organisms that cause disease.
● **Forks** A garden fork useful for dividing perennials. It may be necessary to use two for dividing large clumps. A hand fork can be used for small perennials.
● **Other items** Gravel can be used to improve soil texture and drainage. Wire pegs are useful for securing runners.

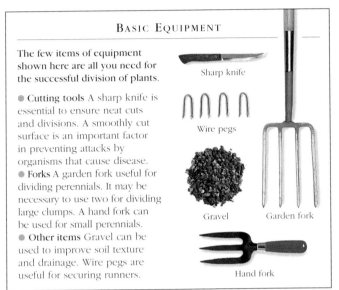

Sharp knife

Wire pegs

Gravel

Garden fork

Hand fork

SUITABLE PLANTS

Achillea, Arum, Anemone hupehensis, Aster, Astilbe, Astrantia, Bergenia, Campanula, Centaurea dealbata, Coreopsis verticillata, Crambe cordifolia, Doronicum, Epilobium, Geranium, Helianthus, Helleborus orientalis, Hemerocallis, Heuchera, Hosta, Liatris, Lobelia cardinalis, Lychnis, Nepeta, Oenothera, Paeonia, Phormium, Polemonium, Pulmonaria, Rheum, Rudbeckia, Sedum spectabile, Sidalcea, Solidago, Thalictrum, Trollius, Veronica.

DIVIDING RHIZOMES

Division provides a chance to rejuvenate old clumps of rhizomes and bulbs and to create new clumps at the same time. Tough plants may require two large forks inserted back-to-back to divide them, but many can be divided by hand or by using a knife.

LIFTING, TRIMMING, AND PLANTING RHIZOMES

Cut out and discard old rhizomes

1 Use a large fork to lift the clump. To reduce the risk of root damage, drive the fork into the ground at an angle and well away from the rhizomes. Shake off excess soil, and split up the clump.

2 Detach any new, healthy rhizomes from the clump, and trim their ends with a sharp knife. Dust the cut surfaces with a sulphur-based fungicide. Discard old or diseased rhizomes.

3 Make a sloping cut on each leaf to about 15 cm (6 in) to minimize root disturbance from windrock. Replant the rhizomes, leaving half above soil level. Ensure that the foliage is upright.

LOOKING AFTER BULBS

Bulbs require some attention if they are to perform well over a long period. Clumps become overcrowded after a few years and need to be divided. It is best to lift clumps during the dormant season, and to replant the bulbs in irregular groups immediately after division.

MAINTAINING BULBS

● **Marking clumps** When clumps begin to flower unreliably, it is a sign that they need to be divided. Mark these clumps with a cane when the foliage starts to die back so that they can be identified easily when dormant.

● **Foliar feeding** Bulbs that need dividing are often considerably undersized. Help to boost their growth by giving them a foliar feed immediately after replanting. Continue to feed regularly during the growing season.

● **Offset bulbs** Do not discard offset bulbs. Plant them in a separate site or nursery bed until they are fully grown.

DIVIDING OVERCROWDED BULBS

Remove offsets from parent bulb, along with loose outer layers of bulb tunic

Lifting a clump
Lift a clump using a hand fork. A large fork may be necessary for big or deep clumps. Try to avoid piercing any bulbs, and discard any that are damaged. Prepare a fresh planting hole, and incorporate fertilizer into it.

Removing offsets
Carefully remove offsets from the parent bulbs. Discard bulbs that appear unhealthy. Replant bulbs that are full-size or near full-size immediately, at the correct depth (see p. 57), and in a suitable site for the bulb type.

SCALING BULBS

Bulb scaling is a method of propagation for any bulbs with scales. It is most frequently used for lilies and *Fritillaria*, and it is carried out in late summer or early autumn. Look for scales with bulbils (miniature bulbs), which form between the bases of scales and bulbs.

PROPAGATING WITH LILY SCALES AND BULBILS

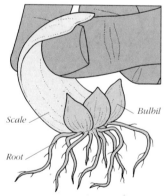

Scale
Root
Bulbil

Shake scales in sulphur to deter fungal infections

1 Remove any soil and damaged or diseased scales from around the bulb. Gently pull off any healthy scales that have bulbils at the bases. Be careful not to separate the scales from the bulbils.

2 Shake the scales in a bag containing sulphur. Remove the scales, and tap gently. Put them in a bag of peat substitute and perlite. Seal, and keep in the dark at 21°C (70°F) for three months.

3 Put the scales into individual pots of sandy potting compost. The tops of the scales should be just beneath the compost surface. Keep in a cold greenhouse or well-shaded cold frame.

PROPAGATING BY DIVISION

Most plants will reproduce readily in their natural habitats, and propagation often takes advantage of this process. Propagation by division produces sizeable plants very quickly. Correct timing and the proper aftercare of new plants are the key to guaranteed success.

DIVIDING SUCCESSFULLY

● **Timing** Choose the time of day carefully for this task. Divisions are likely to fail if they become dehydrated. Try to divide plants during the coolest part of the day – if possible early in the evening.

● **Cool spot** Replant any divisions as soon as possible to minimize moisture loss. Keep the new plants in a cool spot out of direct sunlight.

● **Healthy material** Use only healthy stock as propagating material. When dividing plants, take the opportunity to discard weak or old sections.

● **Weeds** Before replanting divided sections, remove any weeds that are growing through the roots.

USING RUNNERS

Dividing strawberry plants
Strawberry plants produce runners that make propagation very easy. Space the runners out around the plant, and peg them down. When they are rooted and showing signs of strong growth, sever the runners from the plant, and plant out.

USING OFFSETS

Dividing *Sempervivum*
These plants produce many small plants in clusters. Carefully remove these from the parent plant. Some may have already grown small root systems, but even those that do not will readily root when potted up in sandy potting compost.

DIVIDING RASPBERRY PLANTS

Raspberry canes naturally form suckers. If they are healthy and free from viruses, these can be used to replace old stock or for adding to the existing crop. In late autumn, you can lift any suckers that have developed around vigorous, healthy plants.

1 Select suckers from a healthy plant. Use a fork to lift suckers, taking care not to damage the roots. Sever each sucker with secateurs or a sharp knife. Ensure that each sucker has a good root system.

2 Remove the remaining leaves, and replant the rooted suckers on a well-prepared site. Choose a fresh site to limit the risk of soil-borne pests and diseases. Water the suckers in well.

DIVIDING PERENNIALS

● **Clumps** Perennials respond particularly well to propagation by division. Once a clump has become well established, there are few herbaceous plants that will not benefit from this method of propagation.

● **Timing** Division is usually carried out while the plant is dormant in autumn or early spring. Spring division is usually most successful on heavy soils (see p. 60).

GENERAL MAINTENANCE

PLANTS ARE NOT THE ONLY FEATURES in a garden that benefit from care and attention. Tools, structures, and buildings should be kept in good condition. The materials from which they are made determine the type and frequency of maintenance. Use the chart below to assess the pros and cons of each material.

GARDEN MATERIALS

MATERIAL	PROS	CONS
HARDWOODS Hardwoods – such as beech, mahogany, and teak – are used in the construction of most garden structures and furniture.	Hardwoods are strong, long lasting, and do not damage easily. They retain their finish with relatively little maintenance and are not prone to rot.	Hardwoods are supplied mainly by specialist merchants, and items made from them can be costly. Check that the wood comes from a sustainable source.
SOFTWOODS Softwoods – such as cedar, fir, pine, and spruce – are used principally to make garden furniture, arches, pergolas, gates, and fences. They can be stained or painted.	Production of softwoods is widespread and, as a result, they are cheaper and easier to obtain than hardwoods, and come in a wide variety of sizes. Their light density and equivalent weight make them easy to work with.	Softwoods have a shorter lifespan and are more prone to damage than hardwoods. Regular treatment with a preservative is essential if these woods are to last, particularly if kept outside over winter.
PLASTIC Injection-moulded plastic is a popular construction material for garden furniture, as well as for windowboxes, pots, and other plant containers.	Plastic does not rot, warp, or corrode, it is not affected by cold or damp weather, and it requires little maintenance. One of a gardener's less expensive options, it is also lightweight.	The colours in which plastic is manufactured can seem too bright and artificial for a small or traditional garden. The colour of some plastics will fade after prolonged exposure to the sun.
CAST IRON Cast iron was used in the last century to make garden furniture and ornaments.	Cast iron is very heavy, making it ideal for areas in which stability is required. It is easy to paint with a brush, aerosol, or spray gun.	Cast iron needs regular painting to stop rust forming. Its weight makes it difficult to move, and it may break on sudden impact.
ALUMINIUM This alloy is used for structures such as frames and greenhouses.	Aluminium can be painted with enamel for a consistent colour. It is lightweight and easy to move.	Weathered aluminium surfaces can become covered with a white and powdery corrosion.
STEEL Steel is used for items such as children's play equipment.	Steel is strong, sturdy, and is not easily damaged, so it requires a minimum of maintenance.	Paint coatings on galvanized steel surfaces may chip and peel off after a time.

BASIC EQUIPMENT

The maintenance of garden features is a varied task that may require a range of tools. Assess the nature of the work before deciding whether to purchase or hire expensive equipment.

● **Removing deposits** Use a stiff wire brush for demanding cleaning jobs, such as removing rust, paint, algae, and other deposits from hard surfaces.
● **Cleaning surfaces** Use a stiff hair brush to clean surfaces that may be marked by wire.
● **Painting** Select paint brushes in a range of sizes to apply wood treatments and stains, paints, and other liquids.
● **Filling small areas** Clear out rotten wood or crumbling mortar with a chisel, then level the hole with wood filler or cement. Apply these with a filling knife for a smooth finish.
● **Filling large areas** Fill in and smooth large areas of concrete or mortar with a mortar trowel.
● **Replacing nails** Remove old nails with the claw of a hammer. Replace with galvanized nails.
● **Hammering** Strike fence posts and paving stones into position using a club hammer.
● **Handling** Wear sturdy gloves when moving rough or sharp materials and objects.

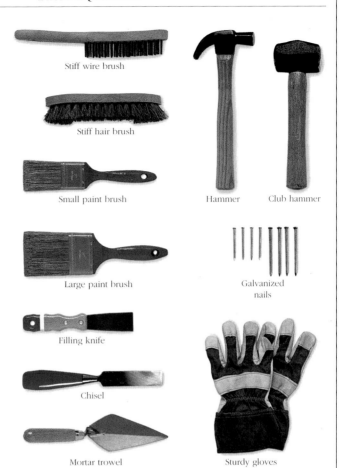

Stiff wire brush

Stiff hair brush

Small paint brush

Large paint brush

Filling knife

Chisel

Mortar trowel

Hammer

Club hammer

Galvanized nails

Sturdy gloves

ADHESIVES, PRESERVATIVES, AND SEALANTS

Liquid treatments can often be customized to your needs by mixing with paints and other materials.

● **Protection** Apply wood preservative regularly to extend the life of a wooden structure.
● **Colour** Select a wood filler that matches the wood in colour.
● **Strength** PVA adhesive is a sealant and bonding agent. It can be mixed with materials that need strengthening.
● **Repairs** Sealants and bitumen are available for particular repairs, including mending roofs and ponds.

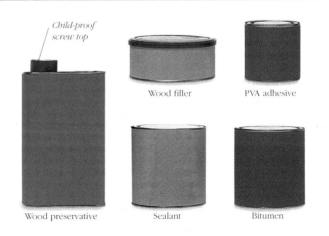

Child-proof screw top

Wood preservative

Wood filler

PVA adhesive

Sealant

Bitumen

WOODEN STRUCTURES

WOOD COMPLEMENTS ALMOST ANY GARDEN. Soft- and hardwoods are available in a range of colours, weights, sizes, and prices. They can be stained, treated, or painted to alter their colour and blend in with their environment.

REPAIRING SHEDS

A shed will potentially last for many years. It should not need a considerable amount of maintenance, but routine jobs such as timber treatment will extend a shed's life considerably. Repairs, including mending roofing material and replacing glass, may also be necessary.

REPAIRING ROOFS

● **Refelting** Do this in warm weather when felt is unlikely to crack. If repairs require you to climb on to the roof, kneel on a plank to spread your weight.
● **Roofing felt** Select a thick grade of roofing felt, making sure that it is sufficiently flexible for easy handling.
● **Old nails** Remove old nails from the roof with a claw hammer before replacing felt. If any break, hammer them in before securing the new felt with rustproof, galvanized nails.
● **Timber** Strip off the roofing felt arch, and check that the timber beneath is sound.

REPLACING DAMAGED ROOFING FELT

 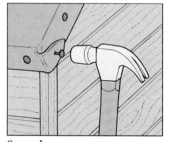

Eliminating air pockets
Place the first sheet of felt so that it extends over the eaves by about 2.5 cm (1 in) and the ends overlap the fascia boards by about 2.5 cm (1 in). Press down with a wooden batten to smooth out air pockets in the felt.

Securing a corner
Where the eaves and fascia boards meet, tuck the felt into a triangle, and fold it towards the fascia board, fixing it in position with galvanized nails. Tuck the corner in to ensure that it does not collect rain water.

REPAIRING WOOD CLADDING

Wood cladding on external walls has a tendency to splinter, crack, and rot. If a small area is affected, it is a relatively simple process to replace the wood. Once fitted, it is essential that you protect the new cladding against damp by filling gaps with putty, then treat the board with wood preservative.

 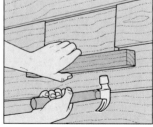

1 Drive wedges under the damaged area, levering out the cladding with a crowbar. Insert a thin, wooden plank to protect the timber below, then cut out the damaged area with a saw.

2 Measure and cut a replacement section, and drive it in, protecting the new board from the hammer with a block of wood. Nail the cladding in with galvanized nails.

USING TIMBER
● **Cut ends** Treat freshly cut ends before using the wood.
● **Drying** After treating timber, allow it to dry before use.
● **Damaged boards** If more than one area of a board is damaged, replace the whole board.
● **Cladding** Use pressure-treated timber to increase the life of cladding. This wood resists insects and fungi, and is ideal for damp locations.
● **Wood putty** For filling gaps, select wood putty that matches the colour of the cladding.

MAINTAINING GUTTERING

I t is essential that guttering and downpipes on greenhouses, conservatories, and sheds are maintained in good condition. Pipes are liable to become blocked and may leak or overflow, causing serious damage to the structure, which will take time and money to repair.

PREVENTING PROBLEMS

● **Rust** Scrape off rust as soon as it appears, and apply an anti-rust solution. Allow this to dry before painting the affected area with gloss paint.

● **Plastic guttering** Replacing a damaged section of plastic guttering is more effective in the long term than mending. However, minor damage can be repaired with bitumen or PVA adhesive. Waterproof tape is also useful for short periods.

● **Chicken wire** If inspecting or repairing guttering, take the opportunity to fix a narrow-gauge chicken wire along the length of the guttering to prevent it from becoming blocked with debris.

REPAIRING PLASTIC AND METAL GUTTERING

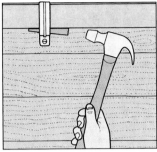

Repairing a sagging gutter
Loose or sagging plastic guttering will not drain properly, and this may cause its contents to overflow. As a temporary measure, hammer in a wooden wedge between each bracket and the gutter to hold each section in position until you can replace it.

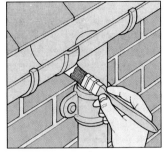

Sealing a crack
If metal guttering cracks and develops leaks, scrape off any rust, then paint the affected area with a sealing compound. Protect from rain until the sealant has dried. If the guttering is damaged at several points, replace the entire section.

INSULATING AND SECURING SHEDS

T o serve its purpose effectively, a shed must be dry and watertight. It should also be a safe, secure, and comfortable place in which to work and store tools and equipment. With a little effort, an unwelcoming, damp shed can be transformed into a warm, dry workplace.

FITTING INSULATION

Using polystyrene
Nail expanded polystyrene sheeting between the supporting struts of the roof and walls on the inside of a shed. Use short nails to avoid damaging the outer surface of the cladding or the roofing felt. Cover the polystyrene with hardboard.

MAINTAINING SHEDS

● **Wood preservative** If the timber on your shed needs to be treated with preservative, do this in the summer months. In warm weather, the shed door and windows can be left open to diffuse any noxious fumes.
● **Curtains** Hang a curtain over a shed door for added insulation against draughts.
● **Draughts** Fit draught-excluding foam strips around the door and window frames.
● **Heating** If working in a shed during cold and wet winter months, use a paraffin heater to keep it warm and dry. Ensure that the heater is well serviced and operated according to its instructions so that it does not pose a fire or health risk.

SECURING SHEDS

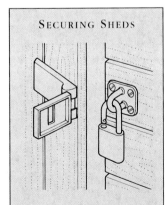

Many locks on sheds are easily broken. Fit a strong locking bar with screws drilled through the back of the door. Fasten with a good-quality padlock. Block out windows with blinds or cardboard if a shed is used for storing valuable tools.

PREVENTING WOOD ROT

Garden structures and items of furniture are continually exposed to the adverse effects of the weather. Seasonal changes and damp conditions encourage rot to become established. If wood comes in contact with soil or any other moist material, the damage can be far-reaching.

PRESERVING WOOD

Wear gloves to protect hands

Cleaning and applying
Prevent the onset or spread of wood rot by applying a coat of suitable wood preservative. Clean the timber of all loose material and debris, and ensure that it is thoroughly dry before painting on the preservative.

DISCOURAGING ROT
● **Using preservative** Place the legs of wooden furniture in saucers of wood preservative for several hours to ensure that the solution is absorbed.
● **Positioning furniture** Stand garden furniture on a flat, even surface that does not collect rainwater. Avoid positioning wooden furniture on grass.
● **Treating corners** Wood rot is likely to develop in the corners of structures. Prevent this by regularly treating these areas with wood preservative.
● **Removing debris** The accumulation of debris on or around wood encourages decay. Clear away fallen leaves and encroaching undergrowth.

FUNGAL ROT

Fungal rot – dry and wet – is not difficult to identify but, apart from treatable patches of wet rot, should be dealt with by a professional.

● **Dry rot** The first signs of dry rot are white, fibrous growths that become dusty red. Wood surfaces split into cubes and are covered by grey mould; if probed with a knife, the wood will crumble. Plaster bulges and cracks.
● **Wet rot** This affects only areas into which moisture has penetrated. It produces narrow, brown strips of fungus, and causes wood to crack, and paint to flake.

TREATING WET ROT

It is best to prevent the development of wood rot, but occasional treatment of damaged areas will still be necessary. Before carrying out repairs, make sure that the wood is as dry as possible – bring wooden furniture under cover for a few weeks prior to starting work.

REMOVING DAMAGED WOOD AND FILLING HOLES

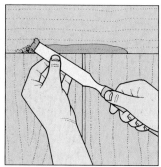

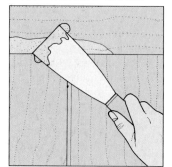

1 Remove damaged wood with a chisel or sturdy kitchen knife. Cut back to the healthy wood, removing any discoloured or decayed areas. If in doubt, cut away, but check that you have not compromised the inherent strength of the structure.

2 If possible, select a wood filler that dries to the same colour as the structure being repaired. Smooth the filler into the hole, firmly pressing it in to expel any air bubbles. To deter moisture accumulation, angle the surface. When dry, paint on a wood preservative.

DRYING TIMBER

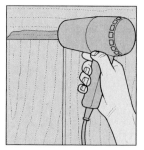

Treating a small area
Frequently, a small patch of timber on a large structure will be in need of repair. To save the time that would be spent waiting for the entire structure to dry out naturally, quickly dry the cleared surface with a hair dryer or hot-air gun.

LOOKING AFTER FENCES

Fences must remain outside, no matter what the weather. The location of some sections may expose them permanently to the effects of cold and damp. Dense planting of climbers and shrubs also encourages the build up of moist air. Ultimately, deterioration is inevitable.

REPAIRING FENCES

● **Hardcore** Drive hardcore firmly into place using the base of a concrete spur or a spare wooden post.
● **Concrete** If you have only a few posts to replace and are short of time, use a quick-setting concrete mix.
● **Winter protection** In cold and wet weather, create a screen to protect fence posts from frost and to prevent water from accumulating on the surface of any concrete.
● **Decayed wood** Do not repair a fence post that shows signs of deterioration; its effectiveness as a weight-bearing support will have been weakened, and the whole post will need to be replaced.
● **Corrosion** Check metal bolts and nails for corrosion, which may reduce their strength.
● **Treatment** Regularly treat fences with wood preservative.

REPLACING A PANEL

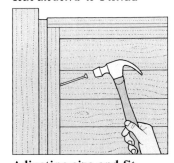

Adjusting size and fit
Fence panels are available in standard sizes, making their replacement relatively easy. However, if a new panel is too thin, insert a section of plank or a small strip of pressure-treated wood between the fence post and the panel edge. Nail the panel in position with galvanized nails.

REPOSITIONING AND MENDING POSTS

● **Loose foundations** Repair a loose post promptly to avoid damage to the fence panels. Avoid disturbing nearby plants.

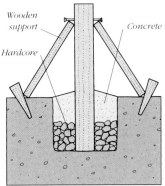

Restoring a wooden post
Dig a hole 20 x 20 cm (8 x 8 in) around the post. Reposition the post, using a spirit level if necessary, and hold it in place with wooden supports. Pour hardcore around the base, force it down, then set in concrete.

● **Concrete spurs** Wood rot can make a fence unstable. Replace the base with concrete, which is impervious to moisture.

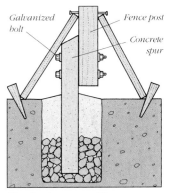

Replacing a section
Replace a rotten post section with a concrete spur and, if necessary, a new post. Attach the post to the spur above the soil with galvanized bolts. Hold in place with temporary supports, and pack with hardcore and concrete.

PROTECTING AND MAINTAINING FENCES

● **Avoiding damp** Fit a concrete or timber board along the base of a fence to protect it from rising damp. Try to keep gravel and soil away from the board.
● **Matching colour** A new panel may appear out of place on an old, weathered fence. After replacing a panel, treat the entire fence with a coloured wood preservative to give it a standard look.
● **Wide panels** Plane the edges of a new panel if it is slightly too wide to fit into the frame of a fence.
● **Plants** To keep damage to nearby plants to a minimum, maintenance and replacement of a fence should be carried out in the autumn or winter.

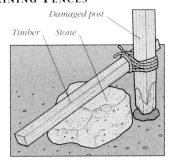

Removing a post
If the remains of a damaged post are difficult to remove, lever them out with a length of sturdy timber and a large stone or pile of bricks. Firmly tie the timber to the damaged post, balancing it over the stone. Push down repeatedly on the timber with your foot until the post is free.

CONCRETE AND BRICKWORK

BRICKWORK AND CONCRETE ARE RESILIENT, long-lasting materials. However, some weather conditions, such as cold or frost, may cause these normally hardy substances to chip and break, making maintenance and repairs necessary.

PREPARING CONCRETE AND MORTAR

MIXING CEMENT
● **Small amounts** Mix the components together by hand if you require only a small amount of concrete. This saves on preparation time and money, enabling you to measure out accurately the required quantities of sand and ballast.
● **Large amounts** If a large amount of concrete is needed, it is worth hiring a cement mixer, which will make the process relatively quick and simple.

MAKING CONCRETE
● **Mixing** Measure out the sand and ballast according to the instructions on the packet. Mix the components together on a flat surface, smooth the top of the heap, make a depression in the centre, and pour in the cement. Combine, and add water if necessary.
● **Consistency** Slap the surface of the mixture with the back of a trowel. If water trickles out, add more sand and ballast.

MAKING MORTAR
● **Ready-mixed mortar** Although this is expensive, ready-mixed mortar is more time- and cost-effective for small jobs than buying separate components.
● **Preparation** Dampen the surface of a mixing board, and pour the mortar powder on to it. Flatten the top of the dry heap, and make a depression in the centre. Add water slowly, mixing thoroughly to produce an even, moist consistency.

MAINTAINING WALLS

The external and dividing walls of a garden, and those on which sheds and greenhouses are built, should both serve a purpose and be attractive. A weathered wall looks good in a garden, but an excessive build up of algae and other deposits can spoil its appearance.

REMOVING DEPOSITS
● **Efflorescence** A salty, white deposit, called efflorescence, may appear on the surface of new bricks. Remove these deposits to prevent ugly marks.

Brushing away sediment
Scrub with a dry wire brush to remove efflorescence. Repeat this process several times. Do not wash the sediment off with water, because extra moisture will make the problem worse.

DEALING WITH DEPOSITS
● **Prevention** Use sealants and treatments on brickwork to help to keep walls dry and avoid deposits collecting.
● **Guttering** Check guttering for debris to ensure that it does not overflow and encourage the build up of algae on walls.
● **Cleaning agents** When clearing deposits with a brush, make sure that you do not use cleaning agents or soaps that can encourage efflorescence.
● **Recurring deposits** If algal deposits recur, remove with a proprietary algicidal product.
● **Pressure washing** Walls that are difficult to clean should be pressure washed. Do this in warm weather when water will evaporate rapidly, and ensure that nearby doors and windows are firmly shut.

BRIGHT IDEA

Restoring bricks
Renovate discoloured, stained, or marked brickwork using an old brick of a matching colour. Keep the old brick wet – place a bucket of water nearby, and rub the brick vigorously over the damaged areas.

REPAIRING BRICKWORK

After a time, the pointing on a brick wall may crack, allowing unwelcome moisture to penetrate through to the interior walls of a structure. Extremes of weather can cause the mortar to become loose, crumble, and begin to fall away. Accurate and swift repair is essential.

WEATHERPROOFING

● **Loose mortar** Remove all loose mortar from a wall to a depth of 1–2.5 cm (⅜–1 in) before attempting to replace with fresh mortar.
● **Power drill** Remove large amounts of loose mortar with a power drill. Protective goggles are essential.
● **Depth** If in doubt, chip away between the bricks until all loose mortar has been removed, but make sure that you do not damage the surrounding brickwork.
● **PVA adhesive** Increase the strength of the new mortar by adding PVA adhesive. This will also increase the bonding ability of the mixture.
● **Cleaning** Make sure that all excess mortar is cleared off the brickwork immediately. Use a wet brush or stiff cloth.

CHOOSING A FINISH

● **Matching mortars** Try to match the finish of new pointing with that of the old. This will help to disguise repairs made to the brickwork.

REPOINTING BRICKS

● **Preparation** Chip away any loose mortar with a screwdriver or a slim chisel and a club hammer. Wear goggles to protect your eyes.

Removing loose mortar
Use a soft brush to wipe away sandy deposits after removing loose mortar. Wipe the affected area with a sponge soaked in water before repointing. This will encourage better adhesion of the new mortar to the bricks.

ANGLING POINTING

● **Trowel** To achieve angled pointing, use a trowel to project the mortar over the top of a brick and recess into the base of the brick above.

APPLYING MORTAR

● **Equipment** Repoint a wall using a good-quality pointing trowel. Ensure that it is small enough to manoeuvre and that it will give a smooth finish.

Renovating brickwork
Begin by replacing the pointing in the vertical joints. When a section is completed, move on to the horizontal joints. Wet the wall again if it starts to dry out. Press the mortar in firmly, and trim away excess mortar.

TIME-SAVING TIP

Harmonizing colours
The colour of new mortar may change considerably when it dries. To avoid colour clashes on a wall, mix up a small quantity of the new mortar and allow it to dry, then scoop it on to a trowel, and compare it with the old.

Using old piping
Use a piece of old piping to achieve an even, concave pointing finish. Bend the pipe into a slight curve, making it easy to handle. A piece of garden hose makes an ideal alternative.

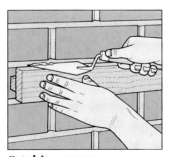

Catching excess
Nail a square-cut length of wood to a plank. Position the plank level with the edge of the mortar, and draw a trowel across the plank, in line with the bricks. Excess mortar will fall on to the wood.

REPAIRING CRACKS IN CONCRETE

Concrete paths and steps may develop cracks and even break up, particularly if they have been subject to heavy use. Weathering and the impact of feet, heavily laden wheelbarrows, and other weighty burdens will all eventually take their toll on these essential garden features.

MAINTAINING CONCRETE

● **Hairline cracks** Do not immediately fill a thin crack. Wait for a month or two to see whether it increases in size before carrying out necessary repairs.

● **Large cracks** These can be caused by a weakness in the material on which a step or path is laid, the sub-base. Take up the area, and lay it again on a strong sub-base.

● **Drying** Cover a repaired area with a polythene sheet to protect the concrete filler from rain. Allow it to dry gradually.

● **Insulating** If freezing weather conditions are forecast, cover a newly filled surface with newspaper, cloth, or other insulating material.

PREPARING AND FILLING CRACKS IN CONCRETE

● **Enlarging areas** Repair any crack or hole that is more than 1.5 cm (⅝ in) in depth. Enlarge the area to ensure that the filler is packed in firmly.

● **Preparation** Remove debris that may have accumulated in the affected area, since it will prevent the filler from adhering to the concrete.

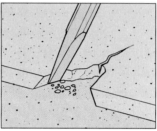

1 Use a chisel to chip away material in the affected area. Angle the chisel to make the hole larger at its base than at its surface, ensuring that the filler will be held firmly in place.

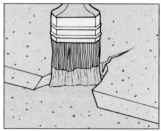

2 Brush away any debris, then paint the sides of the crack or hole with PVA adhesive. Plug the hole with concrete filler, making it level with the surrounding area.

REPAIRING CONCRETE EDGES

The edges of a concrete path or steps are subject to potentially damaging wear and tear. Air pockets beneath the surface, formed when the concrete was first laid, can cause the material to decay and crumble. For this reason, edges require early and frequent maintenance.

MENDING EDGES

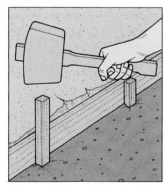

Using timber edging
Hammer blocks of wood into the ground with a mallet to secure a temporary timber edge. Make sure that the top of the timber is level with the concrete. Fill the space with fresh cement.

MAINTAINING EDGES

● **Loose material** Clear away any loose or crumbling material from around a broken edge, leaving a stable rim. If in doubt, remove more material than is necessary.

● **Hardcore** If any of the base material, the hardcore, is exposed during repairs, pack it down firmly with a timber post or concrete spur. Ram a new layer of hardcore into any weak areas.

● **Protective covering** If small children or pets are likely to use a freshly repaired area, cover the new edge with a sheet of polythene and a layer of chicken wire until the concrete has dried.

SAFETY MEASURES

It is essential that the eyes, skin, and lungs are fully covered and protected when carrying out any repairs to concrete structures.

● **Goggles** Wear goggles when working with concrete, stone, and hardcore. Small fragments of debris can seriously injure the eyes. Ensure that the surfaces are clean, providing clear vision.

● **Gloves** Wear rubber gloves to protect your hands from the caustic effects of cement.

● **Face mask** Cement dust is harmful to the lungs. Wear a face mask when mixing the components together.

REPLACING PAVING SLABS

Patio paving slabs can be exposed to a great deal of stress, especially during periods of warm weather. Eventually they will require repair as cracks appear or mortar crumbles, but if carried out promptly there should be no need for extensive and costly work.

FITTING SLABS

● **Individual slabs** Replace any single slabs that have shattered or cracked. Use the opportunity to check that the hardcore below is firm and level.

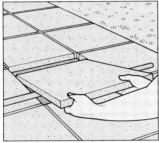

Easing into position
To prevent the surrounding slabs from being damaged, lay a broom handle or section of pipe across the gap to be filled. Use this as a support to ease the replacement paving stone into position.

WORKING WITH SLABS

● **Safety** The edges of paving slabs can be very sharp, particularly if cut using a chisel or bolster. Wear goggles when cutting, and use thick gloves when handling sharp slabs.
● **Cutting surface** Place a slab on a solid, flat surface to ensure an accurate cut.
● **Level surface** When a new slab is in place, use a spirit level to check that the surface is completely level before replacing the mortar.
● **Uneven slabs** To realign an uneven slab, place a block of wood on the surface to prevent damage to the slab, and lightly strike it with a club hammer until level.
● **Cleaning** When the mortar is dry, wash the entire paved surface with a proprietary path and patio cleaning agent.

FILLING JOINTS

● **Positioning** Before filling in a joint with mortar, leave the replacement paving stone to settle on the hardcore for a miminum of two days.

Using a wooden jigger
Fill the joints using a wooden jigger. Align the narrow central opening to the joint, and push the mortar through. Used correctly, a jigger prevents excess mortar from spilling on to the slabs.

PLACING AND CLEANING

● **Spacing** If existing slabs are separated by mortar, use a wooden spacer of the same width as the mortar to position a new slab. Remove the spacer when laying mortar in the joint.
● **Cleaning** Clean up excess mortar with water and a stiff brush or yard broom as promptly as possible. Mortar sets quickly and can be difficult to remove once dry.
● **Planting up** If a paving slab is badly damaged and you are unable to find a suitable replacement, consider removing the damaged slab and planting into the soil beneath (see p. 20).
● **Stains** Paving slabs can be marked by oil, rust, and moss. Use a proprietary cleaning agent to remove the stain.

CUTTING A PAVING SLAB

Paving slabs are available in a wide range of sizes. However, the shape of a patio or terrace may require a slab to be cut to fit. Hire an angle grinder if you have a number of slabs to alter.

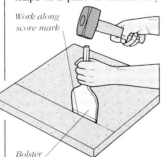

Work along score mark

Bolster

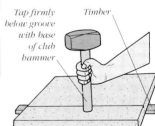

Tap firmly below groove with base of club hammer   *Timber*

1 Score both faces of the slab with a bolster. Work along the score mark with a club hammer and bolster to make a groove 3 mm (⅛ in) deep. If the slab has to fit tightly, cut it to size, less 6 mm (¼ in) all around to allow for uneven edges.

2 Rest the paving slab on a firm surface. Place a section of timber under the groove. Tap the surface of the slab with the base of a club hammer, to one side of the score mark. Repeat until the slab breaks. Shield your eyes from flying debris.

REPAIRING BRICK PATHS

Individual bricks are not easily broken in a path or patio, but occasionally one will crack or shatter. A damaged brick should be replaced promptly because, once the brick is cracked, moisture may penetrate and freeze in cold weather, making the problem worse.

DESIGNING WITH BRICKS
● **Colour** Try to match the colour of a new brick to its surroundings. Although it will stand out when new, the brick will weather with age.
● **Used bricks** Buy second-hand bricks for an instant weathered effect. Make sure that the bricks are frostproof before purchasing them.
● **Combinations** If you cannot locate new bricks that match the old, use the originals to replace broken sections, and position the new bricks in less conspicuous places.
● **Contrast** Place different bricks in among the originals to emphasize the contrast between the old and new bricks, and raise some above the others to create a pattern.

REPLACING BRICKS
● **Removing** Chip away any surrounding mortar, then use a pointed trowel to lever out the broken brick, taking care not to damage adjacent paving.

Inserting a new brick
Tamp down a replacement brick with a club hammer, laying a piece of wood over the top of the brick to avoid damaging the surface. Fill in any gaps between the bricks with silver sand.

BRIGHT IDEA

Storing bricks
If bricks become damp, they will not adhere to mortar. Store them in a dry place, or cover with a tarpaulin sheet. Stack bricks on a wooden plank that has been placed on a level, firm surface. To prevent the pile from collapsing, position the bricks in a pyramid shape so that the outer layer leans inwards.

RECONSTRUCTING CONCRETE STEPS

If the main body of a set of steps begins to fall down, the entire set should be replaced because the steps may be unsafe and collapse without warning. However, it is normally the fronts of steps, and occasionally the sides, that are most likely to incur damage.

MAINTAINING AND RESTORING CONCRETE STEPS
● **Preparation** Remove the damaged area. Brush off all dust and other loose material, then paint the newly prepared surface with PVA adhesive.
● **Concrete** Ensure that a good replacement edge is formed by using a dry mixture of concrete made up from one part cement to five parts ballast.
● **Prevention** Avoid further damage to a set of steps by occasionally varying your path, especially if carrying a heavy load or pushing a heavily laden wheelbarrow. Simple measures such as steering the wheel away from the centre of a step will help.

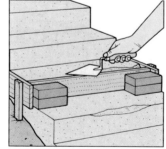

Using a timber mould
A new step edge must be straight. Hold timber boards in place with bricks and wooden stakes hammered into the ground. Firmly pack concrete mixture into this mould, and smooth over with a trowel.

COMPLETING REPAIRS
● **Moulding** Check that timber boards used to form a concrete mould are not warped or marked with knots.
● **Setting** Leave the supporting boards in place for a minimum of four weeks after carrying out a repair. This gives the concrete time to set completely.
● **Protecting** To protect a newly repaired concrete step from rain or frost, cover it with a polythene sheet.
● **Ageing** Dust the surface of wet concrete with sifted soil to give the edge an aged look. When the concrete is set, brush off any excess soil.

GARDEN FURNITURE

I F LEFT OUTSIDE THROUGH THE YEAR, garden furniture will rapidly start to show signs of ageing. If possible, shelter these items in wet or windy weather. Alternatively, cover bulky furniture with plastic sheeting to avoid using valuable storage space.

MAINTAINING FURNITURE

The nature of the maintenance your garden furniture requires will depend upon the material from which the item is made, and how it has been treated in the past. The appearance of old garden furniture can be greatly improved or altered with a coat of paint or a stain.

CARING FOR WOOD

● **Softwood** To prolong the life and condition of softwood, apply a coating of wood preservative every year.
● **Hardwood** Treat hardwood with an annual application of teak oil. Although hardwood has a long life expectancy and is not prone to rot, it will benefit from treatment.
● **Preparation** Before treating or painting wood, rub the surface down to remove any loose material, and allow the timber to dry thoroughly.

PAINTING AND STAINING WOODEN FURNITURE

● **Colour** Wooden furniture can be painted or stained using coloured wood preservative or a coat of paint followed by a coat of wood preservative.

Pour paint into measured quantity of preservative

Creating a colour
Create your own colour by mixing emulsion paint with clear wood preservative. Line a container with foil, pour in the two components, and stir thoroughly.

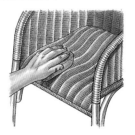
LOOKING AFTER PLASTIC

● **Cleaning** Wash down plastic garden furniture regularly to keep it clean and comfortable, and to help minimize scratching on the surface.
● **Painting** Restore a stained or discoloured item using paints formulated for plastic furniture. Ask for advice at a hardware store or DIY outlet.

LOOKING AFTER METAL

● **Light metal** If purchasing furniture made of light metal, ensure that it is strong and stable. Dents in metal are difficult to remove successfully.
● **Weatherproofing** If a metal item is to remain in the garden throughout the winter, protect all the exposed surfaces with an application of heavy oil. Wipe off the residue before using the furniture again.

OILING FURNITURE

● **Dealing with rust** Choose an aerosol product that inhibits rust when sprayed on metal. If it has an extension tube, it can also be used as a lubricant for springs, hinges, and rivets. Wipe off the oil before use.
● **Using paint** If rust does appear, rub it off with a wire brush. Treat the cleared area with anti-rust paint, and allow it to dry before painting with the colour of your choice.

GARDEN TOOLS

GARDEN TOOLS ARE VALUABLE PIECES OF EQUIPMENT and are well worth keeping in good condition by regularly carrying out the little maintenance they require. Such attention will ensure that your tools continue to perform efficiently.

MAINTAINING TOOLS

Routine maintenance needs to be carried out only once a year if tools are handled with care, cleaned, oiled if necessary, and repaired promptly and accurately. Regular care ensures that damage and deterioration of valuable equipment are kept to a minimum.

CLEANING A FORK

Scrape away lumps of soil

Making digging easier
When working in soil that is heavy and sticky, periodically clear soil from the tines of a fork. At the same time, remove any stones that are jammed between the tines that may cause the metal to bend.

REMOVING SOIL

● **Dried soil** An old but sturdy kitchen knife makes an excellent tool for manually removing lumps of soil that have dried on garden tools.
● **Clay soil** To remove sticky lumps of clay from a fork or spade, drive the tool into a compost heap or a bucket of oily, sharp sand. Much of the adhering clay will be removed and incorporated instead into the compost or sand.
● **Tyres** Clean the tyres of a wheelbarrow regularly – a heavy coating of mud may conceal sharp stones that could cause punctures when the wheelbarrow is next used.

LOOKING AFTER BLADES

Thoroughly wipe blades with oil

Oiling blades
Cutting blades must be clean and dry before oiling. Put plenty of oil on a clean rag, and use this to wipe over the blades and other metal parts. This should be done several times a year at least, and preferably after each use.

LOOKING AFTER WOOD

● **Drying** Before putting tools away, stand them in an upright position to dry, preferably in the sun. If the tools are still damp, store them vertically to prevent water from accumulating.
● **Removing splinters** To remove scratches or splintered areas on wooden handles, rub down the whole handle with fine-grade sandpaper, following the grain of the wood.
● **Applying oil** When storing equipment for a period of time, rub linseed oil into the handles or shafts of wooden tools. Allow the oil to penetrate, and remove any excess with a dry rag.

COVERING UNCOMFORTABLE TOOL HANDLES

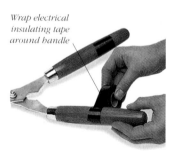

Wrap electrical insulating tape around handle

Taping around wood
Wrap a layer of insulating tape around wooden tool handles that have become rough or splintered. Make sure that the wood is completely dry, allowing the tape to adhere properly. The tape should last for several months and can be easily replaced.

Foam pipe insulation

Making a foam handle
Small sections of foam, such as pre-formed, pipe-insulating material, can form a soft covering for an uncomfortable handle. Hold the foam in place with insulating tape at each end. Make sure that the foam is not too bulky for a comfortable grip.

PREPARING TOOLS FOR STORAGE

For much of the winter, many tools will be required only occasionally, unless digging and soil preparation need to be done during this time. Before putting equipment away in an appropriate place, ensure that it is clean, dry, and prepared for a period of storage.

CHECKING EQUIPMENT
● **Dried debris** Rub dried garden debris off metal blades using a clean cloth soaked in methylated spirit.
● **Fuel tanks** Cold weather may cause petrol to freeze. Before storing petrol-driven equipment, check that all fuel tanks are emptied.
● **Cables** Check the cables of electrically driven equipment for signs of wear and tear. Replace cables if necessary.
● **Clean blades** To keep blades and tines in good condition, scrub them with a wire brush and warm water. Allow to dry, then file the cutting edges if they have deteriorated.

PREVENTING RUST

Oily sand

Cleaning and oiling
Mix a little oil into a bucket of sharp sand. To clean and oil large tools before storage, plunge them into the sand several times. Use oily sand to clean non-electrical equipment, such as forks, spades, and other tools with metal heads.

SHARPENING BLADES

Caring for cutting tools
Cutting tools, such as secateurs and shears, need regular sharpening if they are to continue to perform well. Run the blades regularly through a sharpener, or take the equipment to a professional for servicing.

STORING TOOLS

When the gardening season comes to an end, tools should be placed in a suitable storage place. Before storing the tools, ensure that the area is dry to avoid problems such as rust, wood rot, and frost damage. If in doubt, check the condition of the tools regularly.

HANGING TOOLS
● **Hand tools** Store hand tools off the ground to avoid exposing them to damp and to reduce the possibility of knocking them over.

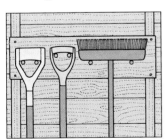

Constructing a tool rack
Make a tool rack by laying the tools to be stored flat on a piece of wood. The tools will be hung on galvanized nails, so mark their positions with a pencil. Remove the tools, and hammer in nails.

STORING CORRECTLY
● **Polythene wrap** Never wrap tools tightly in polythene, since condensation may build up and encourage rot and rust.
● **Hooks** Heavy tools can be suspended above the ground on sturdy hooks such as those used for storing bicycles.
● **Soil** Never store tools on soil. If they cannot be hung up, stand them on a wooden board wrapped in polythene.
● **Shed** Before using a shed as a storage area for tools, check that it is in good condition, and not damp.
● **Power tools** Keep electrically powered garden tools in a dry environment. If the storage area is damp, consider storing such equipment in the house.

TRADITIONAL TIP

Maintaining a lawnmower
To ensure that a lawnmower works efficiently at the beginning of a new gardening season, have the machine professionally serviced before putting it into storage, and make sure that it is kept on a level, wooden base when it is not in use.

GREENHOUSES

Buying, constructing, and filling a new greenhouse can be an exciting experience. However, greenhouses also represent a considerable financial investment, making appropriate and thorough maintenance essential.

CLEANING GREENHOUSES

The type of maintenance needed to keep a greenhouse in pristine condition will vary according to its construction. However, there are tasks common to all types that should be carried out annually in autumn, in order to prolong the effectiveness of a greenhouse.

LOOKING AFTER PLANTS
● **Providing light** Clean both sides of the glazing to remove debris. This is essential if plants are to benefit from natural light during dark winter months.
● **Protecting plants** If using a proprietary cleaner, remove all plants from the area, or cover them with a polythene sheet.

WARNING!

Before cleaning a greenhouse with water, it is essential that the electricity supply is turned off and that sockets are covered with plastic sheets.

MONEY-SAVING TIP

Keeping drainpipes clear
Wedge a plastic scouring pad or a ball of galvanized wire netting into the opening of a drainpipe. This will act as a filter and prevent falling leaves and other debris from clogging up the pipe or entering a water butt.

CLEANING A ROOF

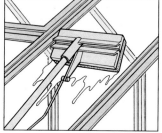

Reaching roof glazing
Use a long-handled floor mop to clean the upper sections of roof glazing on the inside and outside of a greenhouse. If the glazing is very dirty, add washing-up liquid or detergent to the water.

PROTECTING METAL
● **Fittings** Although aluminium frames should not rust, treat fittings of any other metal to prevent possible corrosion.

Preventing rust
To avoid stiffness and rust, apply a thin film of light oil or a layer of anti-rust paint regularly to metal fittings. Substitute corroded hinges and screws with galvanized replacements.

REMOVING PESTS

Scrubbing T-bars
Pests may lurk in the T-bars of aluminium greenhouses and remain there unless removed. Use a water spray and a scrubbing brush to clean out these areas. If pests persist, rub with wire wool.

PREPARING INTERIORS
● **Contents** Sort through the contents of your greenhouse every year, and throw away anything that is not needed.
● **Plants** When cleaning a greenhouse interior, use the opportunity to remove dead flowerheads and leaves.
● **Surfaces** Clean flooring using garden disinfectant. Rinse with clean water. Paint or spray on diluted disinfectant to clean shelves and other surfaces.
● **Draughts** Check vents and doors for draughts, and replace insulation tape if necessary.
● **Insulation** To reduce heat loss during winter months, fit strips of bubble plastic along the bottom panels of a greenhouse, and put sheets of polystyrene on the floor.

REPLACING GLAZING

Clean, undamaged glazing is essential for a productive greenhouse. Cracked panes will make it impossible to maintain temperatures accurately and can be dangerous. Most metal frames use a system of clips to secure the glass panes; putty is necessary for wooden frames.

FIXING GLASS
● **Positioning** Replace broken glass in wooden frames only if you feel confident handling and positioning glass. If in doubt, call in a professional.

Fitting replacement glass
Chisel away any old putty, and replace with a fresh layer. Press the edges, not the middle, of the pane to make contact with the paste. Fix in place with a second application of putty.

WORKING WITH GLAZING
● **Damaged glass** Do not delay replacing a pane of glass that is damaged or broken. Once it is damaged, the whole pane may fall out, with dangerous consequences.
● **Selecting panes** Use special horticultural or greenhouse glass to replace any panes that are broken.
● **Glazing clips** To replace glazing held in place with clips, unhook the clips and remove the pane, then slide in the new glass and fasten the clips.
● **Cleaning** Remove dirty marks from a new pane of glass with a cloth soaked in methylated spirit.
● **Trees** If you cannot prune a tree that regularly damages a roof, replace the roof glazing with polycarbonate sheeting.

USING PUTTY

● **Storing** Roll unused putty into balls and store in jars of water. Label the storage jars carefully, and keep out of the reach of children.
● **Positioning** Apply putty at an angle to ensure that rain and condensation do not collect on a wooden frame, which may lead to wet rot.

MAINTAINING FRAMES AND GLAZING

Greenhouse frames are available in a variety of materials, the properties of which will determine the maintenance required. All glazing needs regular cleaning, since debris or a film of algae reduces the penetration of light. Dirt inside may also provide a hiding place for pests.

TREATING FRAMES
● **Aluminium** Do not remove the grey patina that forms on aluminium. It will protect a frame against damp weather.
● **Steel** Although steel greenhouse frames are strong, they are also prone to rust. Treat them regularly with a coat of anti-rust paint. Replace the paint promptly if the surface is scratched.
● **Wood** Hardwood frames need little maintenance. Treat softwood frames with wood preservative every two years (see p. 162). Use a plant-friendly solution, or remove plants until the solution is dry.

REMOVING DEPOSITS

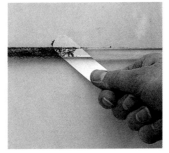

Cleaning between panes
To remove all deposits from overlapping panes of glass, slide a plastic plant label or a piece of thin, flexible plastic in between the panes. Wash off the loose debris with a clean, damp cloth.

CLEANING GLAZING
● **Timing** Avoid cleaning glazing on hot days; loosened dirt may dry in the heat.
● **Cleaners** Use a proprietary garden disinfectant or cleaner on persistently dirty areas or those harbouring pests. Ensure that plants are cleared from the area beforehand.
● **Ventilation** After cleaning interior glazing, ventilate the greenhouse thoroughly to reduce moisture in the air.
● **Leaves** If roof glazing is often covered with leaves, drape lightweight garden netting over the affected area. Empty the netting regularly.

SPRING TASKS

AREA OF THE GARDEN	EARLY SPRING
THE ORNAMENTAL GARDEN Once weather conditions improve and plants begin to grow, there is a great deal to do. There are many seeds that can be sown now, especially those that are sown directly into open ground. Some transplanting and dividing is also possible. The mild conditions of spring stimulate the germination and growth of weeds, as well as the development of many pests and diseases. Prompt action is therefore essential in order to prevent serious problems from developing later in the year.  Snowdrops	● Fork over, remove weeds, and fertilize soil before sowing annuals. Those that can be sown now include *Adonis aestivalis, Brachycome, Centaurea cyanus, Clarkia elegans, Convolvulus tricolor,* and *Eschscholzia californica*. ● Plant out hardy bulbs that have been grown inside over winter. Feed and water them well. ● Lift, divide, and replant congested clumps of snowdrops as soon as the flowers have faded. ● Lift, divide, and replant established or over-sized herbaceous plants, discarding any weak sections. ● Plant summer-flowering bulbs and perennials if the ground is not frozen or waterlogged. ● Prune hybrid bush roses, cutting out any frost-damaged, dead, or crossing stems.
THE VEGETABLE GARDEN Warm weather encourages the growth of many vegetables. Towards the end of spring, many tender vegetables can be planted outside, provided that the frosts are over. Pests and weeds may multiply rapidly, so keep a close watch on all crops.  Broccoli	● Sow broad beans, cauliflowers, Brussels sprouts, carrots, onions, radishes, summer spinach, and parsnips. Make a second sowing of early peas. ● Dig well-rotted manure into celery trenches. ● Plant early potatoes and onion sets. ● Apply a balanced fertilizer to lettuces that will be harvested in early or late spring. ● Prepare runner-bean trenches by digging in garden compost or well-rotted manure.
THE FRUIT GARDEN Although the first garden-grown fruit does not ripen until towards the end of spring, there is still a lot of watering and feeding to be done to ensure that fruiting trees, bushes, and canes are to perform well.  Strawberries	● Prune back the stems of newly planted and two-year-old gooseberries by about 50 per cent. ● Plant currant bushes and raspberry canes, and water in thoroughly. Cut the canes down to 30 cm (12 in) above the soil. ● Spray gooseberries and blackcurrants against American gooseberry mildew. ● Protect strawberry plants with cloches or fleece. ● Spray apples and pears prone to scab infection.
THE GREENHOUSE As the days become warm, windows and doors will need to be left open on sunny days. They should, however, still be closed up at night. The overall atmosphere should be reasonably dry. Throughly clean all the glass, both inside and out, to let in the maximum amount of light.	● Begin sowing herbs. ● Take cuttings of bedding plants such as fuchsias, heliotropes, marguerites, and pelargoniums. ● Sow seeds of *Anemone coronaria, Antirrhinum majus, Aster novi-belgii, Dianthus chinensis, Lobelia erinus, Petunia, Salvia, Tropaeolum peregrinum,* and *Verbena*.
THE LAWN Having spent most of the winter virtually dormant, the lawn grasses will suddenly start to grow. Any damage incurred during the winter must be put right before summer arrives. Now is the time to begin a regular programme of lawn maintenance.	● Rake the lawn clear of twigs, leaves, and other debris that may be clogging the surface. ● To prevent scalping, cut the lawn with the lawnmower blades set reasonably high. ● Neaten up lawn edges with edging shears. ● Brush off worm casts regularly.

MID SPRING	LATE SPRING
• Continue to direct-sow annuals such as *Linaria*, *Mesembryanthemum*, annual *Rudbeckia*, sunflowers, *Tagetes*, and Virginian stocks. • Prune shrubs grown for their decorative winter stems, such as willows and dogwoods. Prune *Forsythia* as soon as it has finished flowering. • Plant out *Antirrhinum* and *Penstemon* raised from autumn cuttings or sowings. Make sure to harden them off gradually first. • Take root cuttings of *Delphinium*, *Lupinus*, and herbaceous *Phlox*. • Apply a high-potash feed around the bases of summer-flowering shrubs, including roses. • Layer shrubs and climbers such as *Carpenteria*, *Fothergilla*, *Kalmia*, *Lonicera*, and *Syringa*.	• Stake young, herbaceous perennials. • Harden off bedding plants in preparation for planting them in open ground. • Plant young perennials grown from seed into a nursery bed where they can grow until autumn. • Begin to thin out seedlings of any annuals sown directly into the ground. • Tie new, vigorous rambler-rose growths gently but securely into their supports. • Sow *Achillea* spp., *Alcea rosea*, *Aquilegia vulgaris*, *Delphinium elatum*, *Erigeron speciosus*, and *Lychnis chalcedonica* seeds. • Plant up hanging baskets, tubs, and other containers. Leave them in a greenhouse or cold-frame until all danger from late frosts has passed.
• Thin out overcrowded vegetable seedlings. • Harden off young plants from winter sowings of cauliflower, leeks, onions, lettuce, peas, and broad beans before planting out. • Prepare and plant new asparagus beds. • Support peas with sticks or netting. • Sow broccoli, leeks, and kohlrabi, and also cauliflowers for planting out in early summer. • Sow winter cabbage in fertile soil.	• Thin seedlings from root crops and onions. • Direct-sow runner beans, sweetcorn, asparagus, peas, endive, French beans, leaf lettuce, Chinese cabbage, and chicory. • Transplant Brussels sprouts and leeks. Water in. • Draw up a little mound of soil over young potato shoots to protect them from frost. • Sow ridge cucumbers on to mounds enriched with plenty of well-rotted manure and compost.
• Feed summer-fruiting plants with sulphate of potash to promote good flowering and fruit. • Control weeds around bush and cane fruit. • Check for pests and diseases. Use sprays at dusk to avoid harming pollinating insects. • Thin heavy-cropping nectarines and peaches when the fruit is 1–1.5 cm (½ in) in diameter. • Feed blackberry and hybrid berry plants with sulphate of ammonia or other high-nitrogen feed.	• Mulch raspberries and other cane fruit. • Carefully remove runners from strawberries. Place mats or straw beneath stems with developing fruit to keep them off the ground. • Control slugs and snails in strawberry beds before they start to attack the fruit. • Tie in new raspberry canes. • Keep all fruit well watered, especially those on light soils, and those that are trained against a wall.
• Plant greenhouse tomato plants in large pots, or plant them in grow bags. • Start to harden off bedding plants. • Introduce biological controls to keep down pests such as glasshouse whitefly and red spider mite. • Pot on established begonias, chrysanthemums, *Cyclamen*, and gloxinias as necessary.	• Apply a high-potash liquid fertilizer to any tomato plants with setting fruit. • Protect greenhouse plants from heat with greenhouse shading or special shading paint. • Water seedlings with a copper-based fungicide. • Check for powdery mildew, grey mould, aphids, and other problems. Take immediate action.
• Apply a spring fertilizer to stimulate growth. • Remove weeds such as dandelions. • Thoroughly prepare ground to be seeded or turfed. Fertilize it with a complete fertilizer. Sow grass seed unless the soil is still very wet. • Protect new seed from birds, and water regularly.	• Control lawn weeds. Remove by hand or use an appropriate weedkiller. • Level off uneven areas of the lawn. • Repair or replace worn-out or bare areas of turf. • Use a lawn edger to neaten up any untidy, squashed, or damaged lawn edges.

SUMMER TASKS

AREA OF THE GARDEN	EARLY SUMMER
THE ORNAMENTAL GARDEN Warm weather continues to encourage plants to grow rapidly, although this gro may be set back considerably if it becomes very hot and dry. To ensure that the garden stays full of colour and crops throughout the summer, regular watering and feeding are essential. Many plants will need tying in to supports, and prompt action must be taken with any outbreaks of pests and diseases. Lilac	• Continue to plant out annual bedding and to fill baskets and other containers. Hang up and display any baskets that have been kept in the greenhouse. • Prune back *Arabis, Aubrieta,* and perennial candytuft as soon as they have finished flowering. • Divide congested clumps of primulas, primroses, and flag irises as soon as flowering is over. • Remove flowerheads from lilac and late-flowering camellias as soon as the flowers fade. • Remove suckers from roses. Make sure to cut them off close to the rootstock. • Water all ornamental plants regularly to prevent developing buds from dropping off. • Sow biennals and perennials, including *Aubrietia, Coreopsis,* delphiniums, and wallflowers.
THE VEGETABLE GARDEN There is a great deal to do in the vegetable garden in summer. In order for vegetables to crop as they should, they need a constant supply of water and careful feeding. Weeds compete for water and nutrients, so weed control, although time consuming, is vital for a healthy crop. Asparagus	• Make successional sowings of lettuce, turnips, runner beans, French beans, endive, radish, and kohlrabi. Sow Chinese cabbage. • Pinch out the tips on broad beans to encourage good pod set and to deter attack from aphids. • Stop picking asparagus so that the plants do not exhaust themselves. • Plant outdoor tomatoes, and tie them gently but firmly to canes to secure them.
THE FRUIT GARDEN Summer is when you can begin to enjoy the crops from many of your fruit trees, bushes, and canes. The plants themselves need relatively little maintenance, except for regular watering, some feeding, and possible spraying against pests and diseases. Peaches	• Spray raspberries against raspberry beetle. Apply the first spray as soon as the first fruit turns pink. • Hang codling-moth traps on apple trees. • Spray against apple scab, mildew, and aphids. • Tie in new canes of blackberries and hybrid berries to a system of support wires, allowing a maximum of eight canes per plant. • Summer-prune gooseberries by cutting back side shoots to five leaves.
THE GREENHOUSE Prevent high temperatures in the greenhouse from damaging plants. Open doors, vents, and windows, and damp down regularly to increase humidity.	• Water and feed tomatoes, cucumbers, and peppers, never letting the compost dry out. • Fit slings or nets to melons as they swell. • Continue to remove side shoots from tomatoes.
THE LAWN Lawn grasses grow strongly throughout the summer, so regular mowing is one of the most frequent tasks. Wear and tear is often at its height, too, as the lawn is put to heavy use for parties, sunbathing, barbecues, and play. The amount of mowing and watering required will be strongly influenced by the weather, and this may vary considerably from year to year.	• Mow as often as necessary, ensuring that you do not cut too short, especially in hot, dry weather. • Control broadleaved weeds by handweeding or by using suitable proprietary weedkillers. • Water regularly with a sprinkler, but first check to see if there are any local watering restrictions. • If necessary, apply a nitrogen-rich liquid feed to the lawn to green it up and to encourage the grasses to put on rapid growth.

MID SUMMER	LATE SUMMER
● Feed roses and other flowering plants in open ground and in containers with a high-potash fertilizer to encourage flowering. ● Deadhead faded flowers to promote the formation of new buds and encourage growth. ● Trim hedges regularly to avoid having to cut them back too much at any one time. ● Weed carefully between plants in borders and beneath trees, shrubs, and climbers. ● Layer border carnations and propagate pinks by taking 7.5-cm (3-in) long cuttings. ● Transplant Canterbury bells, sweet Williams, and wallflowers into a nursery bed. Water in well. ● Take semi-ripe cuttings of many shrubs, including *Deutzia* and *Weigela*.	● Plant *Amaryllis belladonna*, autumn crocus, *Colchicum, Fritillaria imperialis, Lilium candidum*, and *Sternbergia* bulbs. ● Continue to deadhead all flowering plants, unless you intend to save seed. ● Control earwigs and powdery mildew on dahlias and chrysanthemums. ● Prune rambler roses once flowering is over. ● Spray roses against fungal attack such as powdery mildew, rust, and black spot. ● Water all plants regularly, giving priority to relatively new plants and those that are particularly intolerant of drought. ● Move layered border carnations into the positions they will occupy permanently.
● Spray outdoor tomatoes and potatoes with a fungicide to protect them from blight. ● Mound soil around celery stems, and tie together. ● Harvest herbs for use in the winter, preferably before they begin to flower. ● Start to make successional sowings of spring cabbage. Sow turnips and swedes. ● Harvest runner and French beans as soon as they are ready. Freeze while they are still tender.	● Ripen onions by lifting them gently and leaving them in position for a couple of weeks. ● Sow onions (for an early crop next year), pickling and red cabbage, spinach, and spinach beets. ● Continue to water regularly, especially crops that bolt or fail if allowed to dry out. ● Weed regularly between rows of crops. ● Use a proprietary spray on all crops, particularly cabbages, to prevent attacks by caterpillars.
● Prune fan-trained cherries and plums to prevent excessive growth towards the wall or fence. ● Remove and dispose of any apples and pears showing signs of pest infestation. ● Water apple trees regularly and thoroughly to decrease the risk of bitter pit developing. Spray developing fruit with calcium nitrate. ● Erect netting around developing fruit to protect them from being attacked by birds.	● Control woolly aphid on apple trees. ● Prune summer-fruiting raspberries. As soon as they have finished cropping, cut all the raspberry canes that have just fruited back to ground level, and tie in new canes to supports. ● Remove old leaves and runners from strawberries once they have finished fruiting. ● Start to prune apples, and continue to prune cherries, plums, apricots, nectarines, and peaches.
● Continue to water tomato plants very frequently to prevent the development of blossom-end rot. ● Remove excessive leaf growth from tomatoes. ● Add extra shading to glazing if necessary.	● Take cuttings of ivy-leaved geraniums, and zonal pelargoniums, and pot up. ● Take semi-ripe cuttings of *Berberis, Camellia, Ceanothus, Cotoneaster, Daphne*, and *Mahonia*.
● Protect areas that are frequently used by children, or move swings and other play equipment around to spread the wear and tear. ● Continue to water regularly if possible. Water in early evening to minimize wastage. ● Control any ants that may be beneath the lawn. ● Drench any areas of lawn that have been urinated on by pets and wildlife. ● Leave grass clippings on the lawn in dry weather.	● Apply a lawn fertilizer with relatively high phosphate and potassium levels to encourage the development of strong roots. ● Trim back herbaceous plants that have grown excessively and flopped over the lawn edges. ● Continue to water regularly and thoroughly during hot, dry weather. Always water well after applying any kind of fertilizer. ● Continue to mow the lawn regularly.

AUTUMN TASKS

AREA OF THE GARDEN	EARLY AUTUMN
THE ORNAMENTAL GARDEN Summer borders have now begun to deteriorate. You will need to tidy up the plants for the winter, weed, and in some cases divide and replant congested clumps. Damp weather often encourages an outbreak of diseases, so you may need to control these, too. Clear up fallen leaves, since they may harbour diseases and swamp small plants. Autumn is a good time to plan next year's planting.  *Schizostylis*	● Plant daffodils and other *Narcissus*, crocus, scillas, iris, and many lilies for a spring display. ● Remove the remains of summer-flowering annuals, and prepare the soil thoroughly for winter-flowering bedding plants. ● In light, well-drained soils, direct sow hardy annuals, including *Alyssum, Calendula,* candytuft, *Clarkia, Nigella,* and poppies. ● Lift and store gladiolus corms. ● Place nets over ponds to prevent the water from becoming polluted by falling leaves. ● Continue to prune rambler roses. ● Ensure that autumn-flowering herbaceous plants are properly staked. ● Rake up autumn leaves regularly.
THE VEGETABLE GARDEN Some vegetables will be used immediately, but others can be harvested carefully and stored. There is also a considerable amount of tidying up to do in preparation for new crops. Ensure that all diseased debris is disposed of, well away from the vegetable garden. 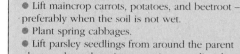 Marrow	● Lift maincrop carrots, potatoes, and beetroot – preferably when the soil is not wet. ● Plant spring cabbages. ● Lift parsley seedlings from around the parent plant, and pot them into containers or directly into a coldframe or cold greenhouse border. ● Lift and store the last of the marrow crop. ● Pick the last of the outdoor tomatoes, and ripen them in a warm spot indoors.
THE FRUIT GARDEN Most fruit trees yield the majority of their harvests during autumn. Late varieties of some bush and cane fruit are productive now, too. Many apples, and some pears, can be stored for use later in the year.  Grapes	● Plant peaches and nectarines, preferably in a sheltered spot, and trained against a sunny wall. ● Begin planting blackberries and hybrid berries. ● Prune raspberry canes that fruited in the summer back to soil level. Carefully tie in new canes to the support system. ● Rake up and dispose of fallen leaves from scab-infected apple and pear trees, and from any rust-infected plum trees.
THE GREENHOUSE As cool weather arrives, put half-hardy plants into the greenhouse for protection over winter. Reduce ventilation and humidity levels.	● Take off all shading from greenhouse glazing. ● Pot up bulbs for winter displays. ● Sow lettuce, radish, and carrot varieties for subsequent growing under cloches.
THE LAWN The lawn can now begin to recover from the heavy use it may have had over the summer months, as well as from any damaging dry periods when adequate watering may not have been possible. As autumn approaches, grass growth slows down, allowing much essential maintenance work to be done. Work carried out now will be of benefit to the lawn throughout the coming year.	● Rake fallen leaves off the grass as soon as possible, especially if the weather is wet. ● Reseed any worn patches in the lawn. ● Prepare areas ready to be turfed or seeded. ● Aerate the lawn to encourage good drainage and to stimulate root growth. Use a garden fork for small areas or a hollow-tine aerator on large areas. ● Apply an insecticide drench if leatherjacket grubs are present in the lawn.

MID AUTUMN	LATE AUTUMN
● Pick and dry attractive seedheads for use in dried-flower arrangements. ● Protect alpines, which are intolerant of-wet conditions, with a pane of glass. ● Cut back chrysanthemums to about 15 cm (6 in) above ground level, lift, and store in boxes. ● To prolong the flowering period of *Schizostylis*, pot up garden-grown plants, and overwinter them in a greenhouse or cold frame. ● Plant winter and spring bedding plants such as *Bellis*, forget-me-nots, *Polyanthus*, universal pansies, and wallflowers. Plant lily-of-the-valley. ● Clear up dead and dying herbaceous plants, leaving enough foliage behind to protect the crowns from severe winter weather.	● If necessary, transplant trees and shrubs while the soil is still warm and moist, but not too wet. ● Prune deciduous hedges, and carry out any necessary major cutting back. ● Protect half-hardy bulbs such as *Agapanthus*. ● Plant tulip bulbs, preferably in a sunny, sheltered border, or into containers. ● Plant spring-flowering plants for added colour to fill any bare gaps between shrubs next spring. ● Continue to remove the last of the weeds, taking care not to distribute seeds. ● To ensure good bud formation for plenty of spring flowers, make sure that all plants have enough water during dry spells. ● Clear fallen leaves from gutters.
● Harvest onions and cauliflowers. ● Remove leaves showing signs of infection from lettuces and brassicas. ● Lift chicory as the foliage dies back, and store in a cool shed in boxes of sand. ● For a winter crop of spinach, put cloches over late spinach sowings to protect them from frost. ● Cut back foliage of asparagus crowns planted in mid spring. Mound up soil over crowns.	● Sow broad beans in a sheltered spot to achieve a very early crop without the aid of a greenhouse. ● Lift and store parsnip, horseradish, and Jerusalem artichoke crops. ● Pick Brussels sprouts when the buttons firm up. ● Harvest leeks, trimming off roots and carefully disposing of any outer, rust-infested foliage. ● Dig over vacant areas thoroughly, and leave the soil to be broken down by winter frosts.
● Plant blackcurrants, red and white currants, and raspberry canes from now until early spring, provided that the soil is not too cold or too wet. ● Take hardwood cuttings from grapevines, blackcurrants, and gooseberries. Root them in sandy soil in a sheltered spot. ● Remove all weeds from between strawberry plants, water well, and apply a mulch. ● Continue to rake up and dispose of fallen leaves.	● Cut canes of blackberry and hybrid berries that fruited this year back to soil level, and tie in newly formed canes to supports. ● Plant gooseberries, apples, and pears, provided that the soil is not too wet or too cold. ● Prune back newly planted apple trees immediately after planting. Reduce all side shoots by about 50 per cent, and cut back maiden trees to approximately 50 cm (20 in) above soil level.
● Pick the last of the tomatoes. Clear up and dispose of all the plant remains. ● Bring in the last of the chrysanthemums for protection during the winter months.	● Water overwintering plants occasionally so that they do not dry out completely. ● Lift crowns of lily-of-the-valley, and pot up for an early, indoor, scented display.
● Seed new lawns or lay turves. ● Scarify the lawn using a spring-tined rake, or a powered rake for very large areas. This removes any dead matter and debris from the surface. ● Continue to rake up autumn leaves regularly. Use them to make leafmould. ● Use a proprietary moss killer for moss-infested lawns. To prevent the spread of moss spores, wait until the moss is completely dead before raking it out.	● Plant *Narcissus* and any other suitable bulbs in drifts or clumps in lawns. ● Repair any humps and hollows created by excessive summer wear and tear. ● Continue to trim back herbaceous plants that have flopped on to the lawn edges. ● Clean up the lawnmower, and carry out any necessary repairs before storing it for the winter. ● Repair broken and crushed lawn edges.

WINTER TASKS

AREA OF THE GARDEN	EARLY WINTER
THE ORNAMENTAL GARDEN Frosts, freezing conditions, and snow may make much of the winter season a time when it is difficult, if not inadvisable, to do much work outside. It is, however, possible to create a winter garden that has plenty of visual interest as well as fragrance. Temporary colour can be introduced in the form of winter-flowering bedding plants as well as a few winter-flowering bulbs. Combine these with a selection of shrubs grown either for their winter bark, flowers, and berries (such as *Skimmia*), or for their evergreen foliage. *Skimmia*	● Protect crowns of herbaceous plants from frost damage with straw or dry leaves. ● Protect rootballs of container-grown plants by wrapping containers in hessian or newspaper. ● Continue to clear vacant beds and borders. ● Where necessary, firm back soil that has been lifted around shrub roots by frost . ● In a windy garden, prune back some of the top-growth on roses to minimize windrock. ● If soil in flowerbeds is very wet, try to avoid walking or treading on it, which could compact it. Stand on a plank or board so that your weight is spread over a large area. ● Sow alpine and tree seeds that benefit from exposure to frost, and leave them outside. ● Begin winter pruning trees and shrubs. ● Browse through seed catalogues, and decide what to buy. Put in orders to seed companies early so that you are not disappointed.
THE VEGETABLE GARDEN A carefully planned vegetable garden will continue to yield some fresh crops throughout winter. Protect crops with horticultural fleece and cloches to gain the maximum benefit. Cauliflower	● Continue to lift trench celery. Check for slug damage, and take appropriate action if necessary. ● Continue to harvest leek, turnip, swede, kohlrabi, and parsnip crops. ● Bend the leaves of cauliflowers over the curds to protect them from frost damage. ● Plant chicory roots into pots, and place them in a dark spot at about 7°C (45°F). Harvest young shoots as they are produced.
THE FRUIT GARDEN Winter weather provides a relatively quiet period in the fruit garden, since fruit trees and bushes are now fully dormant. Check fruit in store, and remove any showing signs of deterioration or disease. Stored apples	● Prune red and white currants from now until late winter. After pruning is complete, apply a mulch of well-rotted manure or garden compost. ● Prune apples and pears. Check branches, stems, and trunks for signs of fungal canker. Prune out and treat affected areas as necessary. ● Check that any stakes and ties around fruit bushes and trees are held firmly in place. ● Apply a tar-oil winter wash to help control overwintering pests and diseases.
THE GREENHOUSE Use a greenhouse to make early sowings of many vegetables and flowers. Check the thermometer regularly, and adjust the heating as necessary.	● Sow the seeds of herbaceous perennials such as anemone, *Canna,* columbine, *Dianthus,* hollyhock, and poppies, ● Prune grapevines grown under glass.
THE LAWN The lawn needs little attention during the winter. Unless any urgent action is required, it is best to avoid working on the lawn too much until spring.	● Continue to rake up any fallen leaves that have been blown on to the lawn. ● Use a brush with stiff bristles to scatter any worm casts that have appeared on the lawn.

MID WINTER	LATE WINTER
● Slugs will be causing damage in mild spells, so control them before they attack any plant crowns that are left in the ground. ● Prevent the sides of ponds from being cracked by pressure from freezing water. Float a ball, empty plastic bottle, or log on the surface. ● Brush heavy snow off branches to prevent the weight from snapping them. ● Protect winter-flowering hellebores from being splashed with mud by covering them with cloches. ● Carefully fork over the surface soil in flowerbeds containing spring-flowering bulbs to break up compaction and to deter the growth of algae, moss, and weeds. ● Dig over the soil in preparation for planting dahlias when all danger from frost has passed. ● Make sure that garden birds have a regular supply of food and water during the cold weather. ● Plant trees and shrubs on dry, warm days.	● Sow a selection of herbaceous perennials to incorporate into your flower borders in the spring. ● Once winter-flowering heathers have finished flowering, trim them back lightly. Do not cut into woody growth – just trim off old flowering stems. ● Plant *Tigridia* bulbs outside in a sheltered, warm spot. Also plant *Crocosmia*. ● Check over dahlias in store, and remove any that are showing signs of rotting. ● Prune winter-flowering jasmine as soon as the last of the flowers have finished. ● Prune and train in stems of ornamental vines such as *Vitis coignetiae*. ● Start to prune *Cornus* (dogwoods), which are grown for their brightly coloured winter stems. ● Plant gladioli, anemones, lilies, *Ranunculus,* and hedges in mild areas. ● Feed established flowerbeds and borders with well-rotted manure.
● Continue to harvest winter cabbage, Brussels sprouts, parsnips, and leeks. ● Spray Brussels sprouts and other winter brassicas against whitefly infestation. ● Lift crops of Jerusalem artichokes. Make sure that you lift every scrap of tuber. Store tubers in a paper bag in a cool, well-ventilated shed or garage. ● Plant early potatoes into pots in a greenhouse or a coldframe to produce a very early crop.	● Choose a sheltered spot with moist soil, and make the first sowing of stump-rooted carrots. ● Sow early peas in a sheltered spot. ● Sow maincrop onions and salad onions. ● Continue to harvest winter brassicas, leeks, celery, and root crops. ● Continue to spray against brassica whitefly. ● In mild areas shallots may be planted. ● Thin lettuces sown in mid summer.
● Spray peaches, nectarines, and almonds with a copper-based fungicide to prevent attacks of peach-leaf curl. Cover fan-trained trees with an open-sided polythene shelter. ● Start forcing rhubarb. Cover the crowns with a deep layer of leaves or leafmould – then cover with a forcing pot or any other pot. ● Apply a mulch of well-rotted manure or garden compost around the bases of gooseberries. ● Complete the last pruning of apples and pears.	● Apply a second spray of copper-based fungicide to trees susceptible to peach-leaf curl about 14 days after the first application. ● Sprinkle sulphate of potash around the root-feeding area of apples, pears, and plums to encourage good fruiting later in the year. ● Prune autumn-fruiting raspberries. Cut back to ground level the canes that fruited last autumn. ● Prune back canes of raspberries planted last year to about 30 cm (12 in) above ground level.
● Start to sow seeds of *Antirrhinum* begonias, pelargoniums, salvias, verbenas, and at 18°C (65°F). ● Take cuttings from perpetual-flowering carnations; root in sandy compost at 10°C (50°F).	● Water trays of seedlings with a copper-based fungicide to prevent damping off disease. ● Ventilate as much as possible to prevent the build up of diseases in the damp atmosphere.
● Have your lawnmower serviced and repaired if you have not already done so. ● Check that all lawn tools are properly cleaned, oiled, and stored for the winter.	● Try to keep off the grass if it is frozen, since stepping on it will encourage the onset of diseases. ● Lift loose or sunken stepping stones in the lawn. Level them, and re-lay.

INDEX

ACKNOWLEDGMENTS

AUTHOR'S ACKNOWLEDGMENTS
I would like to thank Linda Martin and Jayne Carter for their help and patience. Thanks, too, to the rest of the Dorling Kindersley team; to Justina Buswell for her wordprocessing help; Alasdair, Fiona, Simon, John, and various other friends for their advice.

PUBLISHER'S ACKNOWLEDGMENTS
Dorling Kindersley would like to thank the following: Linda Martin for planting up the containers, Debra Whitehead and Kristina Fitzsimmons for additional help, Peter Griffiths for making the model on p. 64, and Ray Jones for making props for photography.

Prop loan Adrian Hall Ltd., Putney Garden Centre, London; The West Hampstead Garden Centre.

Editorial and design assistance Emma Lawson, Adèle Hayward, and Colette Connolly for editorial assistance; Chris Bernstein for the index; Austin Barlow, Jackie Dollar and Darren Hill for design assistance.

ARTWORKS
Illustrators All illustrations by Kuo Kang Chen and John Woodcock, apart from additional illustrations on pages 12–13, 14, 21, 22, 29, 32–33 by Karen Cochrane, and pages 124, 126, 128, 130–131 by David Ashby.

PHOTOGRAPHY
Photographers Andy Crawford, Steve Gorton, Gary Ombler.
Additional photography Jane Stockman, Peter Anderson, Andreas Einsiedel, Graham Kirk, Matthew Ward, Jerry Young.

Picture Researcher Sarah Moule.

PICTURE CREDITS
Key: a above, b below, c centre, l left, r right, t top

Garden Picture Library J. Baker 133c; A. Bedding 19bc; J. Bouchier 74tl; L. Burgess 71bl; T. Candler 71tc; B. Carter 13tr; J. Glover 17tc; 70bc; S. Harte 32br, 133cr; M. Howes 91bl; Lamontagne 70bl; J. Legate 116c; J. Miller 15tl; C. Perry 111bl; J. Wade 112br; S. Wooster 28cl. **John Glover** 16bl, 37bc. **Harpur Garden Library** 32bc, 34bl, 35bl, 37bl; design: Chris Grey-Wilson 24ca; design: Yong Man Kim 27br; design: Mrs. Wethered 28bl; design: G. & F. Whiten 26bl. **Holt Studios International Ltd.** N. Caitlin 104cla, 106clb, 107tl, 107cla, 107clb, 107cbl, 112c, 115c, 115cr. **Frank Lane Picture Agency** B. Borrell 105br, 106cla; E. & A. Hosking 105clb; R. Wilmshurst 110br. **Andrew Lawson Photography** 76cb. **Natural History Photographic Agency** S. Dalton 110bc. **Photos Horticultural** 104bcl, 105cl, 112cr, 116cl. **Harry Smith Photographic Collection** 17tl, 17bl, 28tr, 36, 37bc, 71tr, 74tc, 76bl, 104bl, 122c, 122cr.

Hand models Toby Heran, Katie Martin, Marlon Reddin, and Helen Oyo.